Saint Cuthbert Prayer Book

Also by
The Diocese of St. Cuthbert ...

Prayers and Blessings

Saint Cuthbert Prayer Book

From the Diocese of St. Cuthbert

The Rt. Rev. Robert H. Hoyt, Jr. SC
The Rev. Canon Michael F. Lee

"Scripture quotations marked (ESV) are from The Holy Bible, English Standard Version®, copyright © 2001 by Crossway Bibles, a publishing ministry of Good News Publishers. Used by permission. All rights reserved."

"Scripture quotations marked (NRSV) are from the New Revised Standard Version Bible, copyright 1989, Division of Christian Education of the National Council of the Churches of Christ in the United States of America. Used by permission. All rights reserved."

Scripture texts in this work marked (NAB) are taken from the *New American Bible* © 1991, 1986, 1970 Confraternity of Christian Doctrine, Washington, D.C. and are used by permission of the copyright owner. All Rights Reserved. No part of the *New American Bible* may be reproduced in any form without permission in writing from the copyright owner.

Scripture quotations marked "NKJV" are taken from the New King James Version®. Copyright © 1982 by Thomas Nelson, Inc. Used by permission. All rights reserved

English translations of *Gloria in excelsis, Gloria patri* © 1988 English Language Liturgical Consultation (ELLC), www.englishtexts.org. Used by permission.

The Lord's Prayer, 1789 Book of Common Prayer.

Copyright 2007 by Diocese of Saint Cuthbert
ISBN 978-0-6151-7489-1

Preface

The Morning and Evening Prayer Office of the Saint Cuthbert Prayer Book draws on resources from many traditions as noted in the text. It may be used with any lectionary schema. The use of the Saint Cuthbert Psalter, which is included, is suggested.

The focus of the daily prayer has been developed to reflect values which are held by the Diocese of Saint Cuthbert.

Sunday	Worship
Monday	Journey
Tuesday	Creativity
Wednesday	Community and Relationship
Thursday	The Land
Friday	Healing
Saturday	Unity

We pray that this work will prove to be a valuable resource for you in the years to come.

Morning Prayer
SUNDAY

✠ In the Name of the Father,
  and of the Son,
  and of the Holy Spirit.
Amen.

I arise today
Through a mighty strength:
    God's power to guide me,
    God's might to uphold me,
    God's eyes to watch over me;
    God's ear to hear me,
    God's word to give me speech,
    God's hand to guard me,
    God's way to lie before me,
    God's shield to shelter me,
    God's host to secure me.

Bridgid of gael, From Sandy Stevenson, *Gaelic Blessings*

"I am the resurrection and the life;
whoever believes in me, even if he dies, will live,
and everyone who lives
and believes in me will never die. Do you believe this?"
Amen. Lord, we believe.
                      John 11:25-26 NAB

O come, let us worship and bow down,
  let us kneel before the LORD, our Maker!
For he is our God,
  and we are the people of his pasture,
  and the sheep of his hand.
                      Psalm 95:6-7, NRSV

Morning Prayer

Appointed Psalm

Glory be to the Father, and to the Son, and to the Holy Ghost;
As it was in the beginning, is now, and ever shall be, world without end. Amen.

   Glory to God in the highest,
    and peace to his people on earth.
   Lord God, heavenly King,
   almighty God and Father,
    we worship you, we give you thanks,
    we praise you for your glory.
   Lord Jesus Christ, only Son of the Father,
   Lord God, Lamb of God,
   you take away the sin of the world:
    have mercy on us;
   you are seated at the right hand of the Father:
    receive our prayer.
   For you alone are the Holy One,
   you alone are the Lord,
   you alone are the Most High,
    Jesus Christ,
    with the Holy Spirit,
   in the glory of God the Father.
   Amen.

Readings
Meditation

The Lord be with you.
And with thy spirit.
Let us pray.

Morning Prayer

Our Father, who art in heaven,
   hallowed be thy Name,
   thy kingdom come,
   thy will be done,
      on earth as it is in heaven.
Give us this day our daily bread.
And forgive us our trespasses,
   as we forgive those
   who trespass against us.
And lead us not into temptation,
   but deliver us from evil.
For thine is the kingdom,
   and the power, and the glory,
   for ever and ever.
   Amen.

Intercessions

Thanks be to You, Jesus Christ
Who brought us up from last night,
To the gladsome light of this day,
To win everlasting life for our souls,
Through the blood You shed for us.

Praise be to You, O God, for ever,
For the blessings You bestow on us –
Our food, Our speech, Our work, Our health.
Praise be to You, O God, for ever.

From the Carmina gadelica

✠ In the Name of the Father,
   and of the Son,
   and of the Holy Spirit.
   Amen.

Morning Prayer

MONDAY

✠ In the Name of the Father,
and of the Son,
and of the Holy Spirit.
Amen.

I arise today
Through a mighty strength:
> **God's power to guide me,**
> God's might to uphold me,
> **God's eyes to watch over me;**
> God's ear to hear me,
> **God's word to give me speech,**
> God's hand to guard me,
> **God's way to lie before me,**
> God's shield to shelter me,
> **God's host to secure me.**

> *Bridgid of gael*, From Sandy Stevenson, *Gaelic Blessings*

Without any doubt, the mystery of our religion is great:
> He was revealed in flesh,
> vindicated in spirit,
> seen by angels,
> proclaimed among Gentiles,
> believed in throughout the world,
> taken up in glory.

Amen. Lord, we believe.

1 Tim 3:16 NRSV

You will show me the path to life,
abounding joy in your presence,
the delights at your right hand forever.

Psalm 16:11 NAB

Morning Prayer

Appointed Psalm

Glory be to the Father, and to the Son, and to the Holy Ghost;
As it was in the beginning, is now, and ever shall be, world without end. Amen.

Blessed are you, LORD God of Israel our Father,
for ever and ever.
Yours, O LORD, is the greatness, and the power, and the glory, and the victory, and the majesty:
for all that is in the heaven and in the earth is yours; yours is the kingdom, O LORD, and you are exalted as head above all.
Both riches and honour come from you, and you reign over all;
and in your hand is power and might; and in yours hand it is to make great, and to give strength unto all.
Now therefore, our God, we thank you,
and praise your glorious name.
But who am I, and what is my people, that we should be able to offer so willingly as this?
For all things come from you, and of your own have we given you.
For we are strangers and sojourners, as were all our fathers:
our days on the earth are as a shadow, and there is none abiding.

1 Chr 29:10b-15, ESV

Readings
Meditation

The Lord be with you.
And with thy spirit.
Let us pray.

Morning Prayer

Our Father, who art in heaven,
  hallowed be thy Name,
  thy kingdom come,
  thy will be done,
    on earth as it is in heaven.
Give us this day our daily bread.
And forgive us our trespasses,
  as we forgive those
  who trespass against us.
And lead us not into temptation,
  but deliver us from evil.
For thine is the kingdom,
  and the power, and the glory,
  for ever and ever.
  Amen.

Intercessions

Thanks be to You, Jesus Christ
Who brought us up from last night,
To the gladsome light of this day,
To win everlasting life for our souls,
Through the blood You shed for us.

Praise be to You, O God, for ever,
For the blessings You bestow on us –
Our food, Our speech, Our work, Our health.
Praise be to You, O God, for ever.

From the Carmina gadelica

✠ In the Name of the Father,
  and of the Son,
  and of the Holy Spirit.
  Amen.

Morning Prayer

TUESDAY

✠ In the Name of the Father,
and of the Son,
and of the Holy Spirit.
Amen.

I arise today
Through a mighty strength:
> **God's power to guide me,**
> God's might to uphold me,
> **God's eyes to watch over me;**
> God's ear to hear me,
> **God's word to give me speech,**
> God's hand to guard me,
> **God's way to lie before me,**
> God's shield to shelter me,
> **God's host to secure me.**

Bridgid of gael, From Sandy Stevenson, *Gaelic Blessings*

He is the image – of the invisible God, the firstborn of all creation.
For in him – were created all things in heaven and on earth, the visible and the invisible, whether thrones or dominions or principalities or powers; all things were created through him and for him.
He is before all things, and in him all things hold together.
He is the head of the body, the church. – He is the beginning, the firstborn from the dead, that in all things he himself might be preeminent.
For in him all the fullness – was pleased to dwell, and through him to reconcile all things for him, making peace by the blood of his cross
   Amen. Lord, we believe.

Col 1:15-20a NAB

Morning Prayer

When I see your heavens, the work of your fingers,
the moon and stars that you set in place—
What are humans that you are mindful of them,
mere mortals that you care for them?
Yet you have made them little less than a god,
crowned them with glory and honor.
You have given them rule over the works of your hands,
put all things at their feet:

Psalm 8:4-7 NAB

Appointed Psalm

Glory be to the Father, and to the Son, and to the Holy Ghost;
As it was in the beginning, is now, and ever shall be, world without end. Amen.

Splendor and honor and kingly power
are yours by right, O Lord our God,
For you created everything that is,
and by your will they were created and have their being;
And yours by right, O Lamb that was slain,
For with your blood you have redeemed for God,
From every family, language, people, and nation,
a kingdom of priests to serve our God.
And so, to him who sits upon the throne,
and to Christ the Lamb,
Be worship and praise, dominion and splendor,
For ever and for evermore.

A Song to the Lamb, BCP

Readings
Meditation

Morning Prayer

The Lord be with you.
And with thy spirit.
Let us pray.

  Our Father, who art in heaven,
   hallowed be thy Name,
   thy kingdom come,
   thy will be done,
    on earth as it is in heaven.
  Give us this day our daily bread.
  And forgive us our trespasses,
   as we forgive those
   who trespass against us.
  And lead us not into temptation,
   but deliver us from evil.
  For thine is the kingdom,
   and the power, and the glory,
   for ever and ever.
  Amen.

Intercessions

Thanks be to You, Jesus Christ
Who brought us up from last night,
To the gladsome light of this day,
To win everlasting life for our souls,
Through the blood You shed for us.

 Praise be to You, O God, for ever,
For the blessings You bestow on us –
Our food, Our speech, Our work, Our health.
 Praise be to You, O God, for ever.

From the Carmina gadelica

✠ In the Name of the Father,
  and of the Son,
  and of the Holy Spirit.
  Amen.

Morning Prayer

WEDNESDAY

✠ In the Name of the Father,
and of the Son,
and of the Holy Spirit.
Amen.

I arise today
Through a mighty strength:
> **God's power to guide me,**
> God's might to uphold me,
> **God's eyes to watch over me;**
> God's ear to hear me,
> **God's word to give me speech,**
> God's hand to guard me,
> **God's way to lie before me,**
> God's shield to shelter me,
> **God's host to secure me.**
>> *Bridgid of gael*, from Sandy Stevenson, *Gaelic Blessings*

The cup of blessing that we bless, is it not a participation in the blood of Christ?
The bread that we break, is it not a participation in the body of Christ?
Because the loaf of bread is one, we, though many, are one body, for we all partake of the one loaf.
Amen. Lord, we believe.
>> 1 Cor 10:16-17 NAB

How good it is, how pleasant,
where the people dwell as one!
Like precious ointment on the head, running down upon the beard,
Upon the beard of Aaron, upon the collar of his robe.
Like dew of Hermon coming down upon the mountains of Zion.
There the LORD has lavished blessings, life for evermore!
>> Psalm 133 NAB

Morning Prayer

Appointed Psalm

Glory be to the Father, and to the Son, and to the Holy Ghost;
As it was in the beginning, is now, and ever shall be, world without end. Amen.

Now this is the message that we have heard from him and proclaim to you:
God is light, and in him there is no darkness at all.
If we say, "We have fellowship with him," while we continue to walk in darkness,
we lie and do not act in truth.
But if we walk in the light as he is in the light, then we have fellowship with one another,
and the blood of his Son Jesus cleanses us from all sin.
See what love the Father has bestowed on us that we may be called the children of God.
Yet so we are.
For this is the message you have heard from the beginning:
we should love one another,
We know that we have passed from death to life
because we love our brothers.
The way we came to know love was that he laid down his life for us;
so we ought to lay down our lives for our brothers.
Beloved, let us love one another, because love is of God;
everyone who loves is begotten by God and knows God.
1 John 1:5-7; 3:1a,11,14a,16; 4:7 NAB

Readings
Meditation

Morning Prayer

The Lord be with you.
And with thy spirit.
Let us pray.

> Our Father, who art in heaven,
>   hallowed be thy Name,
>   thy kingdom come,
>   thy will be done,
>   on earth as it is in heaven.
>   Give us this day our daily bread.
>   And forgive us our trespasses,
>   as we forgive those
>   who trespass against us.
>   And lead us not into temptation,
>   but deliver us from evil.
>   For thine is the kingdom,
>   and the power, and the glory,
>   For ever and ever.
>   Amen.

Intercessions

Thanks be to You, Jesus Christ
Who brought us up from last night,
To the gladsome light of this day,
To win everlasting life for our souls,
Through the blood You shed for us.

Praise be to You, O God, for ever,
For the blessings You bestow on us –
Our food, our speech, our work, our health.
Praise be to You, O God, for ever,

From the Carmina gadelica

✠ In the Name of the Father,
   and of the Son,
   and of the Holy Spirit.
   Amen.

Morning Prayer

THURSDAY

✠ In the Name of the Father,
and of the Son,
and of the Holy Spirit.
Amen.

I arise today
Through a mighty strength:
> **God's power to guide me,**
> God's might to uphold me,
> **God's eyes to watch over me;**
> God's ear to hear me,
> **God's word to give me speech,**
> God's hand to guard me,
> **God's way to lie before me,**
> God's shield to shelter me,
> **God's host to secure me.**
>> *Bridgid of gael*, From Sandy Stevenson, *Gaelic Blessings*

Show us your steadfast love, O LORD,
and grant us your salvation.
Faithfulness will spring up from the ground,
and righteousness will look down from the sky.
The LORD will give what is good,
and our land will yield its increase.
Righteousness will go before him,
and will make a path for his steps.
Amen. Lord, we believe.
> Psalm 85:7,10-13 NRSV

Morning Prayer

May God be gracious to us and bless us;
may God's face shine upon us.
So shall your rule be known upon the earth,
your saving power among all the nations.
May the peoples praise you, God;
may all the peoples praise you!
May the nations be glad and shout for joy;
for you govern the peoples justly, you guide the nations upon the earth.
May the peoples praise you, God;
may all the peoples praise you!
The earth has yielded its harvest;
God, our God, blesses us.
May God bless us still;
that the ends of the earth may revere our God.
Psalm 67 NAB

Appointed Psalm

Glory be to the Father, and to the Son, and to the Holy Ghost;
As it was in the beginning, is now, and ever shall be, world without end. Amen.

"My soul proclaims the greatness of the Lord;
my spirit rejoices in God my savior.
For he has looked upon his handmaid's lowliness;
behold, from now on will all ages call me blessed.
The Mighty One has done great things for me, and holy is his name.
His mercy is from age to age to those who fear him.
He has shown might with his arm,
dispersed the arrogant of mind and heart.
He has thrown down the rulers from their thrones
but lifted up the lowly.
The hungry he has filled with good things;
the rich he has sent away empty.

Morning Prayer

He has helped Israel his servant, remembering his mercy,
according to his promise to our fathers, to Abraham and to his descendants forever."
Glory be to the Father, and to the Son, and to the Holy Ghost;
As it was in the beginning, is now, and ever shall be, world without end. Amen.

Luke 1:46-54 NAB

Readings
Meditation

The Lord be with you.
And with thy spirit.
Let us pray.

**Our Father, who art in heaven,
hallowed be thy Name,
thy kingdom come,
thy will be done,
 on earth as it is in heaven.
Give us this day our daily bread.
And forgive us our trespasses,
 as we forgive those
 who trespass against us.
And lead us not into temptation,
 but deliver us from evil.
For thine is the kingdom,
 and the power, and the glory,
for ever and ever.
Amen.**

Morning Prayer

Intercessions

Thanks be to You, Jesus Christ
Who brought us up from last night,
To the gladsome light of this day,
To win everlasting life for our souls,
Through the blood You shed for us.

Praise be to You, O God, for ever,
For the blessings You bestow on us –
Our food, Our speech, Our work, Our health.
Praise be to You, O God, for ever,

From the Carmina gadelica

✠ In the Name of the Father,
   and of the Son,
   and of the Holy Spirit.
   Amen.

Morning Prayer

FRIDAY

✠ In the Name of the Father,
and of the Son,
and of the Holy Spirit.
Amen.

I arise today
Through a mighty strength:
    God's power to guide me,
    God's might to uphold me,
    God's eyes to watch over me;
    God's ear to hear me,
    God's word to give me speech,
    God's hand to guard me,
    God's way to lie before me,
    God's shield to shelter me,
    God's host to secure me.
        Bridgid of gael, From Sandy Stevenson, *Gaelic Blessings*

He himself bore our sins in his body upon the cross,
so that, free from sin, we might live for
righteousness. By his wounds you have been healed.
Amen. Lord, we believe.
        1 Peter 2:24 NAB

Bless the LORD, my soul;
all my being, bless his holy name!
Bless the LORD, my soul;
do not forget all the gifts of God,
Who pardons all your sins,
heals all your ills,
Delivers your life from the pit,
surrounds you with love and compassion,
Fills your days with good things;
your youth is renewed like the eagle's.
        Psalm 103:1-5 NAB

Morning Prayer

Appointed Psalm

Glory be to the Father, and to the Son, and to the Holy Ghost;
As it was in the beginning, is now, and ever shall be, world without end. Amen.

Build up, build up, prepare the way,
remove the stumbling blocks from my people's path.
For thus says he who is high and exalted, living eternally, whose name is the Holy One:
On high I dwell, and in holiness, and with the crushed and dejected in spirit, To revive the spirits of the dejected, to revive the hearts of the crushed.
I will not accuse forever, nor always be angry;
For their spirits would faint before me, the souls that I have made.
Because of their wicked avarice I was angry, and struck them,
hiding myself in wrath, as they went their own rebellious way.
I saw their ways, but I will heal them and lead them;
I will give full comfort to them and to those who mourn for them, I, the Creator, who gave them life.
Peace, peace to the far and the near, says the LORD; and I will heal them.

Isaiah 57:14-19 NAB

Readings
Meditation

The Lord be with you.
And with thy spirit.
Let us pray.

Morning Prayer

Our Father, who art in heaven,
  hallowed be thy Name,
  thy kingdom come,
  thy will be done,
    on earth as it is in heaven.
Give us this day our daily bread.
And forgive us our trespasses,
  as we forgive those
  who trespass against us.
And lead us not into temptation,
  but deliver us from evil.
For thine is the kingdom,
  and the power, and the glory,
for ever and ever.
Amen.

Intercessions

Thanks be to You, Jesus Christ
Who brought us up from last night,
To the gladsome light of this day,
To win everlasting life for our souls,
Through the blood You shed for us.

Praise be to You, O God, for ever,
For the blessings You bestow on us –
Our food, Our speech, Our work, Our health.
Praise be to You, O God, for ever,

from the Carmina gadelica

✠ In the Name of the Father,
   and of the Son,
   and of the Holy Spirit.
  Amen.

Morning Prayer

SATURDAY

✠ In the Name of the Father,
and of the Son,
and of the Holy Spirit.
Amen.

I arise today
Through a mighty strength:
> **God's power to guide me,**
> God's might to uphold me,
> **God's eyes to watch over me;**
> God's ear to hear me,
> **God's word to give me speech,**
> God's hand to guard me,
> **God's way to lie before me,**
> God's shield to shelter me,
> **God's host to secure me.**

Bridgid of gael, From Sandy Stevenson, *Gaelic Blessings*

There is one body and one Spirit,
just as you were called in one hope of your calling;
one Lord, one faith, one baptism;
one God and Father of all,
who is above all, and through all, and in you all.
Amen. Lord, we believe.

Eph 4:4-6 NKJV

Make a joyful shout to the LORD, all you lands!
Serve the LORD with gladness;
Come before His presence with singing.
Know that the LORD, He is God;
It is He who has made us, and not we ourselves;

Morning Prayer

We are His people and the sheep of His pasture.
Enter into His gates with thanksgiving,
And into His courts with praise.
Be thankful to Him, and bless His name.
For the LORD is good;
His mercy is everlasting,
And His truth endures to all generations.
Ps 100 NKJV

Appointed Psalm

Glory be to the Father, and to the Son, and to the Holy Ghost;
As it was in the beginning, is now, and ever shall be, world without end. Amen.

Blessed be the Lord, the God of Israel,
for he has visited and brought redemption to his people.
He has raised up a horn for our salvation
within the house of David his servant,
 even as he promised through the mouth of his holy prophets from of old:
salvation from our enemies and from the hand of all who hate us,
to show mercy to our fathers and to be mindful of his holy covenant
and of the oath he swore to Abraham our father, and to grant us that,
rescued from the hand of enemies, without fear we might worship him
in holiness and righteousness before him all our days.
And you, child, will be called prophet of the Most High, for you will go before the Lord to prepare his ways,
to give his people knowledge of salvation through the forgiveness of their sins,

Morning Prayer

because of the tender mercy of our God by which the
daybreak from on high will visit us
to shine on those who sit in darkness and death's
shadow, to guide our feet into the path of peace."
Glory be to the Father, and to the Son, and to the
Holy Ghost;
As it was in the beginning, is now, and ever shall be,
world without end. Amen.

Luke 1:68-79 NAB

Readings
Meditation

The Lord be with you.
And with thy spirit.
Let us pray.

> Our Father, who art in heaven,
> hallowed be thy Name,
> thy kingdom come,
> thy will be done,
>   on earth as it is in heaven.
> Give us this day our daily bread.
> And forgive us our trespasses,
>   as we forgive those
>   who trespass against us.
> And lead us not into temptation,
>   but deliver us from evil.
> For thine is the kingdom,
>   and the power, and the glory,
>   for ever and ever.
> Amen.

Intercessions

Morning Prayer

Thanks be to You, Jesus Christ
Who brought us up from last night,
To the gladsome light of this day,
To win everlasting life for our souls,
Through the blood You shed for us.

**Praise be to You, O God, for ever,
For the blessings You bestow on us –
Our food, Our speech, Our work, Our health.
Praise be to You, O God, for ever,**
From the Carmina gadelica

✠ In the Name of the Father,
  and of the Son,
  and of the Holy Spirit.
  Amen.

Evening Prayer
SUNDAY

✠ In the Name of the Father,
and of the Son,
and of the Holy Spirit.
Amen.

My soul thirst for God, the living God
When shall I come and appear before God?

In the night His song shall be with me,
A prayer to the God of my life.
Psalm 42:3,8 NKJV

O Gladsome Light

O gladsome light, O grace of our Creator's face,
The eternal splendor wearing; celestial, holy blessed,
Our Savior Jesus Christ, joyful in Your appearing!

As fades the day's last light we see the lamps of night,
Our common hymn outpouring, O God of might unknown,
You, the incarnate Son, and Spirit blessed adoring.

To You of right belongs all praise of holy songs,
O Son of God, life giver. You, therefore, O Most High,
The world does glorify and shall exalt forever.

Evening Prayer

"Great and wonderful are your works,
Lord God almighty.
Just and true are your ways,
O king of the nations.
Who will not fear you, Lord,
or glorify your name?
For you alone are holy.
All the nations will come and worship before you,
for your righteous acts have been revealed."

Rev 15:3b-4 NAB

Appointed Psalm

"My soul proclaims the greatness of the Lord;
my spirit rejoices in God my savior.
For he has looked upon his handmaid's lowliness; behold,
from now on will all ages call me blessed.
The Mighty One has done great things for me, and
holy is his name.
His mercy is from age to age to those who fear him.
He has shown might with his arm, dispersed the
arrogant of mind and heart.
He has thrown down the rulers from their thrones but
lifted up the lowly.
The hungry he has filled with good things; the rich he
has sent away empty.
He has helped Israel his servant, remembering his
mercy,
according to his promise to our fathers, to Abraham
and to his descendants forever."
Glory be to the Father, and to the Son, and to the
Holy Ghost;
As it was in the beginning, is now, and ever shall be,
world without end. Amen.

Luke 1:46-54 NAB

Evening Prayer

Readings
Meditation

I am bending my knee
In the eye of the Father who created me,
In the eye of the Son who purchased me,
In the eye of the Spirit who cleansed me,
In friendship and affection.
Through Thine own Anointed One, O God,
Bestow upon us fullness in our need,
Love towards God,
The affection of God,
The smile of God,
The wisdom of God.
The grace of God,
The fear of God,
And the will of God
To do on the world of the Three,
As angels and saints
Do in heaven;
Each shade and light,
Each day and night,
Each time in kindness,
Give Thou us Thy Spirit.

Rune Before Prayer, From the Carmina Gadelica

The Lord be with you.
And with thy spirit.
Let us pray.

Evening Prayer

Our Father, who art in heaven,
hallowed be thy Name,
thy kingdom come,
thy will be done,
　on earth as it is in heaven.
Give us this day our daily bread.
And forgive us our trespasses,
as we forgive those
who trespass against us.
And lead us not into temptation,
but deliver us from evil.
For thine is the kingdom,
and the power, and the glory,
for ever and ever.
Amen.

Intercessions

"Now, Master, you may let your servant go in peace, according to your word,
for my eyes have seen your salvation,
which you prepared in sight of all the peoples,
a light for revelation to the Gentiles, and glory for your people Israel."
Glory be to the Father, and to the Son, and to the Holy Ghost;
As it was in the beginning, is now, and ever shall be, world without end. Amen.

Luke 2:29-32 NAB

Thanks be to you, Lord Christ.
You have given us this day,
And brought us safely to this night.
We place our lives into your hands:
All that we are and hope to be.
Walk with us through the deep of night
And keep us safe.
Amen.

Evening Prayer

Heavenly Father,
You give fire in the night,
And light in the darkness,
Visit us this night.
Grant us rest
And guide us to your peace,
Through Jesus Christ our Lord. Amen.

✠ In the Name of the Father,
  and of the Son,
  and of the Holy Spirit.
  Amen.

Evening Prayer

MONDAY

✠ In the Name of the Father,
and of the Son,
and of the Holy Spirit.
Amen.

My soul thirst for God, the living God
When shall I come and appear before God?

In the night His song shall be with me,
A prayer to the God of my life.
                                      Psalm 42:3,8 NKJV

<u>O Gladsome Light</u>

O gladsome light, O grace of our Creator's face,
The eternal splendor wearing; celestial, holy blessed,
Our Savior Jesus Christ, joyful in Your appearing!

As fades the day's last light we see the lamps of night,
Our common hymn outpouring, O God of might unknown,
You, the incarnate Son, and Spirit blessed adoring.

To You of right belongs all praise of holy songs,
O Son of God, life giver. You, therefore, O Most High,
The world does glorify and shall exalt forever.

Evening Prayer

Blessed are those who dwell in your house;
> they are ever praising you.

Blessed are those whose strength is in you,
> who have set their hearts on pilgrimage.

Hear my prayer, O LORD God Almighty;
> listen to me, O God of Jacob.

Ps 84:4-5,8 NIV

Appointed Psalm

"My soul proclaims the greatness of the Lord;
my spirit rejoices in God my savior.
For he has looked upon his handmaid's lowliness; behold, from now on will all ages call me blessed.
The Mighty One has done great things for me, and holy is his name.
His mercy is from age to age to those who fear him.
He has shown might with his arm, dispersed the arrogant of mind and heart.
He has thrown down the rulers from their thrones but lifted up the lowly.
The hungry he has filled with good things; the rich he has sent away empty.
He has helped Israel his servant, remembering his mercy,
according to his promise to our fathers, to Abraham and to his descendants forever."
Glory be to the Father, and to the Son, and to the Holy Ghost;
As it was in the beginning, is now, and ever shall be, world without end. Amen.

Luke 1:46-54 NAB

Evening Prayer

Readings
Meditation

I am bending my knee
In the eye of the Father who created me,
In the eye of the Son who purchased me,
In the eye of the Spirit who cleansed me,
In friendship and affection.
Through Thine own Anointed One, O God,
Bestow upon us fullness in our need,
Love towards God,
The affection of God,
The smile of God,
The wisdom of God.
The grace of God,
The fear of God,
And the will of God
To do on the world of the Three,
As angels and saints
Do in heaven;
Each shade and light,
Each day and night,
Each time in kindness,
Give Thou us Thy Spirit.
    Rune Before Prayer, From the Carmina Gadelica

The Lord be with you.
And with thy spirit.
Let us pray.

Our Father, who art in heaven,
hallowed be thy Name,
thy kingdom come,
thy will be done,
  on earth as it is in heaven.

Evening Prayer

Give us this day our daily bread.
And forgive us our trespasses,
 as we forgive those
 who trespass against us.
And lead us not into temptation,
 but deliver us from evil.
For thine is the kingdom,
 and the power, and the glory,
 for ever and ever.
 Amen.

Intercessions

"Now, Master, you may let your servant go in peace, according to your word,
For my eyes have seen your salvation,
which you prepared in sight of all the peoples,
a light for revelation to the Gentiles, and glory for your people Israel."
Glory be to the Father, and to the Son, and to the Holy Ghost;
As it was in the beginning, is now, and ever shall be, world without end. Amen.

Luke 2:29-32 NAB

Thanks be to you, Lord Christ.
You have given us this day,
And brought us safely to this night.
We place our lives into your hands:
All that we are and hope to be.
Walk with us through the deep of night
And keep us safe.
Amen.

Evening Prayer

Heavenly Father,
You give fire in the night,
And light in the darkness,
Visit us this night.
Grant us rest
And guide us to your peace,
Through Jesus Christ our Lord. Amen.

✠ In the Name of the Father,
and of the Son,
and of the Holy Spirit.
Amen.

Evening Prayer

TUESDAY

✠ In the Name of the Father,
and of the Son,
and of the Holy Spirit.
Amen.

My soul thirst for God, the living God
When shall I come and appear before God?

In the night His song shall be with me,
A prayer to the God of my life.

Psalm 42:3,8 NKJV

O Gladsome Light

O gladsome light, O grace of our Creator's face,
The eternal splendor wearing; celestial, holy blessed,
Our Savior Jesus Christ, joyful in Your appearing!

As fades the day's last light we see the lamps of night,
Our common hymn outpouring, O God of might unknown,
You, the incarnate Son, and Spirit blessed adoring.

To You of right belongs all praise of holy songs,
O Son of God, life giver. You, therefore, O Most High,
The world does glorify and shall exalt forever.

I WILL lift up mine eyes unto the hills;
From whence cometh my help?
My help cometh even from the LORD,
who hath made heaven and earth.
He will not suffer thy foot to be moved;
and he that keepeth thee will not sleep.
Behold, he that keepeth Israel
shall neither slumber nor sleep.

Evening Prayer

The LORD himself is thy keeper;
the LORD is thy defence upon thy right hand;
So that the sun shall not burn thee by day,
neither the moon by night.
The LORD shall preserve thee from all evil;
yea, it is even he that shall keep thy soul.
The LORD shall preserve thy going out, and thy coming in,
from this time forth for evermore.

Ps 121; 1928 BCP Psalter

Appointed Psalm

"My soul proclaims the greatness of the Lord;
my spirit rejoices in God my savior.
For he has looked upon his handmaid's lowliness; behold, from now on will all ages call me blessed.
The Mighty One has done great things for me, and holy is his name.
His mercy is from age to age to those who fear him.
He has shown might with his arm, dispersed the arrogant of mind and heart.
He has thrown down the rulers from their thrones but lifted up the lowly.
The hungry he has filled with good things; the rich he has sent away empty.
He has helped Israel his servant, remembering his mercy,
according to his promise to our fathers, to Abraham and to his descendants forever."
Glory be to the Father, and to the Son, and to the Holy Ghost;
As it was in the beginning, is now, and ever shall be, world without end. Amen.

Luke 1:46-54 NAB

Readings
Meditation

Evening Prayer

I am bending my knee
In the eye of the Father who created me,
In the eye of the Son who purchased me,
In the eye of the Spirit who cleansed me,
In friendship and affection.
Through Thine own Anointed One, O God,
Bestow upon us fullness in our need,
Love towards God,
The affection of God,
The smile of God,
The wisdom of God.
The grace of God,
The fear of God,
And the will of God
To do on the world of the Three,
As angels and saints
Do in heaven;
Each shade and light,
Each day and night,
Each time in kindness,
Give Thou us Thy Spirit.

Rune Before Prayer, From the Carmina Gadelica

The Lord be with you.
And with thy spirit.
Let us pray.

Our Father, who art in heaven,
  hallowed be thy Name,
  thy kingdom come,
  thy will be done,
    on earth as it is in heaven.

Evening Prayer

Give us this day our daily bread.
And forgive us our trespasses,
 as we forgive those
 who trespass against us.
And lead us not into temptation,
 but deliver us from evil.
For thine is the kingdom,
 and the power, and the glory,
For ever and ever.
Amen.

Intercessions

"Now, Master, you may let your servant go in peace,
according to your word,
For my eyes have seen your salvation,
which you prepared in sight of all the peoples,
a light for revelation to the Gentiles, and glory for
your people Israel."
Glory be to the Father, and to the Son, and to the
Holy Ghost;
As it was in the beginning, is now, and ever shall be,
world without end. Amen.

Luke 2:29-32 NAB

Thanks be to you, Lord Christ.
You have given us this day,
And brought us safely to this night.
We place our lives into your hands:
All that we are and hope to be.
Walk with us through the deep of night
And keep us safe.
Amen.

Evening Prayer

Heavenly Father,
You give fire in the night,
And light in the darkness,
Visit us this night.
Grant us rest
And guide us to your peace,
Through Jesus Christ our Lord. Amen.

✠ In the Name of the Father,
and of the Son,
and of the Holy Spirit.
Amen.

Evening Prayer

WEDNESDAY

✠ In the Name of the Father,
and of the Son,
and of the Holy Spirit.
Amen.

My soul thirst for God, the living God
When shall I come and appear before God?

In the night His song shall be with me,
A prayer to the God of my life.

Psalm 42:3,8 NKJV

<u>O Gladsome Light</u>

O gladsome light, O grace of our Creator's face,
The eternal splendor wearing; celestial, holy blessed,
Our Savior Jesus Christ, joyful in Your appearing!

As fades the day's last light we see the lamps of night,
Our common hymn outpouring, O God of might unknown,
You, the incarnate Son, and Spirit blessed adoring.

To You of right belongs all praise of holy songs,
O Son of God, life giver. You, therefore, O Most High,
The world does glorify and shall exalt forever.

Let love be sincere;
hate what is evil, hold on to what is good;
love one another with mutual affection;
anticipate one another in showing honor.
Do not grow slack in zeal, be fervent in spirit,
serve the Lord.

Evening Prayer

Rejoice in hope, endure in affliction,
persevere in prayer.
Contribute to the needs of the holy ones,
exercise hospitality.
Bless those who persecute (you),
bless and do not curse them.
Rejoice with those who rejoice,
weep with those who weep.
Have the same regard for one another;
do not be haughty but associate with the lowly; do not be wise in your own estimation.
Do not repay anyone evil for evil;
be concerned for what is noble in the sight of all.
If possible, on your part,
live at peace with all.
Do not be conquered by evil
but conquer evil with good.

Romans 12:9-18,21 NAB

Appointed Psalm

"My soul proclaims the greatness of the Lord;
my spirit rejoices in God my savior.
For he has looked upon his handmaid's lowliness; behold, from now on will all ages call me blessed.
The Mighty One has done great things for me, and holy is his name.
His mercy is from age to age to those who fear him.
He has shown might with his arm, dispersed the arrogant of mind and heart.
He has thrown down the rulers from their thrones but lifted up the lowly.
The hungry he has filled with good things; the rich he has sent away empty.
He has helped Israel his servant, remembering his mercy,
according to his promise to our fathers, to Abraham and to his descendants forever."

Evening Prayer

Glory be to the Father, and to the Son, and to the Holy Ghost;
As it was in the beginning, is now, and ever shall be, world without end. Amen.

Luke 1:46-54 NAB

Readings
Meditation

I am bending my knee
In the eye of the Father who created me,
In the eye of the Son who purchased me,
In the eye of the Spirit who cleansed me,
In friendship and affection.
Through Thine own Anointed One, O God,
Bestow upon us fullness in our need,
Love towards God,
The affection of God,
The smile of God,
The wisdom of God.
The grace of God,
The fear of God,
And the will of God
To do on the world of the Three,
As angels and saints
Do in heaven;
Each shade and light,
Each day and night,
Each time in kindness,
Give Thou us Thy Spirit.

Rune Before Prayer, From the Carmina Gadelica

The Lord be with you.
And with thy spirit.
Let us pray.

Evening Prayer

Our Father, who art in heaven,
hallowed be thy Name,
thy kingdom come,
thy will be done,
  on earth as it is in heaven.
Give us this day our daily bread.
And forgive us our trespasses,
  as we forgive those
  who trespass against us.
And lead us not into temptation,
  but deliver us from evil.
For thine is the kingdom,
  and the power, and the glory,
For ever and ever.
Amen.

Intercessions

"Now, Master, you may let your servant go in peace,
according to your word,
for my eyes have seen your salvation,
which you prepared in sight of all the peoples,
a light for revelation to the Gentiles, and glory for
your people Israel."
Glory be to the Father, and to the Son, and to the
Holy Ghost;
As it was in the beginning, is now, and ever shall be,
world without end. Amen.

Luke 2:29-32 NAB

Thanks be to you, Lord Christ.
You have given us this day,
And brought us safely to this night.
We place our lives into your hands:
All that we are and hope to be.
Walk with us through the deep of night
And keep us safe.
Amen.

Evening Prayer

Heavenly Father,
You give fire in the night,
And light in the darkness,
Visit us this night.
Grant us rest
And guide us to your peace,
Through Jesus Christ our Lord. Amen.

✠ In the Name of the Father,
and of the Son,
and of the Holy Spirit.
Amen.

Evening Prayer

THURSDAY

✠ In the Name of the Father,
and of the Son,
and of the Holy Spirit.
Amen.

My soul thirst for God, the living God
When shall I come and appear before God?

In the night His song shall be with me,
A prayer to the God of my life.

Psalm 42:3,8 NKJV

O Gladsome Light

O gladsome light, O grace of our Creator's face,
The eternal splendor wearing; celestial, holy blessed,
Our Savior Jesus Christ, joyful in Your appearing!

As fades the day's last light we see the lamps of night,
Our common hymn outpouring, O God of might unknown,
You, the incarnate Son, and Spirit blessed adoring.

To You of right belongs all praise of holy songs,
O Son of God, life giver. You, therefore, O Most High,
The world does glorify and shall exalt forever.

Happy are they whom you choose and draw to your courts to dwell there!
they will be satisfied by the beauty of your house,
by the holiness of your temple.

Evening Prayer

Awesome things will you show us in your righteousness,
O God of our salvation, *
O Hope of all the ends of the earth
and of the seas that are far away.
You make fast the mountains by your power; *
they are girded about with might.
You still the roaring of the seas,
the roaring of their waves,
and the clamor of the peoples..
Those who dwell at the ends of the earth will
 tremble
at your marvelous signs;
you make the dawn and the dusk to sing for joy.
You visit the earth and water it abundantly;
you make it very plenteous;
the river of God is full of water.
You prepare the grain,
for so you provide for the earth.
You drench the furrows and smooth out the ridges;
with heavy rain you soften the ground and bless its increase.
You crown the year with your goodness,
and your paths overflow with plenty.
May the fields of the wilderness be rich for grazing,
and the hills be clothed with joy.
May the meadows cover themselves with flocks, and the valleys cloak themselves with grain;
let them shout for joy and sing.

Psalm 65:4-14 , The Psalter BCP

Appointed Psalm

Evening Prayer

"My soul proclaims the greatness of the Lord;
my spirit rejoices in God my savior.
For he has looked upon his handmaid's lowliness; behold,
from now on will all ages call me blessed.
The Mighty One has done great things for me, and
holy is his name.
His mercy is from age to age to those who fear him.
He has shown might with his arm, dispersed the
arrogant of mind and heart.
He has thrown down the rulers from their thrones but
lifted up the lowly.
The hungry he has filled with good things; the rich he
has sent away empty.
He has helped Israel his servant, remembering his
mercy,
according to his promise to our fathers, to Abraham
and to his descendants forever."
Glory be to the Father, and to the Son, and to the
Holy Ghost;
As it was in the beginning, is now, and ever shall be,
world without end. Amen.

Luke 1:46-54 NAB

Readings
Meditation

I am bending my knee
In the eye of the Father who created me,
In the eye of the Son who purchased me,
In the eye of the Spirit who cleansed me,
In friendship and affection.
Through Thine own Anointed One, O God,
Bestow upon us fullness in our need,
Love towards God,
The affection of God,
The smile of God,
The wisdom of God.

Evening Prayer

The grace of God,
The fear of God,
And the will of God
To do on the world of the Three,
As angels and saints
Do in heaven;
Each shade and light,
Each day and night,
Each time in kindness,
Give Thou us Thy Spirit.

Rune Before Prayer, From the Carmina Gadelica

The Lord be with you.
And with thy spirit.
Let us pray.

Our Father, who art in heaven,
 hallowed be thy Name,
 thy kingdom come,
 thy will be done,
  on earth as it is in heaven.
Give us this day our daily bread.
And forgive us our trespasses,
 as we forgive those
 who trespass against us.
And lead us not into temptation,
 but deliver us from evil.
For thine is the kingdom,
 and the power, and the glory,
 for ever and ever.
 Amen.

Intercessions

Evening Prayer

"Now, Master, you may let your servant go in peace,
according to your word,
For my eyes have seen your salvation,
which you prepared in sight of all the peoples,
a light for revelation to the Gentiles, and glory for
your people Israel."
Glory be to the Father, and to the Son, and to the
Holy Ghost;
As it was in the beginning, is now, and ever shall be,
world without end. Amen.
Luke 2:29-32 NAB

Thanks be to you, Lord Christ.
You have given us this day,
And brought us safely to this night.
We place our lives into your hands:
All that we are and hope to be.
Walk with us through the deep of night
And keep us safe.
Amen.

Heavenly Father,
You give fire in the night,
And light in the darkness,
Visit us this night.
Grant us rest
And guide us to your peace,
Through Jesus Christ our Lord. Amen.

✠ In the Name of the Father,
  and of the Son,
  and of the Holy Spirit.
  Amen.

Evening Prayer

FRIDAY

✠ In the Name of the Father,
and of the Son,
and of the Holy Spirit.
Amen.

My soul thirst for God, the living God
When shall I come and appear before God?

In the night His song shall be with me,
A prayer to the God of my life.
Psalm 42:3,8 NKJV

O Gladsome Light

O gladsome light, O grace of our Creator's face,
The eternal splendor wearing; celestial, holy blessed,
Our Savior Jesus Christ, joyful in Your appearing!

As fades the day's last light we see the lamps of night,
Our common hymn outpouring, O God of might unknown,
You, the incarnate Son, and Spirit blessed adoring.

To You of right belongs all praise of holy songs,
O Son of God, life giver. You, therefore, O Most High,
The world does glorify and shall exalt forever.

I praise you, LORD,
For you raised me up and did not let my enemies rejoice over me.
O LORD, my God, I cried out to you and you healed me.

Evening Prayer

LORD, you brought me up from Sheol;
you kept me from going down to the pit.
Sing praise to the LORD, you faithful;
give thanks to God's holy name.
For divine anger lasts but a moment;
divine favor lasts a lifetime.
At dusk weeping comes for the night;
but at dawn there is rejoicing.
You changed my mourning into dancing;
you took off my sackcloth and clothed me with gladness.
With my whole being I sing endless praise to you.
O LORD, my God, forever will I give you thanks.

Psalm 30: 1- 7,12-13   NAB

Appointed Psalm

"My soul proclaims the greatness of the Lord;
my spirit rejoices in God my savior.
For he has looked upon his handmaid's lowliness; behold, from now on will all ages call me blessed.
The Mighty One has done great things for me, and holy is his name.
His mercy is from age to age to those who fear him.
He has shown might with his arm, dispersed the arrogant of mind and heart.
He has thrown down the rulers from their thrones but lifted up the lowly.
The hungry he has filled with good things; the rich he has sent away empty.
He has helped Israel his servant, remembering his mercy,
according to his promise to our fathers, to Abraham and to his descendants forever."
Glory be to the Father, and to the Son, and to the Holy Ghost;
As it was in the beginning, is now, and ever shall be, world without end. Amen.

Luke 1:46-54 NAB

Evening Prayer

Readings
Meditation

I am bending my knee
In the eye of the Father who created me,
In the eye of the Son who purchased me,
In the eye of the Spirit who cleansed me,
In friendship and affection.
Through Thine own Anointed One, O God,
Bestow upon us fullness in our need,
Love towards God,
The affection of God,
The smile of God,
The wisdom of God.
The grace of God,
The fear of God,
And the will of God
To do on the world of the Three,
As angels and saints
Do in heaven;
Each shade and light,
Each day and night,
Each time in kindness,
Give Thou us Thy Spirit.

      Rune Before Prayer, From the Carmina Gadelica

The Lord be with you.
And with thy spirit.
Let us pray.

Evening Prayer

Our Father, who art in heaven,
 hallowed be thy Name,
 thy kingdom come,
 thy will be done,
   on earth as it is in heaven.
Give us this day our daily bread.
And forgive us our trespasses,
 as we forgive those
 who trespass against us.
And lead us not into temptation,
 but deliver us from evil.
For thine is the kingdom,
 and the power, and the glory,
 for ever and ever.
 Amen.

Intercessions

"Now, Master, you may let your servant go in peace, according to your word,
for my eyes have seen your salvation,
which you prepared in sight of all the peoples,
a light for revelation to the Gentiles, and glory for your people Israel."
Glory be to the Father, and to the Son, and to the Holy Ghost;
As it was in the beginning, is now, and ever shall be, world without end. Amen.

Luke 2:29-32 NAB

Thanks be to you, Lord Christ.
You have given us this day,
And brought us safely to this night.
We place our lives into your hands:
All that we are and hope to be.
Walk with us through the deep of night
And keep us safe.
Amen.

Evening Prayer

Heavenly Father,
You give fire in the night,
And light in the darkness,
Visit us this night.
Grant us rest
And guide us to your peace,
Through Jesus Christ our Lord. Amen.

✠ In the Name of the Father,
and of the Son,
and of the Holy Spirit.
Amen.

Evening Prayer

SATURDAY

✠ In the Name of the Father,
and of the Son,
and of the Holy Spirit.
Amen.

My soul thirst for God, the living God
When shall I come and appear before God?

In the night His song shall be with me,
A prayer to the God of my life.
Psalm 42:3,8 NKJV

O Gladsome Light

O gladsome light, O grace of our Creator's face,
The eternal splendor wearing; celestial, holy blessed,
Our Savior Jesus Christ, joyful in Your appearing!

As fades the day's last light we see the lamps of night,
Our common hymn outpouring, O God of might unknown,
You, the incarnate Son, and Spirit blessed adoring.

To You of right belongs all praise of holy songs,
O Son of God, life giver. You, therefore, O Most High,
The world does glorify and shall exalt forever.

Put on then, as God's chosen ones, holy and beloved, heartfelt compassion, kindness, humility, gentleness, and patience,
bearing with one another and forgiving one another, if one has a grievance against another; as the Lord has forgiven you, so must you also do.

Evening Prayer

And over all these put on love, that is, the bond of perfection.
And let the peace of Christ control your hearts, the peace into which you were also called in one body. And be thankful.
Let the word of Christ dwell in you richly, as in all wisdom you teach and admonish one another, singing psalms, hymns, and spiritual songs with gratitude in your hearts to God.
And whatever you do, in word or in deed, do everything in the name of the Lord Jesus, giving thanks to God the Father through him.

Col 3: 12-17 NAB

Appointed Psalm

"My soul proclaims the greatness of the Lord;
my spirit rejoices in God my savior.
For he has looked upon his handmaid's lowliness; behold, from now on will all ages call me blessed.
The Mighty One has done great things for me, and holy is his name.
His mercy is from age to age to those who fear him.
He has shown might with his arm, dispersed the arrogant of mind and heart.
He has thrown down the rulers from their thrones but lifted up the lowly.
The hungry he has filled with good things; the rich he has sent away empty.
He has helped Israel his servant, remembering his mercy,
according to his promise to our fathers, to Abraham and to his descendants forever."
Glory be to the Father, and to the Son, and to the Holy Ghost;
As it was in the beginning, is now, and ever shall be, world without end. Amen.

Luke 1:46-54 NAB

Evening Prayer

Readings
Meditation

I am bending my knee
In the eye of the Father who created me,
In the eye of the Son who purchased me,
In the eye of the Spirit who cleansed me,
In friendship and affection.
Through Thine own Anointed One, O God,
Bestow upon us fullness in our need,
Love towards God,
The affection of God,
The smile of God,
The wisdom of God.
The grace of God,
The fear of God,
And the will of God
To do on the world of the Three,
As angels and saints
Do in heaven;
Each shade and light,
Each day and night,
Each time in kindness,
Give Thou us Thy Spirit.

Rune Before Prayer, From the Carmina Gadelica

The Lord be with you.
And with thy spirit.
Let us pray.

Evening Prayer

Our Father, who art in heaven,
hallowed be thy Name,
thy kingdom come,
thy will be done,
 on earth as it is in heaven.
Give us this day our daily bread.
And forgive us our trespasses,
 as we forgive those
 who trespass against us.
And lead us not into temptation,
 but deliver us from evil.
For thine is the kingdom,
 and the power, and the glory,
 for ever and ever.
 Amen.

Intercessions

"Now, Master, you may let your servant go in peace, according to your word,
for my eyes have seen your salvation,
which you prepared in sight of all the peoples,
a light for revelation to the Gentiles, and glory for your people Israel."
Glory be to the Father, and to the Son, and to the Holy Ghost;
As it was in the beginning, is now, and ever shall be, world without end. Amen.

Luke 2:29-32 NAB

Thanks be to you, Lord Christ.
You have given us this day,
And brought us safely to this night.
We place our lives into your hands:
All that we are and hope to be.
Walk with us through the deep of night
And keep us safe.
Amen.

Evening Prayer

Heavenly Father,
You give fire in the night,
And light in the darkness,
Visit us this night.
Grant us rest
And guide us to your peace,
Through Jesus Christ our Lord. Amen.

✠ In the Name of the Father,
and of the Son,
and of the Holy Spirit.
Amen.

The Psalter

The Psalter

The Saint Cuthbert Psalter is taken from the Douay-Rheims Version of the Bible, the numbering of which differs slightly from the Hebrew (Masoretic) Text with which many are more familiar. The **bold** numbers refer to the numbering in our Psalter. For reference, the numbers in parenthesis are the corresponding psalm numbers according to the Hebrew Text. Where only the **bold** number appears, the numbering is in agreement.

The antiphons regularly appointed for the praying of the Psalter precede each psalm. A separate antiphon is included for each portion of Psalm 118 **(119)**.
Other antiphons may be prescribed by competent authority for feasts, solemnities, and other particular occasions.

The table on the following page outlines the appointed psalms for each day of the month

The Psalter

Day	Morning Prayer	Evening Prayer
1	1,2,3	4,5,6
2	7,8	9 (9,10), 10 (11)
3	11(12), 12(13), 13(14)	14(15), 15(16), 16(17)
4	17(18)	18(19), 19(20), 20(21)
5	21(22), 22(23)	23(24), 24(25), 25(26)
6	26(27), 27(28), 28(29)	29(30), 30(31)
7	31(32), 32(33)	33(34), 34(35)
8	35(36), 36(37)	37(38), 38(39), 39(40)
9	40(41), 41(42), 42(43)	43(44), 44(45), 45(46)
10	46(47), 47(48), 48(49)	49(50), 50(51), 51(52)
11	52(53), 53(54), 54(55)	55(56), 56(57), 57(58)
12	58(59), 59(60), 60(61)	61(62), 62(63), 63(64), 64(65)
13	65(66), 66(67)	67(68), 68(69)
14	69(70), 70(71), 71(72)	72(73), 73(74)
15	74(75), 75(76)	76(77), 77(78)
16	78(79), 79(80)	80(81), 81(82), 82(83), 83(84)
17	84(85), 85(86), 86(87)	87(88), 88(89)
18	89(90), 90(91)	91(92), 92(93), 93(94)
19	94(95), 95(96)	96(97), 97(98), 98(99)
20	99(100), 100(101)	101(102), 102(103)
21	103(104), 104(105)	105(106), 106(107)
22	107(108), 108(109), 109(110)	110(111), 111(112), 112(113)
23	113(114-115), 114(116a), 115(116b)	116(117), 117(118), 118(119) vs 1-16
24	118(119) vs 17-32, & vs 33-48	118(119) vs 49-64, vs 65-80, & vs 81-96
25	118(119) vs 97-112, & vs 113-128	118(119) vs 129-152, & vs 153-176
26	119(120), 120(121), 121(122)	122(123), 123(124), 124(125), 125(126)
27	126(127), 127(128), 128(129), 129(130)	130(131), 131(132), 132(133), 133(134)
28	134(135), 135(136)	136(137), 137(138), 138(139)
29	139(140), 140(141), 141(142)	142(143), 143(144), 144(145)
30	145(146), 146(147a), 147(147b)	148, 149, 150
31	5, 8, 62(63)	15(16), 76(77), 111(112)

The Psalter

Day 1 - Morning Prayer

Psalm 1
Beatus vir

Antiphon:
He shall be as a tree that is planted by the waters,
    that spreadeth out its roots towards moisture;
and it shall not fear when the heat cometh. *(Jer 17:8)*

1 Blessed is the man
    who hath not walked in the counsel of the ungodly,
nor stood in the way of sinners,
    nor sat in the chair of pestilence.
2 But his will is in the law of the Lord,
and on his law he shall meditate day and night.
3 And he shall be like a tree
    which is planted near the running waters,
    which shall bring forth its fruit, in due season.
    And his leaf shall not fall off:
and all whosoever he shall do shall prosper.
4 Not so the wicked, not so:
but like the dust, which the wind driveth from the face
    of the earth.
5 Therefore the wicked shall not rise again in
    judgment:
 nor sinners in the council of the just.
6 For the Lord knoweth the way of the just:
and the way of the wicked shall perish.

Psalm 2
Quare Fremuerunt

Antiphon:
This same God hath fulfilled to our children, raising up
    Jesus, as in the second psalm also is written:
    "Thou art my Son, this day have I begotten Thee."
(Acts 13:33)

The Psalter

1 Why have the Gentiles raged,
and the people devised vain things?
2 The kings of the earth stood up,
    and the princes met together,
against the Lord and against his Christ.
3 Let us break their bonds asunder:
and let us cast away their yoke from us.
4 He that dwelleth in heaven shall laugh at them:
and the Lord shall deride them.
5 Then shall he speak to them in his anger,
and trouble them in his rage.
6 But I am appointed king by him over Sion
his holy mountain, preaching his commandment.
7 The Lord hath said to me:
Thou art my son,
this day have I begotten thee.
8 Ask of me, and I will give thee the Gentiles for thy
            inheritance,
and the utmost parts of the earth for thy possession.
9 Thou shalt rule them with a rod of iron,
and shalt break them in pieces like a potter's vessel.
10 And now, O ye kings, understand:
    receive instruction, you that judge the earth.
11 Serve ye the Lord with fear:
and rejoice unto him with trembling.
12 Embrace discipline,
lest at any time the Lord be angry,
    and you perish from the just way.
13 When his wrath shall be kindled in a short time,
blessed are all they that trust in him.

The Psalter

Psalm 3
Domine, quid multiplicati

Antiphon:
Thou, O Lord, art a shield for me; my glory, and the lifter of my head. *(Ps 3:3)*

1 *The psalm of David when he fled from the face of his son Absalom.*

2 Why, O Lord, are they multiplied that afflict me?
many are they who rise up against me.

3 Many say to my soul:
There is no salvation for him in his God.

4 But thou, O Lord art my protector,
my glory, and the lifter up of my head.

5 I have cried to the Lord with my voice:
and he hath heard me from his holy hill.

6 I have slept and taken my rest:
    and I have risen up,
because the Lord hath protected me.

7 I will not fear thousands of the people, surrounding me:
arise, O Lord;
    save me, O my God.

8 For thou hast struck all them who are my adversaries without cause:
thou hast broken the teeth of sinners.

9 Salvation is of the Lord:
and thy blessing is upon thy people.

The Psalter

Day 1 - Evening Prayer

Psalm 4
Cum invocarem

Antiphon:
Be angry, and sin not. Let not the sun go down upon
    your anger.
Give not place to the devil. *(Eph 4:26-27)*

1 Unto the end, in verses. A psalm of David.

2 When I called upon him,
    the God of my justice heard me:
when I was in distress,
    thou hast enlarged me.
Have mercy on me:
    and hear my prayer.

3 O ye sons of men,
    how long will you be dull of heart?
why do you love vanity,
    and seek after lying?

4 Know ye also that the Lord hath made his holy one
        wonderful:
the Lord will hear me when I shall cry unto him.

5 Be angry, and sin not:
the things you say in your hearts,
    be sorry for them upon your beds.

6 Offer up the sacrifice of justice,
    and trust in the Lord:
many say, Who sheweth us good things?

7 The light of thy countenance O Lord,
    is signed upon us:
thou hast given gladness in my heart.

8 By the fruit of their corn, their wine and oil,
they are multiplied.

9 In peace in the selfsame I will sleep,
and I will rest:

The Psalter

10 For thou, O Lord,
singularly hast settled me in hope.

Psalm 5
Verba mea auribul

Antiphon:
God is true and every man is a liar, as it is written:
*That thou mayest be justified in Thy words and
          mayest overcome when thou art judged...*
For all have sinned and do need the glory of God.
          (Rom 3:4,23)

1 *Unto the end, for her that obtaineth the inheritance.
          A psalm of David.*
2 Give ear, O Lord, to my words,
understand my cry.
3 Hearken to the voice of my prayer,
O my King and my God.
4 For to thee will I pray:
O Lord, in the morning thou shalt hear my voice.
5 In the morning I will stand before thee,
     and will see:
because thou art not a God that willest iniquity.
6 Neither shall the wicked dwell near thee:
nor shall the unjust abide before thy eyes.
7 Thou hatest all the workers of iniquity:
Thou wilt destroy all that speak a lie.
The bloody and the deceitful man the Lord will abhor.
8 But as for me in the multitude of thy mercy,
     I will come into thy house;
I will worship towards thy holy temple,
     in thy fear.
9 Conduct me, O Lord, in thy justice:
because of my enemies,
     direct my way in thy sight.

10 For there is no truth in their mouth;
their heart is vain.
11 Their throat is an open sepulchre:
   they dealt deceitfully with their tongues:
   judge them, O God.
Let them fall from their devices:
according to the multitude of their wickedness cast
   them out:
for they have provoked thee, O Lord.
12 But let all them be glad that hope in thee:
they shall rejoice for ever,
   and thou shalt dwell in them.
And all they that love thy name
   shall glory in thee:
13 For thou wilt bless the just.
O Lord, thou hast crowned us,
   as with a shield of thy good will.

Psalm 6
Domine, ne in furore

Antiphon:
Many will say to me in that day: Lord, Lord, have not
   we prophesied in thy name, and cast out devils
   in thy name, and done many miracles in thy
   name?
And then will I profess unto them: I never knew you;
   Depart from me, you that work iniquity.
      (Matt 7:22-23)

1 *Unto the end, in verses, a psalm for David, for the
   octave.*
2 O Lord, rebuke me not in thy indignation,
nor chastise me in thy wrath.
3 Have mercy on me, O Lord,
   for I am weak:
heal me, O Lord,
   for my bones are troubled.

The Psalter

4 And my soul is troubled exceedingly:
   but thou, O Lord, how long?
5 Turn to me, O Lord,
   and deliver my soul:
O save me for thy mercy's sake.
6 For there is no one in death,
   that is mindful of thee:
and who shall confess to thee in hell?
7 I have laboured in my groanings,
   every night I will wash my bed:
I will water my couch with my tears.
8 My eye is troubled through indignation:
I have grown old amongst all my enemies

The Psalter

Day 2 - Morning Prayer

Psalm 7
Domine, Deus meus.

Antiphon:
But Thou, O Lord of Sabaoth, who judgest justly and
    triest the reins and the hearts,
let me see thy revenge on them; for to Thee have I
    revealed my cause. *(Jer 11:20)*

1 *The psalm of David which he sung to the Lord for the
    words of Chusi the son of Jemini. [2 Kgdm
    1:16.]*
2 O Lord my God,
    in thee have I put my trust:
save me from all them that persecute me,
    and deliver me.
3 Lest at any time he seize upon my soul like a lion,
    while there is no one to redeem me, nor to save.
4 O Lord my God,
    if I have done this thing,
    if there be iniquity in my hands:
5 If I have rendered to them that repaid me evils,
    let me deservedly fall empty before my enemies.
6 Let the enemy pursue my soul, and take it,
    and tread down my life on the earth,
    and bring down my glory to the dust.
7 Rise up, O Lord, in thy anger:
    and be thou exalted in the borders of my enemies.
And arise, O Lord my God,
    in the precept which thou hast commanded:
8 and a congregation of people shall surround thee.
    And for their sakes return thou on high.
9 The Lord judgeth the people.
Judge me, O Lord, according to my justice,
    and according to my innocence in me.

10 The wickedness of sinners shall be brought to
   nought:
and thou shalt direct the just:
the searcher of hearts and reins is God.
11 Just is my help from the Lord:
who saveth the upright of heart.
12 God is a just judge, strong and patient:
is he angry every day?
13 Except you will be converted,
   he will brandish his sword:
he hath bent his bow and made it ready.
14 And in it he hath prepared the instruments of
   death,
he hath made ready his arrows for them that burn.
15 Behold he hath been in labour with injustice;
   he hath conceived sorrow,
   and brought forth iniquity.
16 He hath opened a pit and dug it;
   and he is fallen into the hole he made.
17 His sorrow shall be turned on his own head:
   and his iniquity shall come down upon his crown.
18 I will give glory to the Lord according to his justice:
and will sing to the name of the Lord the most high.

Psalm 8
Domine, Dominus noster

Antiphon:
For He must reign *until He hath put all his enemies
   under his feet.*
and the last enemy, death, shall be destroyed last: *For
   He hath put all things under his feet. (1 Cor
   15:25-26)*

1 *Unto the end, for the presses: a psalm of David.*
2 O Lord our Lord,
   how admirable is thy name in the whole earth!
For thy magnificence is elevated above the heavens.

The Psalter

3 Out of the mouth of infants and of sucklings
   thou hast perfected praise,
   because of thy enemies,
that thou mayst destroy the enemy and the avenger.
4 For I will behold thy heavens,
   the works of thy fingers:
the moon and the stars
   which thou hast founded.
5 What is man that thou art mindful of him?
   or the son of man that thou visitest him?
6 Thou hast made him a little less than the angels,
   thou hast crowned him with glory and honour:
7 and hast set him over the works of thy hands.
8 Thou hast subjected all things under his feet,
   all sheep and oxen:
moreover the beasts also of the fields.
9 The birds of the air,
   and the fishes of the sea,
   that pass through the paths of the sea.
10 O Lord our Lord,
how admirable is thy name in all the earth!

The Psalter

Day 2 - Evening Prayer

Psalm 9 (9,10)
Confitebor tibi, Domine

Antiphon:
Now we know that what things soever the law
   speaketh, it speaketh to them that are in the
   law;
that every mouth may be stopped, and all the world
   may be made subject to God. *(Rom 3:19)*

1   *Unto the end, for the hidden things of the Son. A psalm for David.*

2 I will give praise to thee, O Lord,
   with my whole heart:
I will relate all thy wonders.

3 I will be glad and rejoice in thee:
I will sing to thy name,
   O thou most high.

4 When my enemy shall be turned back:
they shall be weakened and perish before thy face.

5 For thou hast maintained my judgment and my cause:
thou hast sat on the throne, who judgest justice.

6 Thou hast rebuked the Gentiles,
   and the wicked one hath perished:
thou hast blotted out their name for ever and ever.

7 The swords of the enemy have failed unto the end:
   and their cities thou hast destroyed.
Their memory hath perished with a noise.

8 But the Lord remaineth for ever.
He hath prepared his throne in judgment:

9 and he shall judge the world in equity,
he shall judge the people in justice.

10 And the Lord is become a refuge for the poor:
a helper in due time in tribulation.

The Psalter

11 And let them trust in thee who know thy name:
for thou hast not forsaken them that seek thee, O
      Lord.
12 Sing ye to the Lord, who dwelleth in Sion:
declare his ways among the Gentiles:
13 For requiring their blood he hath remembered them:
he hath not forgotten the cry of the poor.
14 Have mercy on me, O Lord:
see my humiliation which I suffer from my enemies.
15 Thou that liftest me up from the gates of death,
    that I may declare all thy praises in the gates of the
        daughter of Sion.
16 I will rejoice in thy salvation:
    the Gentiles have stuck fast in the destruction
        which they have prepared.
Their foot hath been taken in the very snare which
    they hid.
17 The Lord shall be known when he executeth
        judgments:
the sinner hath been caught in the works of his own
    hands.
18 The wicked shall be turned into hell,
all the nations that forget God.
19 For the poor man shall not be forgotten to the end:
the patience of the poor shall not perish for ever.
20 Arise, O Lord,
    let not man be strengthened:
let the Gentiles be judged in thy sight.
21 Appoint, O Lord,
    a lawgiver over them:
that the Gentiles may know themselves to be but men.
22 Why, O Lord,
    hast thou retired afar off?
why dost thou slight us in our wants,
    in the time of trouble?

The Psalter

23 Whilst the wicked man is proud,
   the poor is set on fire:
they are caught in the counsels which they devise.
24 For the sinner is praised in the desires of his soul:
and the unjust man is blessed.
25 The sinner hath provoked the Lord
according to the multitude of his wrath he will not
     seek him:
26 God is not before his eyes:
   his ways are filthy at all times.
Thy judgments are removed from his sight:
   he shall rule over all his enemies.
27 For he hath said in his heart:
I shall not be moved from generation to generation,
   and shall be without evil.
28 His mouth is full of cursing, and of bitterness,
   and of deceit:
under his tongue are labour and sorrow.
29 He sitteth in ambush with the rich in private
     places,
that he may kill the innocent.
30 His eyes are upon the poor man:
   He lieth in wait in secret like a lion in his den.
He lieth in ambush that he may catch the poor man:
   to catch the poor, whilst he draweth him to him.
31 In his net he will bring him down,
   he will crouch and fall,
when he shall have power over the poor.
32 For he hath said in his heart:
God hath forgotten,
   he hath turned away his face not to see to the end.
33 Arise, O Lord God,
   let thy hand be exalted:
forget not the poor.
34 Wherefore hath the wicked provoked God?
For he hath said in his heart:
   He will not require it.

35 Thou seest it,
> for thou considerest labour and sorrow:

that thou mayst deliver them into thy hands.
To thee is the poor man left:
> thou wilt be a helper to the orphan.

36 Break thou the arm of the sinner and of the malignant:

his sin shall be sought, and shall not be found.

37 The Lord shall reign to eternity,
> yea, for ever and ever:

ye Gentiles shall perish from his land.

38 The Lord hath heard the desire of the poor:
> thy ear hath heard the preparation of their heart.

39 To judge for the fatherless and for the humble,
that man may no more presume to magnify himself upon earth.

Psalm 10 (11)
In Domino confido

Antiphon:
The Lord is in his holy temple;
let all the earth keep silence before Him. *(Hab 2:20)*

1 *Unto the end. A psalm for David.*
2 In the Lord I put my trust:
> how then do you say to my soul:

Get thee away from hence to the mountain like a sparrow?

3 For, lo, the wicked have bent their bow;
> they have prepared their arrows in the quiver;

to shoot in the dark the upright of heart.

4 For they have destroyed the things which thou hast made:
but what has the just man done?

The Psalter

5 The Lord is in his holy temple,
   the Lord's throne is in heaven.
His eyes look on the poor man:
   his eyelids examine the sons of men.
6 The Lord trieth the just and the wicked:
but he that loveth iniquity hateth his own soul.
7 He shall rain snares upon sinners:
   fire and brimstone and storms of winds
   shall be the portion of their cup.
8 For the Lord is just, and hath loved justice:
his countenance hath beheld righteousness

The Psalter

Day 3 - Morning Prayer

Psalm 11(12)
Salvum me fac

Antiphon:
Every word of God is fire-tried;
He is a buckler to them that hope
      in Him. *(Prov 30:5)*

1 *Unto the end; for the octave, a psalm for David.*
2 Save me, O Lord,
    for there is now no saint:
truths are decayed from among the children of men.
3 They have spoken vain things
    every one to his neighbour:
with deceitful lips,
    and with a double heart have they spoken.
4 May the Lord destroy all deceitful lips,
and the tongue that speaketh proud things.
5 Who have said:
    We will magnify our tongue;
our lips are our own;
    who is Lord over us?
6 By reason of the misery of the needy,
    and the groans of the poor,
    now will I arise, saith the Lord.
I will set him in safety;
    I will deal confidently in his regard.
7 The words of the Lord are pure words:
    as silver tried by the fire,
purged from the earth
    refined seven times.
8 Thou, O Lord, wilt preserve us.:
and keep us from this generation for ever.
9 The wicked walk round about:
    according to thy highness,
thou hast multiplied the children of men.

The Psalter

Psalm 12(13)
Usquequo, Domine

Antiphon:
My God hath sent his angel, and hath shut up the
    mouths of the lions,
and they have not hurt me. *(Dan 6:22a)*

1 *Unto the end, a psalm for David.*
How long, O Lord,
    wilt thou forget me unto the end?
how long dost thou turn away thy face from me?
2 How long shall I take counsels in my soul,
sorrow in my heart all the day?
3 How long shall my enemy be exalted over me?
4 Consider, and hear me,
    O Lord my God.
Enlighten my eyes that I never sleep in death:
5 lest at any time my enemy say:
    I have prevailed against him.
They that trouble me will rejoice when I am moved:
6 but I have trusted in thy mercy.
    My heart shall rejoice in thy salvation:
I will sing to the Lord, who giveth me good things:
    yea I will sing to the name of the Lord the most
        high.

Psalm 13(12)
Dixit insipiens

Antiphon:
All have turned out of the way; they are become
    unprofitable together;
there is none that doth good, there is not so much
    as one. *(Rom 3:13)*

The Psalter

1 *Unto the end, a psalm for David.*
The fool hath said in his heart:
    There is no God,
They are corrupt,
    and are become abominable in their ways:
there is none that doth good, no not one.
2 The Lord hath looked down from heaven
    upon the children of men,
        to see if there be any that understand and seek
            God.
3 They are all gone aside,
    they are become unprofitable together:
there is none that doth good,
    no not one.
Their throat is an open sepulchre:
    with their tongues they acted deceitfully;
    the poison of asps is under their lips.
Their mouth is full of cursing and bitterness;
    their feet are swift to shed blood.
Destruction and unhappiness in their ways:
    and the way of peace they have not known:
there is no fear of God before their eyes.
4 Shall not all they know that work iniquity,
    who devour my people as they eat bread ?
5 They have not called upon the Lord:
    there have they trembled for fear, where there was
        no fear.
6 For the Lord is in the just generation:
    you have confounded the counsel of the poor man,
    but the Lord is his hope.
7 Who shall give out of Sion the salvation of Israel?
    when the Lord shall have turned away the captivity
        of his people,
    Jacob shall rejoice and Israel shall be glad.

The Psalter

Day 3 - Evening Prayer

Psalm 14(13)
Domine, quis habitabit

Antiphon:
It hath been told thee, O man, what is good, and what
    the Lord doth require of thee:
Only to do justly, and to love mercy, and to walk
    humbly with thy God. *(Micah 6:8b)*

1 *A psalm of David.*
Lord, who shall dwell in thy tabernacle?
or who shall rest in thy holy hill?
2 He that walketh without blemish,
and worketh justice:
3 He that speaketh truth in his heart,
    who hath not used deceit in his tongue:
Nor hath done evil to his neighbour:
    nor taken up a reproach against his neighbours.
4 In his sight the malignant is brought to nothing:
    but he glorifieth them that fear the Lord.
He that sweareth to his neighbour,
    and deceiveth not;
5 he that hath not put out his money to usury,
    nor taken bribes against the innocent:
He that doth these things shall not be moved for ever.

Psalm 15(14)
Conserva me, Domine

Antiphon:
David spoke, foreseeing the resurrection of Christ;
for neither was He left in hell; neither did his flesh see
    corruption. *(Acts 2:31)*

The Psalter

1 *The inscription of a title to David himself.*
Preserve me, O Lord,
for I have put trust in thee.
2 I have said to the Lord,
    thou art my God,
for thou hast no need of my goods.
3 To the saints, who are in his land,
 he hath made wonderful all my desires in them.
4 Their infirmities were multiplied:
    afterwards they made haste.
I will not gather together their meetings for blood
        offerings:
    nor will I be mindful of their names by my lips.
5 The Lord is the portion of my inheritance and of my
        cup:
it is thou that wilt restore my inheritance to me.
6 The lines are fallen unto me in goodly places:
    for my inheritance is goodly to me.
7 I will bless the Lord,
    who hath given me understanding:
moreover my reins also have corrected me even till
        night.
8 I set the Lord always in my sight:
    for he is at my right hand, that I be not moved.
9 Therefore my heart hath been glad,
    and my tongue hath rejoiced:
moreover my flesh also shall rest in hope.
10 Because thou wilt not leave my soul in hell;
    nor wilt then give thy holy one to see corruption.
11 Thou hast made known to me the ways of life,
    thou shalt fill me with joy with thy countenance:
at thy right hand are delights even to the end.

The Psalter

Psalm 16(15)
Exaudi, Domine, justitiam

Antiphon:
I will give thee thy life, and save thee
in all places whithersoever thou shalt go.   (Jer 45:5b)

1 *The prayer of David.*
Hear, O Lord, my justice:
　　attend to my supplication.
Give ear unto my prayer,
　　which proceedeth not from deceitful lips.
2 Let my judgment come forth from thy countenance:
let thy eyes behold the things that are equitable.
3 Thou hast proved my heart,
　　and visited it by night,
thou hast tried me by fire:
　　and iniquity hath not been found in me.
4 That my mouth may not speak the works of men:
　　for the sake of the words of thy lips,
　　I have kept hard ways.
5 Perfect thou my goings in thy paths:
　　that my footsteps be not moved.
6 I have cried to thee,
　　for thou, O God, hast heard me:
O incline thy ear unto me, and hear my words.
7 Shew forth thy wonderful mercies;
　　thou who savest them that trust in thee.
8 From them that resist thy right hand keep me,
　　as the apple of thy eye.
Protect me under the shadow of thy wings.
9 From the face of the wicked who have afflicted me.
My enemies have surrounded my soul:
10 they have shut up their fat:
their mouth hath spoken proudly.
11 They have cast me forth
　　and now they have surrounded me:
they have set their eyes bowing down to the earth.

The Psalter

12 They have taken me, as a lion prepared for the prey; and as a young lion dwelling in secret places.

13 Arise, O Lord, disappoint him and supplant him; deliver my soul from the wicked one: thy sword

14 From the enemies of thy hand. O Lord,
> divide them from the few of the earth in their life:
> their belly is filled from thy hidden stores.

They are full of children:
> and they have left to their little ones the rest of their substance.

15 But as for me,
> I will appear before thy sight in justice:

I shall be satisfied when thy glory shall appear.

The Psalter

Day 4 - Morning Prayer

Psalm 17(18)
Diligam te, Domine

Antiphon:
Who is God but the Lord; and who is strong but our
    God?
God who hath girded me with strength, and made my
    way perfect.
    (2 Kings 22:32-33)

1 *Unto the end, for David the servant of the Lord, who spoke to the Lord the words of this canticle, in the day that the Lord delivered him from the hands of all his enemies, and from the hand of Saul. [2Kgdm 1:22.]*

2 I will love thee, O Lord, my strength:

3 The Lord is my firmament,
    my refuge, and my deliverer.
My God is my helper,
    and in him will I put my trust.
My protector and the horn of my salvation,
    and my support.

4 Praising I will call upon the Lord:
and I shall be saved from my enemies.

5 The sorrows of death surrounded me:
and the torrents of iniquity troubled me.

6 The sorrows of hell encompassed me:
and the snares of death prevented me.

7 In my affliction I called upon the Lord,
    and I cried to my God:
And he heard my voice from his holy temple:
    and my cry before him came into his ears.

The Psalter

8 The earth shook and trembled:
   the foundations of the mountains were troubled and
       were moved,
   because he was angry with them.
9 There went up a smoke in his wrath:
   and a fire flamed from his face:
   coals were kindled by it.
10 He bowed the heavens, and came down:
and darkness was under his feet.

11 And he ascended upon the cherubim, and he flew;
he flew upon the wings of the winds.
12 And he made darkness his covert,
   his pavilion round about him:
dark waters in the clouds of the air.
13 At the brightness that was before him
   the clouds passed,
   hail and coals of fire.
14 And the Lord thundered from heaven,
   and the highest gave his voice:
   hail and coals of fire.
15 And he sent forth his arrows,
   and he scattered them:
he multiplied lightnings,
   and troubled them.
16 Then the fountains of waters appeared,
   and the foundations of the world were discovered:
At thy rebuke, O Lord,
   at the blast of the spirit of thy wrath.
17 He sent from on high, and took me:
and received me out of many waters.
18 He delivered me from my strongest enemies,
   and from them that hated me:
   for they were too strong for me.
19 They prevented me in the day of my affliction:
and the Lord became my protector.

20 And he brought me forth into a large place:
he saved me, because he was well pleased with me.
21 And the Lord will reward me according to my justice;
and will repay me according to the cleanness of my hands:
22 Because I have kept the ways of the Lord;
and have not done wickedly against my God.
23 For till his judgments are in my sight:
and his justices I have not put away from me.
24 And I shall be spotless with him:
and shall keep myself from my iniquity.
25 And the Lord will reward me according to my justice;
and according to the cleanness of my hands before his eyes.
26 With the holy, thou wilt be holy;
and with the innocent man thou wilt be innocent.
27 And with the elect thou wilt be elect:
and with the perverse thou wilt be perverted.
28 For thou wilt save the humble people;
but wilt bring down the eyes of the proud.
29 For thou lightest my lamp, O Lord:
O my God enlighten my darkness.
30 For by thee I shall be delivered from temptation;
and through my God I shall go over a wall.
31 As for my God, his way is undefiled:
the words of the Lord are fire tried:
he is the protector of all that trust in him.
32 For who is God but the Lord?
or who is God but our God?
33 God who hath girt me with strength;
and made my way blameless.
34 Who hath made my feet like the feet of harts:
and who setteth me upon high places.
35 Who teacheth my hands to war:
and thou hast made my arms like a brazen bow.

The Psalter

36 And thou hast given me the protection of thy salvation:
and thy right hand hath held me up:
And thy discipline hath corrected me unto the end:
and thy discipline, the same shall teach me.
37 Thou hast enlarged my steps under me;
and my feet are not weakened.
38 I will pursue after my enemies, and overtake them:
and I will not turn again till they are consumed.
39 I will break them,
and they shall not be able to stand:
they shall fall under my feet.
40 And thou hast girded me with strength unto battle;
and hast subdued under me them that rose up against me.
41 And thou hast made my enemies turn their back upon me,
and hast destroyed them that hated me.
42 They cried, but there was none to save them,
to the Lord: but he heard them not.
43 And I shall beat them as small as the dust before the wind;
I shall bring them to nought,
like the dirt in the streets.
44 Thou wilt deliver me from the contradictions of the people:
thou wilt make me head of the Gentiles.
45 A people, which I knew not, hath served me:
at the hearing of the ear they have obeyed me.
46 The children that are strangers have lied to me,
strange children have faded away,
and have halted from their paths.
47 The Lord liveth, and blessed be my God,
and let the God of my salvation be exalted :
48 O God, who avengest me,
and subduest the people under me,
my deliverer from my enemies.

The Psalter

49 And thou wilt lift me up above them that rise up
    against me:
From the unjust man thou wilt deliver me.
50 Therefore will I give glory to thee, O Lord,
    among the nations,
    and I will sing a psalm to thy name.
51 Giving great deliverance to his king,
    and shewing mercy to David his anointed :
    and to his seed for ever.

The Psalter

Day 4 - Evening Prayer

Psalm 18(19)
Coeli enarrant

Antiphon:
Thus it is written, and thus it behoved Christ to suffer
    and to rise again from the dead, the third day;
and that penance and remission of sin should be
    preached in his name unto all nations,
beginning at Jerusalem; and you are witnesses of these
    things.
      (Luke 24:46-48)

1 *Unto the end. A psalm for David.*
2 The heavens shew forth the glory of God,
and the firmament declareth the work of his hands.
3 Day to day uttereth speech,
and night to night sheweth knowledge.
4 There are no speeches nor languages,
where their voices are not heard.
5 Their sound hath gone forth into all the earth:
and their words unto the ends of the world.
6 He hath set his tabernacle in the sun:
    and he, as a bridegroom coming out of his bride
        chamber,
Hath rejoiced as a giant to run the way:
7 His going out is from the end of heaven,
    And his circuit even to the end thereof:
and there is no one that can hide himself from his heat.
8 The law of the Lord is unspotted,
    converting souls:
 the testimony of the Lord is faithful,
    giving wisdom to little ones.
9 The justices of the Lord are right,
    rejoicing hearts:
the commandment of the Lord is lightsome,
    enlightening the eyes.

10 The fear of the Lord is holy,
   enduring for ever and ever:
the judgments of the Lord are true,
   justified in themselves.
11 More to be desired than gold and many precious
      stones: and sweeter than honey and the
      honeycomb.
12 For thy servant keepeth them,
and in keeping them there is a great reward.
13 Who can understand sins?
 From my secret ones cleanse me, O Lord:
14 and from those of others spare thy servant.
If they shall have no dominion over me,
      then shall I be without spot:
      and I shall be cleansed from the greatest sin.
15 And the words of my mouth shall be such as may
      please:
and the meditation of my heart always in thy sight.
      O Lord, my helper, and my redeemer.

Psalm 19(20)
Exaudiat te Dominus

Antiphon:
We were bondmen of Pharaoh in Egypt,
and the Lord brought us out of Egypt with a strong
            hand. *(Deut 6:21)*

1 *Unto the end. A psalm for David.*
2 May the Lord hear thee in the day of tribulation:
may the name of the God of Jacob protect thee.
3 May he send thee help from the sanctuary:
and defend thee out of Sion.
4 May he be mindful of all thy sacrifices:
and may thy whole burnt offering be made fat.
5 May he give thee according to thy own heart;
and confirm all thy counsels.

The Psalter

6 We will rejoice in thy salvation;
and in the name of our God we shall be exalted.
7 The Lord fulfil all thy petitions:
> now have I known that the Lord hath saved his anointed.

He will hear him from his holy heaven:
the salvation of his right hand is in powers.
8 Some trust in chariots, and some in horses:
but we will call upon the name of the Lord our God.
9 They are bound, and have fallen;
> but we are risen, and are set upright.

O Lord, save the king:
> and hear us in the day that we shall call upon thee

Psalm 20(21)
Domine, in virtute

Antiphon:
God also hath exalted Him, and hath given Him a name
> which is above all names;

that in the name of Jesus every knee should bow,
> of those that are in heaven, on earth, and under the earth.
>> (Phil 2:9-10)

1 *Unto the end. A psalm for David.*
2 In thy strength, O Lord, the king shall joy;
and in thy salvation he shall rejoice exceedingly.
3 Thou hast given him his heart's desire:
and hast not withholden from him the will of his lips.
4 For thou hast prevented him with blessings of sweetness:
thou hast set on his head a crown of precious stones.
5 He asked life of thee: and thou hast given him length of days for ever and ever.
6 His glory is great in thy salvation:
glory and great beauty shalt thou lay upon him.

The Psalter

7 For thou shalt give him to be a blessing for ever and ever:
thou shalt make him joyful in gladness with thy countenance.

8 For the king hopeth in the Lord:
and through the mercy of the most High he shall not be moved.

9 Let thy hand be found by all thy enemies:
let thy right hand find out all them that hate thee.

10 Thou shalt make them as an oven of fire, in the time of thy anger:
the Lord shall trouble them in his wrath, and fire shall devour them.

11 Their fruit shalt thou destroy from the earth:
and their seed from among the children of men.

12 For they have intended evils against thee:
they have devised counsels which they have not been able to establish.

13 For thou shalt make them turn their back:
in thy remnants thou shalt prepare their face.

14 Be thou exalted, O Lord, in thy own strength:
we will sing and praise thy power.

The Psalter

Day 5 - Morning Prayer

Psalm 21(22)
Deus Deus meus

Antiphon:
He saved others; Himself He cannot save.
If He be the king of Israel, let Him now come down
 from the cross;
and we will believe Him. *(Matt 27:42)*

1 *Unto the end, for the morning protection, a psalm for David.*

2 O God my God, look upon me:
 why hast thou forsaken me?
Far from my salvation are the words of my sins.

3 O my God, I shall cry by day,
 and thou wilt not hear:
and by night,
 and it shall not be reputed as folly in me.

4 But thou dwellest in the holy place,
the praise of Israel.

5 In thee have our fathers hoped:
they have hoped, and thou hast delivered them.

6 They cried to thee, and they were saved:
they trusted in thee, and were not confounded.

7 But I am a worm, and no man:
the reproach of men, and the outcast of the people.

8 All they that saw me have laughed me to scorn:
they have spoken with the lips, and wagged the head.

9 He hoped in the Lord, let him deliver him:
let him save him, seeing he delighteth in him.

10 For thou art he that hast drawn me out of the womb:
my hope from the breasts of my mother.

11 I was cast upon thee from the womb.
From my mother's womb thou art my God,

The Psalter

12 depart not from me. For tribulation is very near:
for there is none to help me.
13 Many calves have surrounded me:
fat bulls have besieged me.
14 They have opened their mouths against me,
as a lion ravening and roaring.
15 I am poured out like water;
and all my bones are scattered.
My heart is become like wax melting in the midst of
my bowels.
16 My strength is dried up like a potsherd,
and my tongue hath cleaved to my jaws:
and thou hast brought me down into the dust of death.
17 For many dogs have encompassed me:
the council of the malignant hath besieged me.
They have dug my hands and feet.
18 They have numbered all my bones.
And they have looked and stared upon me.
19 They parted my garments amongst them;
and upon my vesture they cast lots.
20 But thou, O Lord,
remove not thy help to a distance from me;
look towards my defence.
21 Deliver, O God, my soul from the sword:
my only one from the hand of the dog.
22 Save me from the lion's mouth;
and my lowness from the horns of the unicorns.
23 I will declare thy name to my brethren:
in the midst of the church will I praise thee.
24 Ye that fear the Lord, praise him:
all ye the seed of Jacob, glorify him.
25 Let all the seed of Israel fear him:
because he hath not slighted nor despised the
supplication of the poor man.
Neither hath he turned away his face from me:
and when I cried to him he heard me.

26 With thee is my praise in a great church:
I will pay my vows in the sight of them that fear him.
27 The poor shall eat and shall be filled:
and they shall praise the Lord that seek him:
their hearts shall live for ever and ever.
28 All the ends of the earth shall remember, and shall
be converted to the Lord:
And all the kindreds of the Gentiles shall adore in his
sight.
29 For the kingdom is the Lord's;
and he shall have dominion over the nations.
30 All the fat ones of the earth have eaten and have
adored:
all they that go down to the earth shall fall before him.
31 And to him my soul shall live:
and my seed shall serve him.
32 There shall be declared to the Lord a generation to
come:
and the heavens shall shew forth his justice to a
people that shall be born,
which the Lord hath made.

Psalm 22(23)
Dominus regit me

Antiphon:
He shall feed his flock like a shepherd;
he shall gather together the lambs with his arm,
and shall take them up in his bosom, and he himself shall
carry them that are with young. *(Isaiah 40:11)*

1 A *psalm for David.*
The Lord ruleth me: and I shall want nothing.
2 He hath set me in a place of pasture.
He hath brought me up,
on the water of refreshment:

The Psalter

3 he hath converted my soul.
He hath led me on the paths of justice,
   for his own name's sake.
4 For though I should walk in the midst of the shadow
      of death,
   I will fear no evils,
for thou art with me.
   Thy rod and thy staff, they have comforted me.
5 Thou hast prepared a table before me against them
      that afflict me.
Thou hast anointed my head with oil;
   and my chalice which inebriateth me,
   how goodly is it!
6 And thy mercy will follow me all the days of my life.
And that I may dwell in the house of the Lord unto
      length of days.

The Psalter

Day 5 - Evening Prayer

Psalm 23(24)
Domini est terra

Antiphon:
And it came to pass, whilst he blessed them,
He departed from them, and was carried up to heaven.
(Lk 24:51)

1 *On the first day of the week, a psalm for David.*
The earth is the Lord's and the fulness thereof:
the world, and all they that dwell therein.
2 For he hath founded it upon the seas;
and hath prepared it upon the rivers.
3 Who shall ascend into the mountain of the Lord:
or who shall stand in his holy place?
4 The innocent in hands, and clean of heart,
    who hath not taken his soul in vain,
    nor sworn deceitfully to his neighbour.
5 He shall receive a blessing from the Lord,
and mercy from God his Saviour.
6 This is the generation of them that seek him,
of them that seek the face of the God of Jacob.
7 Lift up your gates,
    O ye princes, and be ye lifted up,
O eternal gates:
    and the King of Glory shall enter in.
8 Who is this King of Glory?
    the Lord who is strong and mighty:
the Lord mighty in battle.
9 Lift up your gates,
    O ye princes, and be ye lifted up,
O eternal gates:
    and the King of Glory shall enter in.
10 Who is this King of Glory?
    the Lord of hosts, he is the King of Glory.

The Psalter

Psalm 24(25)
Ad te, Domine, levavi

Antiphon:
If you abide in me, and my words abide in you,
you shall ask whatever you will, and it shall be done
unto you. *(John 15:7)*

1 *Unto the end, a psalm for David.*
To thee, O Lord, have I lifted up my soul.
2 In thee, O my God, I put my trust;
let me not be ashamed.
3 Neither let my enemies laugh at me:
for none of them that wait on thee shall be confounded.
4 Let all them be confounded that act unjust things
    without cause.
Shew, O Lord, thy ways to me,
   and teach me thy paths.
5 Direct me in thy truth, and teach me;
   for thou art God my Saviour;
and on thee have I waited all the day long.
6 Remember, O Lord, thy bowels of compassion;
and thy mercies that are from the beginning of the
    world.
7 The sins of my youth and my ignorances do not
    remember.
According to thy mercy remember thou me:
   for thy goodness' sake, O Lord.
8 The Lord is sweet and righteous:
therefore he will give a law to sinners in the way.
9 He will guide the mild in judgment:
he will teach the meek his ways.

The Psalter

10 All the ways of the Lord are mercy and truth,
to them that seek after his covenant and his
      testimonies.

11 For thy name's sake, O Lord,
    thou wilt pardon my sin:
        for it is great.

12 Who is the man that feareth the Lord?
    He hath appointed him a law in the way he hath
        chosen.

13 His soul shall dwell in good things:
and his seed shall inherit the land.

14 The Lord is a firmament to them that fear him:
and his covenant shall be made manifest to them.

15 My eyes are ever towards the Lord:
for he shall pluck my feet out of the snare.

16 Look thou upon me, and have mercy on me;
for I am alone and poor.

17 The troubles of my heart are multiplied:
deliver me from my necessities.

18 See my abjection and my labour;
and forgive me all my sins.

19 Consider my enemies for they are multiplied,
and have hated me with an unjust hatred.

20 Keep thou my soul, and deliver me:
I shall not be ashamed, for I have hoped in thee.

21 The innocent and the upright have adhered to me:
because I have waited on thee.

22 Deliver Israel, O God,
from all his tribulations.

The Psalter

Psalm 25(26)
Judica me, Domine

Antiphon:
We look for new heavens and a new earth...in which justice dwelleth,
...be diligent that you may be found before him unspotted and blameless, in peace. *(2 Peter 3:13-14)*

1 *Unto the end, a psalm for David.*
Judge me, O Lord, for I have walked in my innocence:
and I have put my trust in the Lord,
    and shall not be weakened.
2 Prove me, O Lord, and try me;
burn my reins and my heart.
3 For thy mercy is before my eyes;
and I am well pleased with thy truth.
4 I have not sat with the council of vanity:
neither will I go in with the doers of unjust things.
5 I have hated the assembly of the malignant;
and with the wicked I will not sit.
6 I will wash my hands among the innocent;
and will compass thy altar, O Lord:
7 That I may hear the voice of thy praise:
and tell of all thy wondrous works.
8 I have loved, O Lord, the beauty of thy house;
and the place where thy glory dwelleth.
9 Take not away my soul, O God, with the wicked:
nor my life with bloody men:
10 In whose hands are iniquities:
their right hand is filled with gifts.
11 But as for me, I have walked in my innocence:
redeem me, and have mercy on me.
12 My foot hath stood in the direct way:
in the churches I will bless thee, O Lord.

The Psalter

Day 6 - Morning Prayer

Psalm 26(27)
Dominus illuminatio

Antiphon:
Then shall the just shine as the sun,
in the kingdom of their Father.
(Matt 13:43)

1 *The psalm of David before he was anointed.*
The Lord is my light and my salvation,
 whom shall I fear?
The Lord is the protector of my life:
 of whom shall I be afraid?
2 Whilst the wicked draw near against me,
 to eat my flesh.
My enemies that trouble me,
 have themselves been weakened,
 and have fallen.
3 If armies in camp should stand together against me,
 my heart shall not fear.
If a battle should rise up against me,
 in this will I be confident.
4 One thing I have asked of the Lord,
 this will I seek after;
that I may dwell in the house of the Lord all the days of
 my life.
That I may see the delight of the Lord,
 and may visit his temple.
5 For he hath hidden me in his tabernacle;
in the day of evils,
 he hath protected me in the secret place of his
  tabernacle.
6 He hath exalted me upon a rock:
 and now he hath lifted up my head above my
  enemies.
I have gone round, and have offered up in his tabernacle
 a sacrifice of jubilation:
 I will sing, and recite a psalm to the Lord.

The Psalter

7 Hear, O Lord, my voice,
> with which I have cried to thee:

have mercy on me and hear me.

8 My heart hath said to thee:
My face hath sought thee:
> thy face, O Lord, will I still seek.

9 Turn not away thy face from me;
> decline not in thy wrath from thy servant.

Be thou my helper, forsake me not;
> do not thou despise me, O God my Saviour.

10 For my father and my mother have left me:
but the Lord hath taken me up.

11 Set me, O Lord, a law in thy way,
and guide me in the right path, because of my enemies.

12 Deliver me not over to the will of them that trouble me;
for unjust witnesses have risen up against me;
> and iniquity hath lied to itself.

13 I believe to see the good things of the Lord
in the land of the living.

14 Expect the Lord, do manfully,
> and let thy heart take courage,
> and wait thou for the Lord.

Psalm 27(28)
Ad te, Domine, clamabo

Antiphon:
Be strengthened in the Lord,
> and in the might of his power.
> (Eph 6:10)

1 A psalm for David himself.
Unto thee will I cry, O Lord:
O my God, be not thou silent to me:
> lest thou be silent to me,
> I become like them that go down into the pit.

The Psalter

2 Hear, O Lord, the voice of my supplication,
   when I pray to thee;
when I lift up my hands to thy holy temple.

3 Draw me not away together with the wicked;
   and with the workers of iniquity destroy me not:
Who speak peace with their neighbour,
   but evils are in their hearts.

4 Give them according to their works,
   and according to the wickedness of their inventions.
According to the works of their hands give thou to them:
   render to them their reward.

5 Because they have not understood the works of the Lord,
   and the operations of his hands:
thou shalt destroy them,
   and shalt not build them up.

6 Blessed be the Lord,
for he hath heard the voice of my supplication.

7 The Lord is my helper and my protector:
   in him hath my heart confided,
   and I have been helped.
And my flesh hath flourished again,
   and with my will I will give praise to him.

8 The Lord is the strength of his people,
and the protector of the salvation of his anointed.

9 Save, O Lord, thy people,
   and bless thy inheritance:
and rule them and exalt them for ever.

Psalm 28(29)
Afferte Domino

Antiphon:
When Christ shall appear, who is your life,
then you also shall appear with him in glory. *(Col 3:4)*

The Psalter

1 *A psalm for David, at the finishing of the tabernacle.*
Bring to the Lord, O ye children of God:
bring to the Lord the offspring of rams.
2 Bring to the Lord glory and honour:
    bring to the Lord glory to his name:
    adore ye the Lord in his holy court.
3 The voice of the Lord is upon the waters;
    the God of majesty hath thundered,
The Lord is upon many waters.
4 The voice of the Lord is in power;
the voice of the Lord in magnificence.
5 The voice of the Lord breaketh the cedars:
yea, the Lord shall break the cedars of Libanus.
6 And shall reduce them to pieces,
    as a calf of Libanus,
    and as the beloved son of unicorns.
7 The voice of the Lord divideth the flame of fire:
8 The voice of the Lord shaketh the desert:
and the Lord shall shake the desert of Cades.
9 The voice of the Lord prepareth the stags:
    and he will discover the thick woods:
    and in his temple all shall speak his glory.
10 The Lord maketh the flood to dwell:
    and the Lord shall sit king for ever.
The Lord will give strength to his people:
    the Lord will bless his people with peace.

The Psalter

Day 6 - Evening Prayer

Psalm 29(30)
Exaltabo te, Domine

Antiphon:
For we are buried together with him by baptism into death;
that as Christ is risen from the dead by the glory of the Father,
so we also may walk in newness of life. *(Rom 6:4)*

1 *A psalm of a canticle, at the dedication of David's house.*

2 I will extol thee, O Lord,
   for thou hast upheld me:
and hast not made my enemies to rejoice over me.

3 O Lord my God, I have cried to thee,
and then hast healed me.

4 Thou hast brought forth, O Lord,
   my soul from hell:
thou hast saved me from them that go down into the pit.

5 Sing to the Lord, O ye his saints:
and give praise to the memory of his holiness.

6 For wrath is in his indignation;
   and life in his good will.
In the evening weeping shall have place,
   and in the morning gladness.

7 And in my abundance I said:
   I shall never be moved.

8 O Lord, in thy favour,
   thou gavest strength to my beauty.
Thou turnedst away thy face from me,
   and I became troubled.

9 To thee, O Lord, will I cry:
and I will make supplication to my God.

10 What profit is there in my blood,
   whilst I go down to corruption?
Shall dust confess to thee,
   or declare thy truth?
11 The Lord hath heard, and hath had mercy on me:
the Lord became my helper.
12 Thou hast turned for me my mourning into joy:
thou hast cut my sackcloth,
   and hast compassed me with gladness:
13 To the end that my glory may sing to thee,
   and I may not regret:
O Lord my God,
   I will give praise to thee for ever.

Psalm 30(31)
In te, Domine, speravi

Antiphon:
And Jesus crying with a loud voice, said;
Father, into thy hands I commend my spirit. *(Lk 23:46a)*

1 Unto the end, a psalm for David, in an ecstasy.
2 In thee, O Lord, have I hoped,
   let me never be confounded:
deliver me in thy justice.
3 Bow down thy ear to me:
   make haste to deliver me.
Be thou unto me a God,
   a protector, and a house of refuge, to save me.
4 For thou art my strength and my refuge;
   and for thy name's sake thou wilt lead me,
   and nourish me.
5 Thou wilt bring me out of this snare,
   which they have hidden for me:
for thou art my protector.

The Psalter

6 Into thy hands I commend my spirit:
   thou hast redeemed me,
O Lord, the God of truth.
7 Thou hast hated them that regard vanities,
   to no purpose.
But I have hoped in the Lord:
8 I will be glad and rejoice in thy mercy.
For thou best regarded my humility,
   thou hast saved my soul out of distresses.
9 And thou hast not shut me up in the hands of the
      enemy:
thou hast set my feet in a spacious place.
10 Have mercy on me, O Lord,
   for I am afflicted:
my eye is troubled with wrath,
   my soul, and my belly:
11 For my life is wasted with grief:
   and my years in sighs.
My strength is weakened through poverty
   and my bones are disturbed.
12 I am become a reproach among all my enemies,
   and very much to my neighbours;
   and a fear to my acquaintance.
They that saw me without fled from me.
13 I am forgotten as one dead from the heart.
I am become as a vessel that is destroyed.
14 For I have heard the blame of many that dwell round
      about.
While they assembled together against me,
   they consulted to take away my life.
15 But I have put my trust in thee,
O Lord: I said: Thou art my God.
16 My lots are in thy hands.
Deliver me out of the hands of my enemies;
   and from them that persecute me.
17 Make thy face to shine upon thy servant; save me
      in thy mercy.

The Psalter

18 Let me not be confounded, O Lord,
    for I have called upon thee.
Let the wicked be ashamed,
    and be brought down to hell.
19 Let deceitful lips be made dumb.
Which speak iniquity against the just,
    with pride and abuse.
20 O how great is the multitude of thy sweetness, O Lord,
    which thou hast hidden for them that fear thee!
Which thou hast wrought for them that hope in thee,
    in the sight of the sons of men.
21 Thou shalt hide them in the secret of thy face,
    from the disturbance of men.
Thou shalt protect them in thy tabernacle
    from the contradiction of tongues.
22 Blessed be the Lord,
    for he hath shewn his wonderful mercy to me in a fortified city.
23 But I said in the excess of my mind:
    I am cast away from before thy eyes.
Therefore thou hast heard the voice of my prayer,
    when I cried to thee.
24 O love the Lord, all ye his saints:
    for the Lord will require truth,
    and will repay them abundantly that act proudly.
25 Do ye manfully, and let your heart be strengthened,
all ye that hope in the Lord.

The Psalter

Day 7 - Morning Prayer

Psalm 31(32)
Beati quorum

Antiphon:
And it shall come to pass, that before they call, I will
 hear;
as they are yet speaking, I will hear. *(Isaiah 65:24)*

1 *To David himself, understanding.*
Blessed are they whose iniquities are forgiven,
and whose sins are covered.
2 Blessed is the man to whom the Lord hath not
 imputed sin,
and in whose spirit there is no guile.
3 Because I was silent my bones grew old;
whilst I cried out all the day long.
4 For day and night thy hand was heavy upon me:
 I am turned in my anguish,
  whilst the thorn is fastened.
5 I have acknowledged my sin to thee,
  and my injustice I have not concealed.
I said I will confess against myself my injustice to the
 Lord:
  and thou hast forgiven the wickedness of my sin.
6 For this shall every one that is holy pray to thee in a
 seasonable time.
And yet in a flood of many waters,
 they shall not come nigh unto him.
7 Thou art my refuge from the trouble which hath
 encompassed me:
my joy, deliver me from them that surround me.
8 I will give thee understanding,
  and I will instruct thee in this way,
  in which thou shalt go:
I will fix my eyes upon thee.

The Psalter

9 Do not become like the horse and the mule,
  who have no understanding.
With bit and bridle bind fast their jaws,
  who come not near unto thee.
10 Many are the scourges of the sinner,
  but mercy shall encompass him
  that hopeth in the Lord.
11 Be glad in the Lord, and rejoice, ye just,
and glory, all ye right of heart.

Psalm 32(33)
Exultate, justi

Antiphon:
Let all thy creatures serve thee;
because thou hast spoken, and they were made;
thou didst send forth thy spirit, and they were
  created.
And there is no one that can resist thy voice. *(Judith 16:17)*

1 A psalm for David.
Rejoice in the Lord, O ye just:
praise becometh the upright.
2 Give praise to the Lord on the harp;
  sing to him with the psaltery,
  the instrument of ten strings.
3 Sing to him a new canticle,
sing well unto him with a loud noise.
4 For the word of the Lord is right,
and all his works are done with faithfulness.
5 He loveth mercy and judgment;
the earth is full of the mercy of the Lord.
6 By the word of the Lord the heavens were
    established;
and all the power of them by the spirit of his mouth:
7 Gathering together the waters of the sea,
  as in a vessel;
laying up the depths in storehouses.

The Psalter

8 Let all the earth fear the Lord,
and let all the inhabitants of the world be in awe of him.
9 For he spoke and they were made:
he commanded and they were created.
10 The Lord bringeth to naught the counsels of nations;
and he rejecteth the devices of people,
   and casteth away the counsels of princes.
11 But the counsel of the Lord standeth for ever:
the thoughts of his heart to all generations.
12 Blessed is the nation whose God is the Lord:
the people whom he hath chosen for his inheritance.
13 The Lord hath looked from heaven:
he hath beheld all the sons of men.
14 From his habitation which he hath prepared,
he hath looked upon all that dwell on the earth.
15 He who hath made the hearts of every one of them:
who understandeth all their works.
16 The king is not saved by a great army:
nor shall the giant be saved by his own great strength.
17 Vain is the horse for safety:
neither shall he be saved by the abundance of his strength.
18 Behold the eyes of the Lord are on them that fear him:
and on them that hope in his mercy.
19 To deliver their souls from death;
and feed them in famine.
20 Our soul waiteth for the Lord:
for he is our helper and protector.
21 For in him our heart shall rejoice:
and in his holy name we have trusted.
22 Let thy mercy, O Lord, be upon us,
as we have hoped in thee.

The Psalter

Day 7 - Evening Prayer

Psalm 33(34)
Benedicam Dominum

Antiphon:
He hath shewed might in his arm; he hath scattered
    the proud in the conceit of their heart.
He hath put down the mighty from their seat, and
    hath exalted the humble. *(Lk 1:51-52)*

1 For David, when he changed his countenance before
    Achimelech, who dismissed him, and he went his
    way. [*1Kgdm 1:21.*]
2 I will bless the Lord at all times,
his praise shall be always in my mouth.
3 In the Lord shall my soul be praised:
let the meek hear and rejoice.
4 O magnify the Lord with me;
and let us extol his name together.
5 I sought the Lord, and he heard me;
and he delivered me from all my troubles.
6 Come ye to him and be enlightened:
and your faces shall not be confounded.
7 This poor man cried, and the Lord heard him:
and saved him out of all his troubles.
8 The angel of the Lord shall encamp round about
    them that fear him:
and shall deliver them.
9 O taste, and see that the Lord is sweet:
blessed is the man that hopeth in him.
10 Fear the Lord, all ye his saints:
for there is no want to them that fear him.
11 The rich have wanted, and have suffered hunger:
but they that seek the Lord shall not be deprived of
    any good.

The Psalter

12 Come, children, hearken to me:
I will teach you the fear of the Lord.
13 Who is the man that desireth life:
who loveth to see good days?
14 Keep thy tongue from evil,
and thy lips from speaking guile.
15 Turn away from evil and do good:
seek after peace and pursue it.
16 The eyes of the Lord are upon the just:
and his ears unto their prayers.
17 But the countenance of the Lord is against them
that do evil things:
to cut off the remembrance of them from the earth.
18 The just cried, and the Lord heard them:
and delivered them out of all their troubles.
19 The Lord is nigh unto them that are of a contrite
heart:
and he will save the humble of spirit.
20 Many are the afflictions of the just;
but out of them all will the Lord deliver them.
21 The Lord keepeth all their bones,
not one of them shall be broken.
22 The death of the wicked is very evil:
and they that hate the just shall be guilty.
23 The Lord will redeem the souls of his servants:
and none of them that trust in him shall offend.

Psalm 34(35)
Judica, Domine, nocentes me

Antiphon:
If I had not come and spoken to them, they would not
have sin, but now they have no excuse for their sin.
He that hateth me, hateth my Father also. *(John 15:22-23)*

The Psalter

1 *For David himself.*
Judge thou, O Lord, them that wrong me :
overthrow them that fight against me.
2 Take hold of arms and shield :
and rise up to help me.
3 Bring out the sword,
    and shut up the way against them that persecute
        me :
say to my soul :
    I am thy salvation.
4 Let them be confounded and ashamed
    that seek after my soul.
Let them be turned back and be confounded
    that devise against me.
5 Let them become as dust before the wind :
and let the angel of the Lord straiten them.
6 Let their way become dark and slippery;
and let the angel of the Lord pursue them.
7 For without cause they have hidden their net for me
    unto destruction :
without cause they have upbraided my soul.
8 Let the snare which he knoweth not come upon him :
    and let the net which he hath hidden catch him :
    and let the net which he hath hidden catch him :
    and into that very snare let them fall.
9 But my soul shall rejoice in the Lord;
and shall be delighted in his salvation.
10 All my bones shall say : Lord, who is like to thee?
Who deliverest the poor from the hand of them that
    are stronger than he;
    the needy and the poor from them that strip him.
11 Unjust witnesses rising up
have asked me things I knew not.
12 They repaid me evil for good :
to the depriving me of my soul.

The Psalter

13 But as for me, when they were troublesome to me,
   I was clothed with haircloth.
I humbled my soul with fasting;
   and my prayer shall be turned into my bosom.
14 As a neighbour and as an own brother, so did I please:
as one mourning and sorrowful so was I humbled.
15 But they rejoiced against me, and came together :
scourges were gathered together upon me,
   and I knew not.
      they tempted me, they scoffed at me with scorn :
      they gnashed upon me with their teeth.
17 Lord, when wilt thou look upon me?
   rescue thou soul from their malice :
   my only one from the lions.
18 I will give thanks to thee in a great church;
I will praise thee in a strong people.
19 Let not them that are my enemies wrongfully
      rejoice over me :
who have hated me without cause,
   and wink with the eyes.
20 For they spoke indeed peaceably to me;
and speaking in the anger of the earth they devised
      guile.
21 And they opened their mouth wide against me;
they said :
   Well done, well done,
   our eyes have seen it.
22 Thou hast seen, O Lord, be not thou silent :
O Lord, depart not from me.
23 Arise, and be attentive to my judgment :
to my cause, my God, and my Lord.
24 Judge me, O Lord my God according to thy justice,
and let them not rejoice over me.
25 Let them not say in their hearts :
   It is well, it is well, to our mind :
neither let them say :
We have swallowed him up.

The Psalter

26 Let them blush :
   and be ashamed together, who rejoice at my evils.
Let them be clothed with confusion and shame,
   who speak great things against me.
27 Let them rejoice and be glad, who are well pleased
      with my justice,
and let them say always : The Lord be magnified, who
      delights in the peace of his servant.
28 Any my tongue shall meditate thy justice,
thy praise all the day long.

The Psalter

Day 8 - Morning Prayer

Psalm 35(36)
Dixit injustus

Antiphon:
Unto you that fear my name the Sun of justice shall
 arise, and health in his wings;
and you shall go forth and shall leap like calves of the
 herd. *(Malachi 4:2)*

1 Unto the end, for the servant of God, David himself.
2 The unjust hath said within himself,
 that he would sin :
there is no fear of God before his eyes.
3 For in his sight he hath done deceitfully,
that his iniquity may be found unto hatred.
4 The words of his mouth are iniquity and guile :
he would not understand that he might do well.
5 He hath devised iniquity on his bed,
 he hath set himself on every way that is not good :
but evil he hath not hated.
6 O Lord, thy mercy is in heaven,
and thy truth reacheth, even to the clouds.
7 Thy justice is as the mountains of God,
 thy judgments are a great deep.
Men and beasts thou wilt preserve, O Lord :
8 O how hast thou multiplied thy mercy, O God!
 But the children of men shall put their trust
 under the covert of thy wings.
9 They shall be inebriated with the plenty of thy house;
and thou shalt make them drink of the torrent of thy
 pleasure.
10 For with thee is the fountain of life;
 and in thy light we shall see light.
11 Extend thy mercy to them that know thee,
and thy justice to them that are right in heart.

12 Let not the foot of pride come to me,
and let not the hand of the sinner move me.
13 There the workers of iniquity are fallen,
they are cast out, and could not stand.

Psalm 36(37)
Noli aemulari

Antiphon:
Hearken to me, you that know what is just; my people
 who have my law in your heart;
Fear ye not the reproach of men, and be not afraid of
 their blasphemies. *(Isaiah 51:7)*

1 *A psalm for David himself.*
Be not emulous of evildoers;
nor envy them that work iniquity.
2 For they shall shortly wither away as grass,
and as the green herbs shall quickly fall.
3 Trust in the Lord, and do good,
 and dwell in the land,
and thou shalt be fed with its riches.
4 Delight in the Lord,
and he will give thee the requests of thy heart.
5 Commit thy way to the Lord,
and trust in him, and he will do it.
6 And he will bring forth thy justice as the light,
and thy judgment as the noonday.
7 Be subject to the Lord and pray to him
Envy not the man who prospereth in his way;
 the man who doth unjust things.
8 Cease from anger, and leave rage;
have no emulation to do evil.
9 For the evildoers shall be cut off:
but they that wait upon the Lord shall inherit the
 land.

The Psalter

10 For yet a little while, and the wicked shall not be :
and thou shalt seek his place, and shalt not find it.
11 But the meek shall inherit the land,
and shall delight in abundance of peace.
12 The sinner shall watch the just man :
and shall gnash upon him with his teeth.
13 But the Lord shall laugh at him :
for he foreseeth that his day shall come.
14 The wicked have drawn out the sword :
    they have bent their bow.
To cast down the poor and needy,
    to kill the upright of heart.
15 Let their sword enter into their own hearts,
and let their bow be broken.
16 Better is a little to the just,
than the great riches of the wicked.
17 For the arms of the wicked shall be broken in pieces;
but the Lord strengtheneth the just.
18 The Lord knoweth the days of undefiled;
and their inheritance shall be for ever.
19 They shall not be confounded in the evil time;
and in the days of famine they shall be filled :
20 because the wicked shall perish.
And the enemies of the Lord,
    presently after they shall be honoured and exalted,
shall come to nothing and vanish like smoke.
21 The sinner shall borrow, and not pay again;
but the just sheweth mercy and shall give.
22 For such as bless him shall inherit the land :
but such as curse him shall perish.
23 With the Lord shall the steps of a man be directed,
and he shall like well his way.
24 When he shall fall he shall not be bruised,
for the Lord putteth his hand under him.
25 I have been young, and now am old;
and I have not seen the just forsaken, nor his seed
      seeking bread.

The Psalter

26 He sheweth mercy, and lendeth all the day long;
and his seed shall be in blessing.
27 Decline from evil and do good,
and dwell for ever and ever.
28 For the Lord loveth judgment,
 and will not forsake his saints :
they shall be preserved for ever.
The unjust shall be punished,
 and the seed of the wicked shall perish.
29 But the just shall inherit the land,
and shall dwell therein for evermore.
30 The mouth of the just shall meditate wisdom :
and his tongue shall speak judgment.
31 The law of his God is in his heart,
and his steps shall not be supplanted.
32 The wicked watcheth the just man,
and seeketh to put him to death,
33 But the Lord will not leave in his hands;
nor condemn him when he shall be judged.
34 Expect the Lord and keep his way :
 and he will exalt thee to inherit the land :
 when the sinners shall perish thou shalt see.
35 I have seen the wicked highly exalted,
and lifted up like the cedars of Libanus.
36 And I passed by, and lo, he was not :
and I sought him and his place was not found.
37 Keep innocence, and behold justice :
for there are remnants for the peaceable man.
38 But the unjust shall be destroyed together :
the remnants of the wicked shall perish.
39 But the salvation of the just is from the Lord,
and he is their protector in the time of trouble.
40 And the Lord will help them and deliver them :
 and he will rescue them from the wicked,
 and save them, because they have hoped in him.

The Psalter

Day 8 - Evening Prayer

Psalm 37(38)
Domine, ne in furore

Antiphon:
There is now therefore no condemnation to them that
  are in Christ Jesus, who walk not according to
  the flesh.
For the law of the spirit of life, in Christ Jesus, hath
  delivered me from the law of sin and of death.
  (Rom 8:1-2)

1 A psalm for David, for a remembrance of the
    sabbath.
2 Rebuke me not, O Lord, in thy indignation;
nor chastise me in thy wrath.
3 For thy arrows are fastened in me :
and thy hand hath been strong upon me.
4 There is no health in my flesh, because of thy wrath :
there is no peace for my bones,
    because of my sins.
5 For my iniquities are gone over my head :
and as a heavy burden are become heavy upon me.
6 My sores are putrified and corrupted,
because of my foolishness.
7 I am become miserable, and am bowed down even to
    the end :
I walked sorrowful all the day long.
8 For my loins are filled with illusions;
and there is no health in my flesh.
9 I am afflicted and humbled exceedingly :
I roared with the groaning of my heart.
10 Lord, all my desire is before thee,
and my groaning is not hidden from thee.
11 My heart is troubled, my strength hath left me,
and the light of my eyes itself is not with me.
12 My friends and my neighbours have drawn near,
    and stood against me.
And they that were near me stood afar off :

The Psalter

13 And they that sought my soul used violence.
And they that sought evils to me spoke vain things,
> and studied deceits all the day long.

14 But I, as a deaf man, heard not :
and as a dumb man not opening his mouth.
15 And I became as a man that heareth not :
and that hath no reproofs in his mouth.
16 For in thee, O Lord, have I hoped :
thou wilt hear me, O Lord my God.
17 For I said:
> Lest at any time my enemies rejoice over me :
and whilst my feet are moved,
>> they speak great things against me.

18 For I am ready for scourges :
and my sorrow is continually before me.
19 For I will declare my inequity :
and I will think for my sin.
20 But my enemies live, and are stronger that I :
and they hate me wrongfully are multiplied.
21 They that render evil for good,
have detracted me, because I followed goodness.
22 Forsake me not, O Lord my God :
do not thou depart from me.
23 Attend unto my help,
O Lord, the God of my salvation.

Psalm 38(39)
Dixi custodiam

Antiphon:
The eye of God hath looked upon him for good, and
> hath lifted him up from his low estate, and
hath exalted his head.
And many have wondered at him, and have glorified
> God. *(Ecclus 11:13)*

1 *Unto the end, for Idithun himself, a canticle of
David.*

The Psalter

2 I said: I will take heed to my ways :
  that I sin not with my tongue.
  I have set guard to my mouth,
    when the sinner stood against me.
3 I was dumb, and was humbled,
  and kept silence from good things :
  and my sorrow was renewed.
4 My heart grew hot within me :
and in my meditation a fire shall flame out.
5 I spoke with my tongue :
  O Lord, make me know my end.
And what is the number of my days :
  that I may know what is wanting to me.
6 Behold thou hast made my days measurable :
  and my substance is as nothing before thee.
And indeed all things are vanity :
  every man living.
7 Surely man passeth as an image :
  yea, and he is disquieted in vain.
He storeth up :
  and he knoweth not for whom he shall gather these things.
8 And now what is my hope?
  is it not the Lord?
  and my substance is with thee.
9 Deliver thou me from all my iniquities :
thou hast made me a reproach to the fool.
10 I was dumb, and I opened not my mouth,
because thou hast done it.
11 Remove thy scourges from me.
The strength of thy hand hath made me faint in
    rebukes:
12 thou hast corrected man for iniquity.
And thou hast made his soul to waste away like a
    spider :
  surely in vain is any man disquieted.
13 Hear my prayer, O Lord, and my supplication :
  give ear to my tears.
  Be not silent :
    for I am a stranger with thee,
    and a sojourner as all my fathers were.

14 O forgive me, that I may be refreshed,
before I go hence, and be no more.

Psalm 39(40)
Expectans expectavi

Antiphon:
He trusted in God; let Him now deliver Him if He will
 have Him.
For He said; I am the Son of God. *(Matt 28:43)*

1 *Unto the end, a psalm for David himself.*
2 With expectation I have waited for the Lord,
and he was attentive to me.
3 And he heard my prayers,
 and brought me out of the pit of misery
 and the mire of dregs.
And he set my feet upon a rock,
 and directed my steps.
4 And he put a new canticle into my mouth,
 a song to our God.
Many shall see, and shall fear :
 and they shall hope in the Lord.
5 Blessed is the man whose trust is in the name of the
  Lord;
and who hath not had regard to vanities,
 and lying follies.
6 Thou hast multiplied thy wonderful works, O Lord
  my God :
 and in thy thoughts there is no one like to thee.
I have declared and I have spoken they are multiplied
 above number.
7 Sacrifice and oblation thou didst not desire;
 but thou hast pierced ears for me.
Burnt offering and sin offering thou didst not require :
8 then said I, Behold I come.
In the head of the book it is written of me

The Psalter

9 that I should do thy will :
   O my God, I have desired it,
   and thy law in the midst of my heart.
10 I have declared thy justice in a great church,
   lo, I will not restrain my lips :
O Lord, thou knowest it.
11 I have not hid thy justice within my heart :
   I have declared thy truth and thy salvation.
I have not concealed thy mercy and thy truth
   from a great council.
12 Withhold not thou, O Lord,
   thy tender mercies from me :
thy mercy and thy truth have always upheld me.
13 For evils without number have surrounded me;
   my iniquities have overtaken me,
   and I was not able to see.
They are multiplied above the hairs of my head :
   and my heart hath forsaken me.
14 Be pleased, O Lord, to deliver me,
look down, O Lord, to help me.
15 Let them be confounded and ashamed together,
   that seek after my soul to take it away.
Let them be turned backward and be ashamed
   that desire evils to me.
16 Let them immediately bear their confusion,
   that say to me : 'T is well, 't is well.
17 Let all that seek thee rejoice and be glad in thee :
     and let such as love thy salvation say always :
   The Lord be magnified.
18 But I am a beggar and poor :
   the Lord is careful for me.
Thou art my helper and my protector :
   O my God, be not slack.

The Psalter

Day 9 - Morning Prayer

Psalm 40(41)
Beatus qui intelligit

Antiphon:
Brethren, the scripture must needs be fulfilled, which
   the Holy Ghost spoke before by the mouth of
   David concerning Judas,
who was the leader of them that apprehended Jesus…
   (Acts 1:16)

1 *Unto the end, a psalm for David himself.*
2 Blessed is he that understandeth
   concerning the needy and the poor :
the Lord will deliver him in the evil day.
3 The Lord preserve him and give him life,
   and make him blessed upon the earth :
and deliver him not up to the will of his enemies.
4 The Lord help him on his bed of sorrow :
thou hast turned all his couch in his sickness.
5 I said: O Lord, be thou merciful to me :
heal my soul, for I have sinned against thee.
6 My enemies have spoken evils against me:
when shall he die and his name perish?
7 And if he came in to see me, he spoke vain things :
   his heart gathered together iniquity to itself.
He went out and spoke to the same purpose.
8 All my enemies whispered together against me :
they devised evils to me.
9 They determined against me an unjust word :
shall he that sleepeth rise again no more?
10 For even the man of peace, in whom I trusted,
who ate my bread, hath greatly supplanted me.
11 But thou, O Lord, have mercy on me,
   and raise me up again :
   and I will requite them.
12 By this I know, that thou hast had a good will for
   me :
because my enemy shall not rejoice over me.

The Psalter

13 But thou hast upheld me by reason of my innocence :
and hast established me in thy sight for ever.
14 Blessed be the Lord the God of Israel
>from eternity to eternity.
So be it. So be it.

Psalm 41(42)
Quemadmodum desiderat

Antiphon:
Therefore, my beloved brethren, be ye steadfast and
>unmovable;
always abounding in the work of the Lord, knowing
>that your labour is not in vain in the Lord. *(I Cor 15:58)*

1 Unto the end, understanding for the sons of Core.
2 As the hart panteth after the fountains of water;
so my soul panteth after thee, O God.
3 My soul hath thirsted after the strong living God;
when shall I come and appear before the face of God?
4 My tears have been my bread day and night,
whilst it is said to me daily : Where is thy God?
5 These things I remembered, and poured out my soul
>in me :
>For I shall go over into the place of the wonderful
>>tabernacle, even to the house of God :
With the voice of joy and praise;
>the noise of one feasting.
6 Why art thou sad, O my soul?
>and why dost thou trouble me?
Hope in God, for I will still give praise to him :
>the salvation of my countenance,
7 and my God. My soul is troubled within myself :
therefore will I remember thee from the land of Jordan
>and Hermoniim,
>from the little hill.
8 Deep calleth on deep, at the noise of thy flood-gates.
All thy heights and thy billows have passed over me.

9 In the daytime the Lord hath commanded his mercy;
  and a canticle to him in the night.
With me is prayer to the God of my life.
10 I will say to God : Thou art my support.
  Why hast thou forgotten me?
    and why go I mourning, whilst my enemy afflicteth me?
11 Whilst my bones are broken,
  my enemies who trouble me have reproached me;
Whilst they say to me day be day :
  Where is thy God?
12 Why art thou cast down, O my soul?
  and why dost thou disquiet me?
Hope thou in God, for I will still give praise to him :
  the salvation of my countenance, and my God.

Psalm 42(43)
Judica me, Deus

Antiphon:
And He went down into Capharnaum, a city of Galilee; and there He taught them on the Sabbath days. *(Lk 4:31)*

1 *A psalm for David.*
Judge me, O God,
    and distinguish my cause from the nation that is not holy :
  deliver me from the unjust and deceitful man.
2 For thou art God my strength :
  why hast thou cast me off?
    and why do I go sorrowful whilst the enemy afflicteth me?
3 Send forth thy light and thy truth :
  they have conducted me,
  and brought me unto thy holy hill,
  and into thy tabernacles.
4 And I will go in to the altar of God :
  to God who giveth joy to my youth.

The Psalter

5 To thee, O God my God,
I will give praise upon the harp :
why art thou sad, O my soul?
    and why dost thou disquiet me?
6 Hope in God, for I will still give praise to him :
the salvation of my countenance, and my God.

The Psalter

Day 9 - Evening Prayer

Psalm 43(44)
Deus auribus nostris

Antiphon:
I am sure that neither death, nor life, nor angels, nor
      principalities, nor powers,
not things present, nor things to come, nor might, nor
      height, nor depth, nor any other creature,
shall be able to separate us from the love of God which
      is in Christ Jesus our Lord.
      (Rom 8:38-39)

1 *Unto the end, for the sons of Core, to give
      understanding.*
2 We have heard, O God, with our ears :
      our fathers have declared to us,
The work, thou hast wrought in their days,
      and in the days of old.
3 Thy hand destroyed the Gentiles,
      and thou plantedst them :
thou didst afflict the people and cast them out.
4 For they got not the possession of the land by their
      own sword :
      neither did their own arm save them.
But thy right hand and thy arm,
      and the light of thy countenance :
      because thou wast pleased with them.
5 Thou art thyself my king and my God,
      who commandest the saving of Jacob.
6 Through thee we will push down our enemies with
      the horn :
and through thy name we will despise them that rise up
      against us.
7 For I will not trust in my bow :
neither shall my sword save me.
8 But thou hast saved us from them that afflict us :
and hast put them to shame that hate us.

The Psalter

9 In God shall we glory all the day long :
and in thy name we will give praise for ever.
10 But now thou hast cast us off, and put us to shame :
and thou, O God, wilt not go out with our armies.
11 Thou hast made us turn our back to our enemies :
and they that hated us plundered for themselves.
12 Thou hast given us up like sheep to be eaten :
thou hast scattered us among the nations.
13 Thou hast sold thy people for no price :
and there was no reckoning in the exchange of them.
14 Thou hast made us a reproach to our neighbours,
a scoff and derision to them that are round about us.
15 Thou hast made us a byword among the Gentiles :
a shaking of the head among the people.
16 All the day long my shame is before me : and the
    confusion of my face hath covered me,
17 At the voice of him that reproacheth and
    detracteth me :
at the face of the enemy and persecutor.
18 All these things have come upon us,
    yet we have not forgotten thee :
and we have not done wickedly in they covenant.
19 And our heart hath not turned back :
neither hast thou turned aside our steps from thy way.
20 For thou hast humbled us in the place of affliction :
and the shadow of death hath covered us.
21 If we have forgotten the name of our God,
and if we have spread forth our hands to a strange god:
22 Shall not God search out these things :
    for he knoweth the secrets of the heart.
Because for thy sake we are killed all the day long :
    we are counted as sheep for the slaughter.
23 Arise, why sleepest thou, O Lord?
arise, and cast us not off to the end.
24 Why turnest thou face away?
and forgettest our want and our trouble?
25 For our soul is humbled down to the dust :
our belly cleaveth to the earth.
26 Arise, O Lord,
help us and redeem us for thy name's sake.

The Psalter

Psalm 44(45)
Eructavit cor meum

Antiphon:
And I saw a new heaven and a new earth.
For the first heaven and the first earth was gone; and
    the sea is now no more.
And I, John, saw the holy city, the new Jerusalem,
    coming down out of heaven from God,
prepared as a bride adorned for her husband. *(Rev 21:1-2)*

1 *Unto the end, for them that shall be changed, for the
    sons of Core, for understanding. A canticle for
    the Beloved.*
2 My heart hath uttered a good word
    I speak my works to the king;
My tongue is the pen of a scrivener that writeth
swiftly.
3 Thou art beautiful above the sons of men:
    grace is poured abroad in thy lips;
    therefore hath God blessed thee for ever
4 Gird thy sword upon thy thigh,
O thou most mighty.
5 With thy comeliness and thy beauty set out,
    proceed prosperously, and reign.
Because of truth and meekness and justice:
    and thy right hand shall conduct thee wonderfully.
6 Thy arrows are sharp: under thee shall people fall,
 into the hearts of the king's enemies.
7 Thy throne, O God, is for ever and ever:
the sceptre of thy kingdom is a sceptre of uprightness.
8 Thou hast loved justice, and hated iniquity:
    therefore God, thy God,
        hath anointed thee with the oil of gladness above
            thy fellows.
9 Myrrh and stacte and cassia perfume thy garments,
from the ivory houses: out of which

The Psalter

10 the daughters of kings have delighted thee in thy
 glory.
The queen stood on thy right hand,
 in gilded clothing; surrounded with variety.
11 Hearken, O daughter, and see, and incline thy ear:
and forget thy people and thy father's house.
12 And the king shall greatly desire thy beauty;
for he is the Lord thy God, and him they shall adore.
13 And the daughters of Tyre with gifts,
yea, all the rich among the people, shall entreat thy
 countenance.
14 All the glory of the king's daughter
is within in golden borders,
15 clothed round about with varieties.
After her shall virgins be brought to the king:
 her neighbours shall be brought to thee.
16 They shall be brought with gladness and rejoicing:
they shall be brought into the temple of the king.
17 Instead of thy fathers, sons are born to thee:
thou shalt make them princes over all the earth.
18 They shall remember thy name throughout all
 generations.
Therefore shall people praise thee for ever;
 yea, for ever and ever.

Psalm 45(46)
Deus noster refugium

Antiphon:
And the dragon was angry against the woman; and
 went to make war with the rest of her seed,
who keep the commandments of God and have the
 testimony of Jesus Christ. *(Rev 12:17)*

1 *Unto the end, for the sons of Core, for the hidden.*
2 Our God is our refuge and strength:
a helper in troubles, which have found us exceedingly.
3 Therefore we will not fear, when the earth shall be
 troubled;
and the mountains shall be removed into the heart of
 the sea.

The Psalter

4 Their waters roared and were troubled:
the mountains were troubled with his strength.
5 The stream of the river maketh the city of God
    joyful:
the most High hath sanctified his own tabernacle.
6 God is in the midst thereof, it shall not be moved:
    God will help it in the morning early.
7 Nations were troubled, and kingdoms were bowed
    down:
he uttered his voice, the earth trembled.
8 The Lord of armies is with us:
the God of Jacob is our protector.
9 Come and behold ye the works of the Lord:
what wonders he hath done upon earth,
10 making wars to cease even to the end of the earth.
He shall destroy the bow, and break the weapons:
    and the shield he shall burn in the fire.
11 Be still and see that I am God;
    I will be exalted among the nations,
    and I will be exalted in the earth.
12 The Lord of armies is with us:
the God of Jacob is our protector.

The Psalter

Day 10 - Morning Prayer

Psalm 46(47)
Omnes gentes, plaudite

Antiphon:
And David and all the house of Israel brought the ark
   of the covenant of the Lord
with joyful shouting, and with sound of trumpet. (2
   Kings 6:15)

1 *Unto the end, for the sons of Core.*
2 O clap your hands, all ye nations:
shout unto God with the voice of joy,
3 For the Lord is high, terrible:
a great king over all the earth.
4 He hath subdued the people under us;
and the nations under our feet.
5 He hath chosen for us his inheritance
the beauty of Jacob which he hath loved.
6 God is ascended with jubilee,
and the Lord with the sound of trumpet.
7 Sing praises to our God, sing ye:
sing praises to our king, sing ye.
8 For God is the king of all the earth:
sing ye wisely.
9 God shall reign over the nations:
God sitteth on his holy throne.
10 The princes of the people are gathered together,
   with the God of Abraham:
for the strong gods of the earth are exceedingly
   exalted.

The Psalter

Psalm 47(48)
Magnus Dominus

Antiphon:
All things of His divine power which appertain to life
    and godliness
are given us through the knowledge of Him who hath
    called us by His own proper glory and virtue. *(2 Peter 1:3)*

1 *A psalm of a canticle, for the sons of Core, on the
    second day of the week.*
2 Great is the Lord, and exceedingly to be praised
    in the city of our God,
    in his holy mountain.
3 With the joy of the whole earth is mount Sion
    founded,
    on the sides of the north,
    the city of the great king.
4 In her houses shall God be known,
when he shall protect her.
5 For behold the kings of the earth assembled
    themselves:
they gathered together.
6 So they saw, and they wondered,
they were troubled, they were moved:
7 trembling took hold of them.
There were pains as of a woman in labour.
8 With a vehement wind thou shalt break in pieces
the ships of Tharsis.
9 As we have heard, so have we seen,
    in the city of the Lord of hosts,
in the city of our God:
    God hath founded it for ever.
10 We have received thy mercy, O God,
in the midst of thy temple.
11 According to thy name, O God,
    so also is thy praise unto the ends of the earth:
thy right hand is full of justice.

The Psalter

12 Let mount Sion rejoice,
 and the daughters of Juda be glad;
because of thy judgments, O Lord.
13 Surround Sion, and encompass her:
tell ye in her towers.
14 Set your hearts on her strength;
and distribute her houses,
 that ye may relate it in another generation.
15 For this is God, our God unto eternity,
 and for ever and ever:
he shall rule us for evermore.

Psalm 48(49)
Audite haec, omnes gentes

Antiphon:
All these things Jesus spoke in parables to the
 multitudes; and without parables He did not
 speak to them,
that it might be fulfilled which was spoken by the
 prophet, saying;
I will open my mouth in parables,
I will utter things hidden from the foundation of the
 world. (Matt 13:34-35)

1 Unto the end, a psalm for the sons of Core.
2 Hear these things, all ye nations:
give ear, all ye inhabitants of the world.
3 All you that are earthborn, and you sons of men:
both rich and poor together.
4 My mouth shall speak wisdom:
and the meditation of my heart understanding.
5 I will incline my ear to a parable;
I will open my proposition on the psaltery.
6 Why shall I fear in the evil day?
the iniquity of my heel shall encompass me.
7 They that trust in their own strength,
 and glory in the multitude of their riches,

The Psalter

8 No brother can redeem, nor shall man redeem:
he shall not give to God his ransom,
9 Nor the price of the redemption of his soul:
and shall labour for ever,
10 and shall still live unto the end.
11 He shall not see destruction,
    when he shall see the wise dying:
the senseless and the fool shall perish together:
    And they shall leave their riches to strangers:
12 and their sepulchres shall be their houses for ever.
Their dwelling places to all generations:
    they have called their lands by their names.
13 And man when he was in honour did not understand;
he is compared to senseless beasts,
    and is become like to them.
14 This way of theirs is a stumblingblock to them:
and afterwards they shall delight in their mouth.
15 They are laid in hell like sheep:
    death shall feed upon them.
And the just shall have dominion over them in the morning;
    and their help shall decay in hell from their glory.
16 But God will redeem my soul from the hand of hell,
when he shall receive me.
17 Be not thou afraid,
    when a man shall be made rich,
    and when the glory of his house shall be increased.
18 For when he shall die he shall take nothing away;
nor shall his glory descend with him.
19 For in his lifetime his soul will be blessed:
and he will praise thee when thou shalt do well to him.
20 He shall go in to the generations of his fathers:
and he shall never see light.
21 Man when he was in honour did not understand:
    he hath been compared to senseless beasts,
    and made like to them.

The Psalter

Day 10 - Evening Prayer

Psalm 49(50)
Deus deorum

Antiphon:
How beautiful upon the mountains are the feet of him
    that bringeth good tidings and that preacheth
    peace,
of him that sheweth forth good, that preacheth
    salvation, that saith to Sion;
Thy God shall reign! (Isaiah 52:7)

1 *A psalm for Asaph.*
The God of gods, the Lord hath spoken:
    and he hath called the earth.
From the rising of the sun,
    to the going down thereof:
2 out of Sion the loveliness of his beauty.
3 God shall come manifestly:
    our God shall come, and shall not keep silence.
A fire shall burn before him:
    and a mighty tempest shall be round about him.
4 He shall call heaven from above, and the earth,
to judge his people.
5 Gather ye together his saints to him:
who set his covenant before sacrifices.
6 And the heavens shall declare his justice:
for God is judge.
7 Hear, O my people, and I will speak:
    O Israel, and I will testify to thee:
I am God, thy God.
8 I will not reprove thee for thy sacrifices:
and thy burnt offerings are always in my sight.
9 I will not take calves out of thy house:
nor he goats out of thy flocks.
10 For all the beasts of the woods are mine:
the cattle on the hills, and the oxen.
11 I know all the fowls of the air:
and with me is the beauty of the field.

12 If I should be hungry, I would not tell thee:
for the world is mine, and the fulness thereof.
13 Shall I eat the flesh of bullocks?
or shall I drink the blood of goats?
14 Offer to God the sacrifice of praise:
and pay thy vows to the most High.
15 And call upon me in the day of trouble:
I will deliver thee, and thou shalt glorify me.
16 But to the sinner God hath said:
    Why dost thou declare my justices,
    and take my covenant in thy mouth?
17 Seeing thou hast hated discipline:
and hast cast my words behind thee.
18 If thou didst see a thief thou didst run with him:
and with adulterers thou hast been a partaker.
19 Thy mouth hath abounded with evil,
and thy tongue framed deceits.
20 Sitting thou didst speak against thy brother,
and didst lay a scandal against thy mother's son:
21 these things hast thou done, and I was silent.
Thou thoughtest unjustly that I should be like to thee:
    but I will reprove thee,
    and set before thy face.
22 Understand these things, you that forget God;
    lest he snatch you away,
    and there be none to deliver you.
23 The sacrifice of praise shall glorify me:
    and there is the way by which I will shew him
    the salvation of God.

Psalm 50(51)
Miserere

Antiphon:
For sin shall not have dominion over you;
for you are not under the law, but under grace. *(Rom 6:14)*

1 *Unto the end, a psalm of David,*
2 *when Nathan the prophet came to him after he had sinned with Bethsabee.*

The Psalter

3 Have mercy on me, O God,
　　according to thy great mercy.
And according to the multitude of thy tender mercies
　　blot out my iniquity.
4 Wash me yet more from my iniquity,
and cleanse me from my sin.
5 For I know my iniquity,
and my sin is always before me.
6 To thee only have I sinned,
　　and have done evil before thee:
　　　that thou mayst be justified in thy words and mayst
　　　　overcome when thou art judged.
7 For behold I was conceived in iniquities;
and in sins did my mother conceive me.
8 For behold thou hast loved truth:
　　the uncertain and hidden things of thy wisdom
　　thou hast made manifest to me.
9 Thou shalt sprinkle me with hyssop,
　　and I shall be cleansed:
thou shalt wash me,
　　and I shall be made whiter than snow.
10 To my hearing thou shalt give joy and gladness:
and the bones that have been humbled shall rejoice.
11 Turn away thy face from my sins,
and blot out all my iniquities.
12 Create a clean heart in me, O God:
and renew a right spirit within my bowels.
13 Cast me not away from thy face;
and take not thy holy spirit from me.
14 Restore unto me the joy of thy salvation,
and strengthen me with a perfect spirit.
15 I will teach the unjust thy ways:
and the wicked shall be converted to thee.
16 Deliver me from blood, O God,
　　thou God of my salvation:
　　　and my tongue shall extol thy justice.
17 O Lord, thou wilt open my lips:
and my mouth shall declare thy praise.
18 For if thou hadst desired sacrifice,
　　I would indeed have given it:
with burnt offerings thou wilt not be delighted.

The Psalter

19 A sacrifice to God is an afflicted spirit:
    a contrite and humbled heart, O God,
    thou wilt not despise.
20 Deal favourably, O Lord, in thy good will with Sion;
that the walls of Jerusalem may be built up.
21 Then shalt thou accept the sacrifice of justice,
      oblations and whole burnt offerings:
then shall they lay calves upon thy altar.

Psalm 51(52)
Quid gloriaris

Antiphon:
But I say to you: Love your enemies;
    do good to them that hate you;
    and pray for them that persecute you;
that you may be the children of your Father who is in
    heaven,
who maketh His sun to shine upon the good and the
    bad, and raineth upon the just and the unjust.
    (Matt 5:44-45)

1 *Unto the end, understanding for David,*
2 *when Doeg the Edomite came and told Saul David*
    went to the house of Achimelech
3 Why dost thou glory in malice,
thou that art mighty in iniquity?
4 All the day long thy tongue hath devised injustice:
as a sharp razor, thou hast wrought deceit.
5 Thou hast loved malice more than goodness:
and iniquity rather than to speak righteousness.
6 Thou hast loved all the words of ruin,
O deceitful tongue.
7 Therefore will God destroy thee for ever:
    he will pluck thee out,
and remove thee from thy dwelling place:
    and thy root out of the land of the living.
8 The just shall see and fear,
and shall laugh at him, and say:

The Psalter

9 Behold the man that made not God his helper:
But trusted in the abundance of his riches:
    and prevailed in his vanity.
10 But I, as a fruitful olive tree in the house of God,
    have hoped in the mercy of God for ever,
    yea for ever and ever.
11 I will praise thee for ever, because thou hast done it:
    and I will wait on thy name,
    for it is good in the sight of thy saints.

The Psalter

Day 11 - Morning Prayer

Psalm 52(53)
Dixit insipiens

Antiphon:
By the works of the law no flesh shall be justified before Him;
For by the law is the knowledge of sin. *(Rom 3:20)*

1 *Unto the end, for Maeleth, understandings to David.*
The fool said in his heart:
There is no God.
2 They are corrupted, and become abominable in
        iniquities:
there is none that doth good.
3 God looked down from heaven on the children of men:
    to see if there were any that did understand,
    or did seek God.
4 All have gone aside,
    they are become unprofitable together,
    there is none that doth good, no not one.
5 Shall not all the workers of iniquity know,
who eat up my people as they eat bread?
6 They have not called upon God:
    there have they trembled for fear,
    where there was no fear.
For God hath scattered the bones of them that please men:
    they have been confounded,
    because God hath despised them.
7 Who will give out of Sion the salvation of Israel?
    when God shall bring back the captivity of his
        people,
    Jacob shall rejoice, and Israel shall be glad.

The Psalter

Psalm 53(54)
Deus, in nomine tuo

Antiphon:
Wherefore, casting away all uncleanness,...
with meekness receive the ingrafted Word, which is
    able to save your souls. *(James 1:21)*

1 *Unto the end, In verses, understanding for David.*
2 *When the men of Ziph had come and said to Saul: Is
    not David hidden with us?*
3 Save me, O God, by thy name,
and judge me in thy strength.
4 O God, hear my prayer:
give ear to the words of my mouth.
5 For strangers have risen up against me;
    and the mighty have sought after my soul:
and they have not set God before their eyes.
6 For behold God is my helper:
and the Lord is the protector of my soul.
7 Turn back the evils upon my enemies;
and cut them off in thy truth.
8 I will freely sacrifice to thee,
    and will give praise, O God, to thy name:
    because it is good:
9 For thou hast delivered me out of all trouble:
and my eye hath looked down upon my enemies.

Psalm 54(55)
Exaudi, Deus

Antiphon:
Be you humbled therefore under the mighty hand of
    God, that He may exalt you in the time of
    visitation:
Casting all your care upon Him, for He hath care of
    you. *(I Peter 5:6-7)*

The Psalter

1 *Unto the end, in verses, understanding for David.*
2 Hear, O God, my prayer,
and despise not my supplication:
3 be attentive to me and hear me.
I am grieved in my exercise; and am troubled,
4 at the voice of the enemy,
    and at the tribulation of the sinner.
For they have cast iniquities upon me:
    and in wrath they were troublesome to me.
5 My heart is troubled within me:
and the fear of death is fallen upon me.
6 Fear and trembling are come upon me:
and darkness hath covered me.
7 And I said: Who will give me wings like a dove,
and I will fly and be at rest?
8 Lo, I have gone far off flying away;
and I abode in the wilderness.
9 I waited for him that hath saved me
    from pusillanimity of spirit, and a storm.
10 Cast down, O Lord, and divide their tongues;
for I have seen iniquity and contradiction in the city.
11 Day and night shall iniquity surround it upon its
    walls:
and in the midst thereof are labour,
12 and injustice. And usury and deceit
have not departed from its streets.
13 For if my enemy had reviled me,
    I would verily have borne with it.
And if he that hated me had spoken great things
    against me,
I would perhaps have hidden myself from him.
14 But thou a man of one mind,
my guide, and my familiar,
15 Who didst take sweetmeats together with me:
in the house of God we walked with consent.
16 Let death come upon them,
    and let them go down alive into hell.
For there is wickedness in their dwellings:
    in the midst of them.

The Psalter

17 But I have cried to God:
and the Lord will save me.
18 Evening and morning,
    and at noon I will speak and declare:
and he shall hear my voice.
19 He shall redeem my soul in peace
    from them that draw near to me:
for among many they were with me.
20 God shall hear, and the Eternal shall humble them.
For there is no change with them,
    and they have not feared God:
21 he hath stretched forth his hand to repay.
They have defiled his covenant,
22 they are divided by the wrath of his countenance,
    and his heart hath drawn near.
His words are smoother than oil,
    and the same are darts.
23 Cast thy care upon the Lord,
    and he shall sustain thee:
he shall not suffer the just to waver for ever.
24 But thou, O God,
    shalt bring them down into the pit of destruction.
Bloody and deceitful men shall not live out half their days;
    but I will trust in thee, O Lord.

The Psalter

Day 11 - Evening Prayer

Psalm 55(56)
Miserere mei, Deus

Antiphon:
He will turn again and have mercy on us;
He will put away our iniquities and He will cast all our
 sins into the bottom of the sea.
 (Micah 7:19)

1 *Unto the end, for a people that is removed at a
 distance from the sanctuary for David, for an
 inscription of a title (or pillar) when the
 Philistines held him in Geth.*
2 Have mercy on me, O God,
 for man hath trodden me under foot;
all the day long he hath afflicted me
 fighting against me.
3 My enemies have trodden on me all the day long;
for they are many that make war against me.
4 From the height of the day I shall fear:
but I will trust in thee.
5 In God I will praise my words,
 in God I have put my trust:
I will not fear what flesh can do against me.
6 All the day long they detested my words:
all their thoughts were against me unto evil.
7 They will dwell and hide themselves:
 they will watch my heel.
As they have waited for my soul,
8 for nothing shalt thou save them:
in thy anger thou shalt break the people in pieces, O
 God,
9 I have declared to thee my life:
 thou hast set my tears in thy sight,
As also in thy promise.

The Psalter

10 Then shall my enemies be turned back.
In what day soever I shall call upon thee,
> behold I know thou art my God.
11 In God will I praise the word,
> in the Lord will I praise his speech.
In God have I hoped,
> I will not fear what man can do to me.
12 In me, O God, are vows to thee,
which I will pay, praises to thee:
13 Because thou hast delivered my soul from death,
> my feet from falling:
that I may please in the sight of God,
> in the light of the living.

Psalm 56(57)
Miserere mei, Deus

Antiphon:
Come to me, all you that labour and are burdened; and
> I will refresh you.
Take up my yoke upon you and learn of me, because
> I am meek, and humble of heart;
and you shall find rest to your souls. *(Matt 11:28-29)*

1 *Unto the end, destroy not, for David, for an
> inscription of a title, when he fled from Saul
> into the cave*
2 Have mercy on me, O God, have mercy on me:
> for my soul trusteth in thee.
And in the shadow of thy wings will I hope,
> until iniquity pass away.
3 I will cry to God the most High;
to God who hath done good to me.
4 He hath sent from heaven and delivered me:
> he hath made them a reproach that trod upon me.
God hath sent his mercy and his truth,
5 and he hath delivered my soul from the midst of the
> young lions.
I slept troubled. The sons of men,
> whose teeth are weapons and arrows,
> and their tongue a sharp sword.

The Psalter

6 Be thou exalted, O God, above the heavens,
and thy glory above all the earth.
7 They prepared a snare for my feet;
   and they bowed down my soul.
They dug a pit before my face,
   and they are fallen into it.
8 My heart is ready, O God, my heart is ready:
I will sing, and rehearse a psalm.
9 Arise, O my glory, arise psaltery and harp:
I will arise early.
10 I will give praise to thee, O Lord, among the people:
I will sing a psalm to thee among the nations.
11 For thy mercy is magnified even to the heavens:
and thy truth unto the clouds.
12 Be thou exalted, O God, above the l heavens:
and thy glory above all the earth.

Psalm 57(58)
Si vere utique

Antiphon:
Woe to thee, Corozain! Woe to thee, Bethsaida!
For if in Tyre and Sidon had been wrought the miracles
   that have been wrought in you,
they had long ago done penance in sackcloth and ashes.
But I say unto you, it shall be more tolerable for Tyre
   and Sidon in the day of judgment than for you.
   (Matt 12:21-22)

1 *Unto the end, destroy not, for David, for an
   inscription of a title.*
2 If in very deed you speak justice:
judge right things, ye sons of men.
3 For in your heart you work iniquity:
your hands forge injustice in the earth.
4 The wicked are alienated from the womb;
   they have gone astray from the womb:
   they have spoken false things.
5 Their madness is according to the likeness of a
   serpent:
like the deaf asp that stoppeth her ears:

The Psalter

6 Which will not hear the voice of the charmers;
nor of the wizard that charmeth wisely.
7 God shall break in pieces their teeth in their mouth:
the Lord shall break the grinders of the lions.
8 They shall come to nothing, like water running down;
he hath bent his bow till they be weakened.
9 Like wax that melteth they shall be taken away:
fire hath fallen on them,
    and they shall not see the sun.
10 Before your thorns could know the brier;
he swalloweth them up, as alive, in his wrath.
11 The just shall rejoice when he shall see the revenge:
he shall wash his hands in the blood of the sinner.
12 And man shall say:
    If indeed there be fruit to the just:
there is indeed a God that judgeth them on the earth.

The Psalter

Day 12 - Morning Prayer

Psalm 58(59)
Eripe me

Antiphon:
And Jesus crying with a loud voice, said;
Father, into thy hands I commend my spirit. *(Lk 23:46a)*

1 *Unto the end, destroy not, for David for an inscription of It title, when Saul sent and watched his house to kill him.*
2 Deliver me from my enemies, O my God;
and defend me from them that rise up against me.
3 Deliver me from them that work iniquity,
and save me from bloody men.
4 For behold they have caught my soul:
the mighty have rushed in upon me:
5 Neither is it my iniquity, nor my sin, O Lord:
without iniquity have I run, and directed my steps.
6 Rise up thou to meet me, and behold:
    even thou, O Lord, the God of hosts,
    the God of Israel.
Attend to visit all the nations:
    have no mercy on all them that work iniquity.
7 They shall return at evening,
    and shall suffer hunger like dogs:
    and shall go round about the city.
8 Behold they shall speak with their mouth,
    and a sword is in their lips:
for who, say they, hath heard us ?
9 But thou, O Lord, shalt laugh at them:
thou shalt bring all the nations to nothing.
10 I will keep my strength to thee:
for thou art my protector:
11 my God, his mercy shall prevent me.
12 God shall let me see over my enemies:
    slay them not, lest at any time my people forget.
Scatter them by thy power;
    and bring them down, O Lord, my protector:

The Psalter

13 For the sin of their mouth,
   and the word of their lips:
and let them be taken in their pride.
And for their cursing and lying they shall be talked of,
14 when they are consumed:
   when they are consumed by thy wrath,
   and they shall be no more.
And they shall know that God will rule Jacob,
   and all the ends of the earth.
15 They shall return at evening
   and shall suffer hunger like dogs:
   and shall go round about the city.
16 They shall be scattered abroad to eat,
 and shall murmur if they be not filled.
17 But I will sing thy strength:
   and will extol thy mercy in the morning.
For thou art become my support,
   and my refuge, in the day of my trouble.
18 Unto thee, O my helper, will I sing,
   for thou art God my defence:
   my God my mercy.

Psalm 59(60)
Deus, repulisti nos

Antiphon:
And He said to me: It is done. I am the Alpha and the
   Omega: the Beginning and the End.
To him that thirsteth, I will give of the fountain of the
   water of life freely.
He that shall overcome shall possess these things.
And I will be his God; and he shall be my son. *(Rev 21:6-7)*

1 *Unto the end, for them that shall be changed, for the
   inscription of a title, to David himself, for
   doctrine,*

The Psalter

2 *when he set fire to Mesopotamia of Syria and Sobal and Joab returned and slew of Edom, in the vale of the saltpits, twelve thousand men.*
3 O God, thou hast cast us off,
and hast destroyed us;
thou hast been angry, and hast had mercy on us.
4 Thou hast moved the earth, and hast troubled it:
heal thou the breaches thereof, for it has been moved.
5 Thou hast shewn thy people hard things;
thou hast made us drink wine of sorrow.
6 Thou hast given a warning to them that fear thee:
that they may flee from before the bow:
That thy beloved may be delivered.
7 Save me with thy right hand, and hear me.
8 God hath spoken in his holy place:
I will rejoice, and I will divide Sichem;
and will mete out the vale of tabernacles.
9 Galaad is mine, and Manasses is mine:
and Ephraim is the strength of my head.
Juda is my king:
10 Moab is the pot of my hope.
Into Edom will I stretch out my shoe:
to me the foreigners are made subject.
11 Who will bring me into the strong city?
who will lead me into Edom?
12 Wilt not thou, O God, who hast cast us off?
and wilt not thou, O God, go out with our armies?
13 Give us help from trouble:
for vain is the salvation of man.
14 Through God we shall do mightily:
and he shall bring to nothing them that afflict us.

Psalm 60(61)
Exaudi, Deus

Antiphon:
He that giveth testimony of these things saith;
Surely, I come quickly; Amen. Come, Lord Jesus! (Rev 22:20)

The Psalter

1 *Unto the end, in hymns, for David.*
2 Hear, O God, my supplication:
be attentive to my prayer.
3 To thee have I cried from the ends of the earth:
when my heart was in anguish,
    thou hast exalted me on a rock.
    Thou hast conducted me;
4 For thou hast been my hope;
a tower of strength against the face of the enemy.
5 In thy tabernacle I shall dwell for ever:
I shall be protected under the covert of thy wings.
6 For thou, my God, hast heard my prayer:
thou hast given an inheritance to them that fear thy
    name.
7 Thou wilt add days to the days of the king:
his years even to generation and generation.
8 He abideth for ever in the sight of God:
his mercy and truth who shall search ?
9 So will I sing a psalm to thy name for ever and ever:
that I may pay my vows from day to day.

The Psalter

Day 12 - Evening Prayer

Psalm 61(62)
Nonne Deo

Antiphon:
For the Son of man shall come in the glory of His
    Father with His angels;
and then will He render to every man according to His
    works. *(Matt 16:27)*

1 Unto the end, For Idithun, a psalm of David.
2 Shall not my soul be subject to God?
For from him is my salvation.
3 For he is my God and my saviour:
he is my protector, I shall be moved no more.
4 How long do you rush in upon a man?
you all kill, as if you were thrusting down a leaning wall,
    and a tottering fence.
5 But they have thought to cast away my price;
I ran in thirst: they blessed with their mouth,
    but cursed with their heart.
6 But be thou, O my soul, subject to God:
For from him is my patience.
7 For he is my God and my saviour:
he is my helper, I shall not be moved.
8 In God is my salvation and my glory:
he is the God of my help, and my hope is in God.
9 Trust in him, all ye congregation of people:
    pour out your hearts before him.
God is our helper for ever.
10 But vain are the sons of men,
    the sons of men are liars in the balances:
that by vanity they may together deceive.
11 Trust not in iniquity, and cover not robberies:
if riches abound, set not your heart upon them.
12 God hath spoken once,
    these two things have I heard,
    that power belongeth to God,
13 and mercy to thee, O Lord;
for thou wilt render to every man according to his
    works.

The Psalter

Psalm 62(63)
Deus Deus meus, ad te

Antiphon:
And if I shall go and prepare a place for you,
I will come again and will take you to myself;
   that where I am, you also may be. *(John 14:3)*

1 *A psalm of David when he was in the desert of Edom.*
2 O God, my God, to thee do I watch at break of day.
   For thee my soul hath thirsted;
     for thee my flesh, O how many ways!
3 In a desert land, and where there is no way, and no water:
so in the sanctuary have I come before thee,
   to see thy power and thy glory.
4 For thy mercy is better than lives:
thee my lips shall praise.
5 Thus will I bless thee all my life long:
and in thy name I will lift up my hands.
6 Let my soul be filled as with marrow and fatness:
and my mouth shall praise thee with joyful lips.
7 If I have remembered thee upon my bed,
I will meditate on thee in the morning:
8 because thou hast been my helper.
And I will rejoice under the covert of thy wings:
9 my soul hath stuck close to thee:
thy right hand hath received me.
10 But they have sought my soul in vain,
they shall go into the lower parts of the earth:
11 They shall be delivered into the hands of the sword,
they shall be the portions of foxes.
12 But the king shall rejoice in God,
   all they shall be praised that swear by him:
because the mouth is stopped of them that speak
     wicked things.

The Psalter

Psalm 63(64)
Exaudi Deus orationem

Antiphon:
He hath shewed might in His arm;
> He hath scattered the proud in the conceit of their heart.

He hath put down the mighty from their seat
> and hath exalted the humble. *(Lk 1:51-52)*

1 *Unto the end, a psalm for David.*
2 Hear, O God, my prayer,
> when I make supplication to thee :

deliver my soul from the fear of the enemy.
3 Thou hast protected me from the assembly of the malignant;
from the multitude of the workers of iniquity.
4 For they have whetted their tongues like a sword;
they have bent their bow a bitter thing,
5 to shoot in secret the undefiled.
6 They will shoot at him on a sudden, and will not fear:
> they are resolute in wickedness.

They have talked of hiding snares;
> they have said: Who shall see them?

7 They have searched after iniquities:
> they have failed in their search.

Man shall come to a deep heart:
8 and God shall be exalted.
The arrows of children are their wounds:
9 and their tongues against them are made weak.
All that saw them were troubled;
10 and every man was afraid.
And they declared the works of God:
> and understood his doings.

11 The just shall rejoice in the Lord,
> and shall hope in him:

and all the upright in heart shall be praised.

The Psalter

Psalm 64(65)
Te decet

Antiphon:
My eyes have seen thy salvation, which Thou hast
> prepared before the face of all peoples:
A light to the revelation of the Gentiles and
> the glory of Thy people Israel. *(Lk 2:30-32)*

1 *To the end, a psalm of David. The canticle of Jeremias
> and Ezechhiel to the people of the captivity,
> when they began to go out.*
2 A Hymn, O God, becometh thee in Sion:
and a vow shall be paid to thee in Jerusalem.
3 O hear my prayer: all flesh shall come to thee.
4 The words of the wicked have prevailed over us:
and thou wilt pardon our transgressions.
5 Blessed is he whom thou hast chosen and taken to
> thee:
> he shall dwell in thy courts.
We shall be filled with the good things of thy house;
> holy is thy temple,
6 wonderful in justice.
Hear us, O God our saviour,
> who art the hope of all the ends of the earth,
> and in the sea afar off.
7 Thou who preparest the mountains by thy strength,
being girded with power:
8 who troublest the depth of the sea,
> the noise of its waves.
The Gentiles shall be troubled,
9 and they that dwell in the uttermost borders
> shall be afraid at thy signs:
thou shalt make the outgoings of the morning
> and of the evening to be joyful.
10 Thou hast visited the earth,
> and hast plentifully watered it;
> thou hast many ways enriched it.
The river of God is filled with water,
> thou hast prepared their food:
> for so is its preparation.

The Psalter

11 Fill up plentifully the streams thereof,
   multiply its fruits;
it shall spring up and rejoice in its showers.
12 Thou shalt bless the crown of the year of thy
      goodness:
and thy fields shall be filled with plenty.
13 The beautiful places of the wilderness shall grow fat:
and the hills shall be girded about with joy,
14 The rams of the flock are clothed,
   and the vales shall abound with corn:
they shall shout, yea they shall sing a hymn.

The Psalter

Day 13 - Morning Prayer

Psalm 65(66)
Jubilate Deo

Antiphon:
Blessed be the God and Father of our Lord Jesus
 Christ,
the Father of all mercies and the God of all comfort...
 (2 Cor 1:3)

1 Unto the end, a canticle of a psalm of the
 resurrection.
Shout with joy to God, all the earth,
2 sing ye a psalm to his name;
give glory to his praise.
3 Say unto God, How terrible are thy works, O Lord!
in the multitude of thy strength thy enemies shall lie
 to thee.
4 Let all the earth adore thee, and sing to thee:
let it sing a psalm to thy name.
5 Come and see the works of God;
who is terrible in his counsels over the sons of men.
6 Who turneth the sea into dry land,
 in the river they shall pass on foot:
there shall we rejoice in him.
7 Who by his power ruleth for ever:
his eyes behold the nations;
let not them that provoke him be exalted in
 themselves.
8 O bless our God, ye Gentiles:
and make the voice of his praise to be heard.
9 Who hath set my soul to live:
and hath not suffered my feet to be moved:
10 For thou, O God, hast proved us:
thou hast tried us by fire, as silver is tried.
11 Thou hast brought us into a net,
thou hast laid afflictions on our back:
12 thou hast set men over our heads.
We have passed through fire and water,
 and thou hast brought us out into a refreshment.

13 I will go into thy house with burnt offerings:
I will pay thee my vows,
14 which my lips have uttered,
And my mouth hath spoken, when I was in trouble.
15 I will offer up to thee holocausts full of marrow,
    with burnt offerings of rams:
I will offer to thee bullocks with goats.
16 Come and hear, all ye that fear God,
and I will tell you what great things he hath done for
    my soul.
17 I cried to him with my mouth:
and I extolled him with my tongue.
18 If I have looked at iniquity in my heart,
the Lord will not hear me.
19 Therefore hath God heard me,
and hath attended to the voice of my supplication.
20 Blessed be God, who hath not turned away my
    prayer,
    nor his mercy from me.

Psalm 66(67)
Deus misereatur

Antiphon:
He that is mighty hath done great things to me; and
    Holy is His name.
And His mercy is from generation unto generations, to
    them that fear Him. (Lk 1:49-50)

1 *Unto the end, in, hymns, a psalm of a canticle for
    David.*
2 May God have mercy on us, and bless us:
may he cause the light of his countenance to shine upon
    us,
    and may he have mercy on us.
3 That we may know thy way upon earth:
thy salvation in all nations.
4 Let people confess to thee, O God:
let all people give praise to thee.

The Psalter

5 Let the nations be glad and rejoice:
for thou judgest the people with justice,
 and directest the nations upon earth.
6 Let the people, O God, confess to thee:
let all the people give praise to thee:
7 the earth hath yielded her fruit.
May God, our God bless us,
8 may God bless us:
and all the ends of the earth fear him.

The Psalter

Day 13 - Evening Prayer

Psalm 67(68)
Exurgat Deus

Antiphon:
*My soul doth magnify the Lord, and my spirit hath rejoiced in God my saviour...
He hath received Israel His servant, being mindful of His mercy.* (Lk 1:46-47,54)

1 Unto the end, a psalm of a canticle for David himself.
2 Let God arise, and let his enemies be scattered:
and let them that hate him flee from before his face.
3 As smoke vanisheth, so let them vanish away:
as wax melteth before the fire,
   so let the wicked perish at the presence of God.
4 And let the just feast, and rejoice before God:
and be delighted with gladness.
5 Sing ye to God, sing a psalm to his name,
   make a way for him who ascendeth upon the west:
the Lord is his name. Rejoice ye before him:
   but the wicked shall be troubled at his presence,
6 who is the father of orphans, and the judge of
   widows.
God in his holy place:
7 God who maketh men of one manner to dwell in a
   house:
Who bringeth out them that were bound in strength;
   in like manner them that provoke,
   that dwell in sepulchres.
8 O God, when thou didst go forth in the sight of thy
   people,
when thou didst pass through the desert:
9 The earth was moved,
   and the heavens dropped at the presence of the God
     of Sina,
   at the presence of the God of Israel.

The Psalter

10 Thou shalt set aside for thy inheritance a free rain, O God:
and it was weakened, but thou hast made it perfect.
11 In it shall thy animals dwell;
in thy sweetness, O God,
  thou hast provided for the poor.
12 The Lord shall give the word to them that preach good tidings with great power.

13 The king of powers is of the beloved, of the beloved;
and the beauty of the house shall divide spoils.
14 If you sleep among the midst of lots,
  you shall be as the wings of a dove covered with silver,
  and the hinder parts of her back with the paleness of gold.
15 When he that is in heaven appointeth kings over her,
they shall be whited with snow in Selmon.
16 The mountain of God is a fat mountain.
A curdled mountain, a fat mountain.
17 Why suspect, ye curdled mountains?
A mountain in which God is well pleased to dwell:
  for there the Lord shall dwell unto the end.
18 The chariot of God is attended by ten thousands;
  thousands of them that rejoice:
the Lord is among them in Sina, in the holy place.
19 Thou hast ascended on high,
  thou hast led captivity captive;
  thou hast received gifts in men.
Yea for those also that do not believe,
  the dwelling of the Lord God.
20 Blessed be the Lord day by day:
  the God of our salvation
    will make our journey prosperous to us.
21 Our God is the God of salvation:
and of the Lord, of the Lord are the issues from death.
22 But God shall break the heads of his enemies:
the hairy crown of them that walk on in their sins.
23 The Lord said: I will turn them from Basan,
I will turn them into the depth of the sea:

24 That thy foot may be dipped in the blood of thy enemies;
the tongue of thy dogs be red with the same.
25 They have seen thy goings, O God, the goings of my God:
of my king who is in his sanctuary.
26 Princes went before joined with singers,
in the midst of young damsels playing on timbrels.
27 In the churches bless ye God the Lord,
from the fountains of Israel.
28 There is Benjamin a youth, in ecstasy of mind.
The princes of Juda are their leaders:
> the princes of Zabulon,
> the princes of Nephthali.

29 Command thy strength, O God:
confirm, O God, what thou hast wrought in us.
30 From thy temple in Jerusalem,
kings shall offer presents to thee.
31 Rebuke the wild beasts of the reeds,
> the congregation of bulls with the kine of the people;
> who seek to exclude them who are tried with silver.

Scatter thou the nations that delight in wars:
32 ambassadors shall come out of Egypt:
Ethiopia shall soon stretch out her hands to God.
33 Sing to God, ye kingdoms of the earth:
sing ye to the Lord: Sing ye to God,
34 who mounteth above the heaven of heavens, to the east.
Behold he will give to his voice the voice of power:
35 give ye glory to God for Israel,
his magnificence, and his power is in the clouds.
36 God is wonderful in his saints:
the God of Israel is he who will give power and strength to his people.
Blessed be God.

The Psalter

Psalm 68(69)
Salvum me fac, Deus

Antiphon:
For Christ did not please Himself; but as it is written:
The reproaches of them that reproached thee fell upon
    me. (Rom 15:3)

1 *Unto the end, for them that shall be changed; for
    David.*
2 SAVE me, O God:
for the waters are come in even unto my soul.
3 I stick fast in the mire of the deep:
    and there is no sure standing.
I am come into the depth of the sea:
    and a tempest hath overwhelmed me.
4 I have laboured with crying;
    my jaws are become hoarse:
my eyes have failed, whilst I hope in my God.
5 They are multiplied above the hairs of my head,
    who hate me without cause.
My enemies are grown strong who have wrongfully
persecuted me:
    then did I pay that which I took not away.
6 O God, thou knowest my foolishness;
    and my offences are not hidden from thee:
7 Let not them be ashamed for me, who look for thee,
    O Lord, the Lord of hosts.
Let them not be confounded on my account,
    who seek thee, O God of Israel.
8 Because for thy sake I have borne reproach;
shame hath covered my face.
9 I am become a stranger to my brethren,
and an alien to the sons of my mother.
10 For the zeal of thy house hath eaten me up:
and the reproaches of them that reproached thee are
    fallen upon me.
11 And I covered my soul in fasting:
and it was made a reproach to me.
12 And I made haircloth my garment:
and I became a byword to them.

The Psalter

13 They that sat in the gate spoke against me:
and they that drank wine made me their song.
14 But as for me, my prayer is to thee, O Lord;
> for the time of thy good pleasure, O God.

In the multitude of thy mercy hear me,
> in the truth of thy salvation.

15 Draw me out of the mire, that I may not stick fast:
deliver me from them that hate me,
> and out of the deep waters.

16 Let not the tempest of water drown me,
> nor the deep swallow me up:

and let not the pit shut her mouth upon me.
17 Hear me, O Lord, for thy mercy is kind;
look upon me according to the multitude of thy tender
> mercies.

18 And turn not away thy face from thy servant:
for I am in trouble, hear me speedily.
19 Attend to my soul, and deliver it:
save me because of my enemies.
20 Thou knowest my reproach,
and my confusion, and my shame.
21 In thy sight are all they that afflict me;
> my heart hath expected reproach and misery.

And I looked for one that would grieve together with
> me,
>> but there was none: and for one that would comfort
>> me, and I found none.

22 And they gave me gall for my food,
and in my thirst they gave me vinegar to drink.
23 Let their table become as a snare before them,
and a recompense, and a stumblingblock.
24 Let their eyes be darkened that they see not;
and their back bend thou down always.
25 Pour out thy indignation upon them:
and let thy wrathful anger take hold of them.
26 Let their habitation be made desolate:
and let there be none to dwell in their tabernacles.
27 Because they have persecuted him whom thou hast
> smitten;

and they have added to the grief of my wounds.

The Psalter

28 Add thou iniquity upon their iniquity:
and let them not come into thy justice.
29 Let them be blotted out of the book of the living;
and with the just let them not be written.
30 But I am poor and sorrowful:
thy salvation, O God, hath set me up.
31 I will praise the name of God with a canticle:
and I will magnify him with praise.
32 And it shall please God better than a young calf,
that bringeth forth horns and hoofs.
33 Let the poor see and rejoice:
seek ye God, and your soul shall live.
34 For the Lord hath heard the poor:
and hath not despised his prisoners.
35 Let the heavens and the earth praise him;
the sea, and every thing that creepeth therein.
36 For God will save Sion, and the cities of Juda shall be
 built up.
And they shall dwell there, and acquire it by
 inheritance.
37 And the seed of his servants shall possess it;
and they that love his name shall dwell therein.

The Psalter

Day 14 - Morning Prayer

Psalm 69(70)
Deus in adjutorium

Antiphon:
I will rejoice in the Lord; and I will joy in God my
    Saviour.
The Lord God is my strength and He will make my feet
    like the feet of harts;
and He the conqueror will lead me upon my high places
    singing psalms. *(Hab 3:18-19)*

1 *Unto the end, a psalm for David, to bring to
    remembrance that the Lord saved him.*
2 O God, come to my assistance;
O Lord, make haste to help me.
3 Let them be confounded and ashamed
that seek my soul:
4 Let them be turned backward, and blush for shame
    that desire evils to me:
Let them be presently turned away
    blushing for shame that say to me:
        'T is well, 't is well.
5 Let all that seek thee rejoice and be glad in thee;
    and let such as love thy salvation say always:
        The Lord be magnified.
6 But I am needy and poor; O God, help me.
Thou art my helper and my deliverer:
    O Lord, make no delay.

Psalm 70(71)
In te, Domine

Antiphon:
Thus saith the Lord of hosts, the God of Israel:
There shall not be wanting a man of the race of
    Jonadab the son of Rechab, standing before
    Me for ever. *(Jer 35:19)*

The Psalter

1 *A psalm for David. Of the sons of Jonadab, and the former captives.*
In thee, O Lord, I have hoped,
let me never be put to confusion:
2 deliver me in thy justice, and rescue me.
Incline thy ear unto me, and save me.
3 Be thou unto me a God,
    a protector, and a place of strength:
that thou mayst make me safe.
    For thou art my firmament and my refuge.
4 Deliver me, O my God, out of the hand of the sinner,
and out of the hand of the transgressor of the law and
    of the unjust.
5 For thou art my patience, O Lord:
my hope, O Lord, from my youth;
6 By thee have I been confirmed from the womb:
    from my mother's womb thou art my protector.
Of thee shall I continually sing:
7 I am become unto many as a wonder,
but thou art a strong helper.
8 Let my mouth be filled with praise,
    that I may sing thy glory;
thy greatness all the day long.
9 Cast me not off in the time of old age:
when my strength shall fail, do not thou forsake me.
10 For my enemies have spoken against me;
and they that watched my soul have consulted
    together,
11 Saying: God hath forsaken him:
pursue and take him, for there is none to deliver him.
12 O God, be not thou far from me:
O my God, make haste to my help.
13 Let them be confounded and come to nothing that
    detract my soul;
let them be covered with confusion and shame that
    seek my hurt.
14 But I will always hope;
and will add to all thy praise.
15 My mouth shall shew forth thy justice;
    thy salvation all the day long.
Because I have not knows learning,

The Psalter

16 I will enter into the powers of the Lord:
O Lord, I will be mindful of thy justice alone.
17 Thou hast taught me, O God, from my youth:
and till now I will declare thy wonderful works.
18 And unto old age and grey hairs:
    O God, forsake me not,
Until I shew forth thy arm to all the generation that is to come:
    Thy power,
19 and thy justice, O God,
    even to the highest great things thou hast done:
O God, who is like to thee?
20 How great troubles hast thou shewn me,
    many and grievous:
and turning thou hast brought me to life,
and hast brought me back again from the depths of the earth:
21 Thou hast multiplied thy magnificence; and turning to me thou hast comforted me.
22 For I will also confess to thee thy truth with the instruments of psaltery:
O God, I will sing to thee with the harp, thou holy one of Israel.
23 My lips shall greatly rejoice, when I shall sing to thee;
and my soul which thou hast redeemed.
24 Yea and my tongue shall meditate on thy justice all the day;
when they shall be confounded and put to shame that seek evils to me.

Psalm 71(72)
Deus, judicium tuum

Antiphon:
There shall come forth a rod out of the root of Jesse;
and a flower shall rise up out of his root.
And the spirit of the Lord shall rest upon Him... *(Isaiah 11:1-2a)*

The Psalter

1 *A psalm on Solomon.*
2 Give to the king thy judgment, O God:
    and to the king's son thy justice:
To judge thy people with justice,
    and thy poor with judgment.
3 Let the mountains receive peace for the people:
and the hills justice.
4 He shall judge the poor of the people,
    and he shall save the children of the poor:
    and he shall humble the oppressor.
5 And he shall continue with the sun,
and before the moon, throughout all generations.
6 He shall come down like rain upon the fleece;
and as showers falling gently upon the earth.
7 In his days shall justice spring up,
and abundance of peace, till the moon be taken away.
8 And he shall rule from sea to sea,
and from the river unto the ends of the earth.
9 Before him the Ethiopians shall fall down:
and his enemies shall lick the ground.
10 The kings of Tharsis and the islands shall offer
    presents:
the kings of the Arabians and of Saba shall bring gifts:
11 And all kings of the earth shall adore him:
all nations shall serve him.
12 For he shall deliver the poor from the mighty:
and the needy that had no helper.
13 He shall spare the poor and needy:
and he shall save the souls of the poor.
14 He shall redeem their souls from usuries and
    iniquity:
and their names shall be honourable in his sight.
15 And he shall live, and to him shall be given of the gold
    of Arabia,
    for him they shall always adore:
    they shall bless him all the day.

The Psalter

16 And there shall be a firmament on the earth on the
    tops of mountains,
  above Libanus shall the fruit thereof be exalted :
and they of the city shall flourish like the grass of the
earth.
17 Let his name be blessed for evermore :
    his name continueth before the sun.
And in him shall all the tribes of the earth be blessed:
    all nations shall magnify him.
18 Blessed be the Lord, the God of Israel,
who alone doth wonderful things.
19 And blessed be the name of his majesty for ever:
    and the whole earth shall be filled with his majesty.
    So be it. So be it.
20 The praises of David, the son of Jesse, are ended.

The Psalter

Day 14 - Evening Prayer

Psalm 72(73)
Quam bonus Israel Deus

Antiphon:
Blessed be the Lord God of Israel;
because He hath visited and wrought the redemption
of His people...
Salvation from our enemies and from the hand of all
that hate us. (Lk 1:68,71)

1 *A psalm for Asaph.*
How good is God to Israel,
to them that are of a right heart!
2 But my feet were almost moved;
my steps had well nigh slipped.
3 Because I had a zeal on occasion of the wicked,
seeing the prosperity of sinners.
4 For there is no regard to their death,
nor is there strength in their stripes.
5 They are not in the labour of men:
neither shall they be scourged like other men.
6 Therefore pride hath held them fast:
they are covered with their iniquity and their
wickedness.
7 Their iniquity hath come forth, as it were from
fatness:
they have passed into the affection of the heart.
8 They have thought and spoken wickedness:
they have spoken iniquity on high.
9 They have set their mouth against heaven:
and their tongue hath passed through the earth.
10 Therefore will my people return here
and full days shall be found in them.
11 And they said: How doth God know?
and is there knowledge in the most High?
12 Behold these are sinners;
and yet abounding in the world they have obtained
riches.

The Psalter

13 And I said: Then have I in vain justified my heart,
and washed my hands among the innocent.
14 And I have been scourged all the day;
and my chastisement hath been in the mornings.
15 If I said: I will speak thus;
behold I should condemn the generation of thy children.
16 I studied that I might know this thing,
it is a labour in my sight:
17 Until I go into the sanctuary of God,
and understand concerning their last ends.
18 But indeed for deceits thou hast put it to them:
when they were lifted up thou hast cast them down.
19 How are they brought to desolation?
> they have suddenly ceased to be:
they have perished by reason of their iniquity.
20 As the dream of them that awake, O Lord;
so in thy city thou shalt bring their image to nothing.
21 For my heart hath been inflamed,
and my reins have been changed:
22 and I am brought to nothing,
and I knew not.
23 I am become as a beast before thee:
and I am always with thee.
24 Thou hast held me by my right hand;
> and by thy will thou hast conducted me,
> and with thy glory thou hast received me.
25 For what have I in heaven?
and besides thee what do I desire upon earth?
26 For thee my flesh and my heart hath fainted away:
thou art the God of my heart,
> and the God that is my portion for ever.
27 For behold they that go far from thee shall perish:
thou hast destroyed all them that are disloyal to thee.
28 But it is good for me to adhere to my God,
> to put my hope in the Lord God:
That I may declare all thy praises,
> in the gates of the daughter of Sion.

The Psalter

Psalm 73(74)
Ut quid, Deus

Antiphon:
Thou shalt go before the face of the Lord to prepare
 His ways:
To give knowledge of salvation to His people, unto the
 remission of their sins. (Lk 1:76b-77)

1 *Understanding for Asaph.*
O God, why hast thou cast us off unto the end:
why is thy wrath enkindled against the sheep of thy
 pasture?
2 Remember thy congregation,
 which thou hast possessed from the beginning.
The sceptre of thy inheritance which thou hast
 redeemed:
mount Sion in which thou hast dwelt.
3 Lift up thy hands against their pride unto the end;
see what things the enemy hath done wickedly in the
 sanctuary.
4 And they that hate thee have made their boasts,
 in the midst of thy solemnity.
They have set up their ensigns for signs,
5 and they knew not both in the going out and on the
 highest top.
As with axes in a wood of trees,
6 they have cut down at once the gates thereof,
with axe and hatchet they have brought it down.
7 They have set fire to thy sanctuary:
they have defiled the dwelling place of thy name on the
 earth.
8 They said in their heart, the whole kindred of them
 together:
Let us abolish all the festival days of God from the
 land.
9 Our signs we have not seen,
there is now no prophet: and he will know us no more.
10 How long, O God, shall the enemy reproach:
is the adversary to provoke thy name for ever?

The Psalter

11 Why dost thou turn away thy hand:
and thy right hand out of the midst of thy bosom for ever ?
12 But God is our king before ages:
he hath wrought salvation in the midst of the earth.
13 Thou by thy strength didst make the sea firm:
thou didst crush the heads of the dragons in the waters.
14 Thou hast broken the heads of the dragon:
thou hast given him to be meat for the people of the Ethiopians.
15 Thou hast broken up the fountains and the torrents:
thou hast dried up the Ethan rivers.
16 Thine is the day, and thine is the night:
thou hast made the morning light and the sun.
17 Thou hast made all the borders of the earth:
the summer and the spring were formed by thee.
18 Remember this, the enemy hath reproached the Lord:
and a foolish people hath provoked thy name.
19 Deliver not up to beasts the souls that confess to thee: and forget not to the end the souls of thy poor.
20 Have regard to thy covenant:
for they that are the obscure of the earth have been filled with dwellings of iniquity.
21 Let not the humble be turned away with confusion:
the poor and needy shall praise thy name.
22 Arise, O God, judge thy own cause:
remember thy reproaches with which the foolish man hath reproached thee all the day.
23 Forget not the voices of thy enemies:
the pride of them that hate thee ascendeth continually.

The Psalter

Day 15 - Morning Prayer

Psalm 74(75)
Confitebimur tibi

Antiphon:
Behold the fear of the Lord; that is wisdom. And to depart from evil is understanding. (Job 28:28)

1 *Unto the end, corrupt not, a psalm of a canticle for Asaph.*
2 We will praise thee, O God:
   we will praise, and we will call upon thy name.
We will relate thy wondrous works:
3 when I shall take a time, I will judge justices.
4 The earth is melted, and all that dwell therein:
I have established the pillars thereof.
5 I said to the wicked: Do not act wickedly:
and to the sinners: Lift not up the horn.
6 Lift not up your horn on high:
speak not iniquity against God.
7 For neither from the east, nor from the west,
nor from the desert hills:
8 For God is the judge.
One he putteth down, and another he lifteth up:
9 For in the hand of the Lord there is a cup of strong
       wine full of mixture.
And he hath poured it out from this to that:
   but the dregs thereof are not emptied:
   all the sinners of the earth shall drink.
10 But I will declare for ever:
I will sing to the God of Jacob.
11 And I will break all the horns of sinners:
but the horns of the just shall be exalted.

The Psalter

Psalm 75(76)
Notus in Judaea

Antiphon:
The ways of the Lord are right, and the just shall walk
 in them;
but the transgressors shall fall in them. (Hosea 14:10 b)

1 *Unto the end, in praises, a psalm for Asaph: a canticle
 to the Assyrians.*
2 In Judea God is known:
his name is great in Israel.
3 And his place is in peace:
and his abode in Sion:
4 There hath he broken the powers of bows,
the shield, the sword, and the battle.
5 Thou enlightenest wonderfully
from the everlasting hills.
6 All the foolish of heart were troubled.
They have slept their sleep;
 and all the men of riches have found nothing in
 their hands.
7 At thy rebuke, O God of Jacob,
they have all slumbered that mounted on horseback.
8 Thou art terrible, and who shall resist thee?
From that time thy wrath.
9 Thou hast caused judgment to be heard from heaven:
the earth trembled and was still,
10 When God arose in judgment,
to save all the meek of the earth.
11 For the thought of man shall give praise to thee:
and the remainders of the thought shall keep holiday to
 thee.
12 Vow ye, and pay to the Lord your God:
 all you that are round about him bring presents.
To him that is terrible,
13 even to him who taketh away the spirit of princes:
to the terrible with the kings of the earth.

The Psalter

Day 15 - Evening Prayer

Psalm 76(77)
Voce mea

Antiphon:
The children of Israel marched through the midst of
    the sea upon dry land;
and the waters were to them as a wall on the right
    hand and on the left.
And the Lord delivered Israel on that day out of the
    hands of the Egyptians. (Exodus 14:29-30)

1 Unto the end, for Idithun, a psalm of Asaph.
2 I cried to the Lord with my voice;
to God with my voice, and he gave ear to me.
3 In the day of my trouble I sought God,
    with my hands lifted up to him in the night,
    and I was not deceived.
My soul refused to be comforted:
4 I remembered God, and was delighted,
and was exercised, and my spirit swooned away.
5 My eyes prevented the watches:
I was troubled, and I spoke not.
6 I thought upon the days of old:
and I had in my mind the eternal years.
7 And I meditated in the night with my own heart:
and I was exercised and I swept my spirit.
8 Will God then cast off for ever?
or will he never be more favourable again?
9 Or will he cut off his mercy for ever,
from generation to generation?
10 Or will God forget to shew mercy?
or will he in his anger shut up his mercies?
11 And I said, Now have I begun:
this is the change of the right hand of the most High.
12 I remembered the works of the Lord:
for I will be mindful of thy wonders from the beginning.
13 And I will meditate on all thy works:
and will be employed in thy inventions.

14 Thy way, O God, is in the holy place:
who is the great God like our God?
15 Thou art the God that dost wonders.
Thou hast made thy power known among the nations:
16 with thy arm thou hast redeemed thy people
the children of Jacob and of Joseph.
17 The waters saw thee, O God, the waters saw thee:
and they were afraid, and the depths were troubled.

18 Great was the noise of the waters:
the clouds sent out a sound. For thy arrows pass:
19 the voice of thy thunder in a wheel.
Thy lightnings enlightened the world:
   the earth shook and trembled.
20 Thy way is in the sea, and thy paths in many
      waters:
and thy footsteps shall not be known.
21 Thou hast conducted thy people like sheep,
by the hand of Moses and Aaron

Psalm 77(78)
Attendite

Antiphon:
Then Jesus said to them: Amen, amen, I say to you;
  Moses gave you not bread from heaven, but my
      Father giveth you the true bread from heaven.
      (John 6:32)

1 *Understanding for Asaph.*
Attend, O my people, to my law:
incline your ears to the words of my mouth.
2 I will open my mouth in parables:
I will utter propositions from the beginning.
3 How great things have we heard and known,
and our fathers have told us.
4 They have not been hidden from their children,
   in another generation.
Declaring the praises of the Lord,
     and his powers, and his wonders which he hath done.

The Psalter

5 And he set up a testimony in Jacob:
and made a law in Israel.
How great things he commanded our fathers,
that they should make the same known to their
　　　children:
6 that another generation might know them.
The children that should be born and should rise up,
and declare them to their children.
7 That they may put their hope in God and may not
　　　forget the works of God:
and may seek his commandments.
8 That they may not become like their fathers,
　　a perverse end exasperating generation.
A generation that set not their heart aright:
and whose spirit was not faithful to God.
9 The sons of Ephraim who bend and shoot with the
　　　bow:
they have turned back in the day of battle.
10 They kept not the covenant of God:
and in his law they would not walk.
11 And they forgot his benefits,
and his wonders that he had shewn them.
12 Wonderful things did he do in the sight of their
　　　fathers,
in the land of Egypt, in the field of Tanis.
13 He divided the sea and brought them through:
and he made the waters to stand as in a vessel.
14 And he conducted them with a cloud by day:
and all the night with a light of
15 He struck the rock in the wilderness:
and gave them to drink, as out of the great deep.
16 He brought forth water out of the rock:
and made streams run down as rivers.
17 And they added yet more sin against him:
they provoked the most High to wrath in the place
　　　without water.
18 And they tempted God in their hearts,
by asking meat for their desires.
19 And they spoke ill of God: they said:
Can God furnish a table in the wilderness?

The Psalter

20 Because he struck the rock, and the waters gushed out, and the streams overflowed.
Can he also give bread, or provide a table for his people?
21 Therefore the Lord heard, and was angry:
and a fire was kindled against Jacob,
and wrath came up against Israel.
22 Because they believed not in God:
and trusted not in his salvation.
23 And he had commanded the clouds from above,
and had opened the doors of heaven.
24 And had rained down manna upon them to eat,
and had given them the bread of heaven.
25 Man ate the bread of angels:
he sent them provisions in abundance.
26 He removed the south wind from heaven:
and by his power brought in the southwest wind.
27 And he rained upon them flesh as dust:
and feathered fowls like as the sand of the sea.
28 And they fell in the midst of their camp,
round about their pavilions.
29 So they did eat, and were filled exceedingly,
and he gave them their desire:
30 they were not defrauded of that which they craved.
As yet their meat was in their mouth:
31 and the wrath of God came upon them.
And he slew the fat ones amongst them,
and brought down the chosen men of Israel.
32 In all these things they sinned still:
and they believed not for his wondrous works.
33 And their days were consumed in vanity,
and their years in haste.
34 When he slew them, then they sought him:
and they returned, and came to him early in the morning.
35 And they remembered that God was their helper:
and the most high God their redeemer.
36 And they loved him with their mouth:
and with their tongue they lied unto him:
37 But their heart was not right with him:
nor were they counted faithful in his covenant.

The Psalter

38 But he is merciful, and will forgive their sins:
   and will not destroy them.
And many a time did he turn away his anger:
   and did not kindle all his wrath.
39 And he remembered that they are flesh:
a wind that goeth and returneth not.
40 How often did they provoke him in the desert:
and move him to wrath in the place without water?
41 And they turned back and tempted God:
and grieved the holy one of Israel.
42 They remembered not his hand,
in the day that he redeemed them from the hand of him
   that afflicted them:
43 How he wrought his signs in Egypt,
and his wonders in the field of Tanis.
44 And he turned their rivers into blood,
and their showers that they might not drink.
45 He sent amongst them divers sores of flies,
which devoured them: and frogs which destroyed them.
46 And he gave up their fruits to the blast,
and their labours to the locust.
47 And he destroyed their vineyards with hail,
and their mulberry trees with hoarfrost.
48 And he gave up their cattle to the hail,
and their stock to the fire.
49 And he sent upon them the wrath of his
   indignation:
indignation and wrath and trouble,
   which he sent by evil angels.
50 He made a way for a path to his anger:
he spared not their souls from death,
   and their cattle he shut up in death.
51 And he killed all the firstborn in the land of Egypt:
the firstfruits of all their labour in the tabernacles of
   Cham.
52 And he took away his own people as sheep:
and guided them in the wilderness like a flock.
53 And he brought them out in hope, and they feared
   not:
and the sea overwhelmed their enemies.

The Psalter

54 And he brought them into the mountain of his sanctuary:
    the mountain which his right hand had purchased.
And he cast out the Gentiles before them:
    and by lot divided to them their land by a line of distribution.
55 And he made the tribes of Israel
to dwell in their tabernacles.
56 Yet they tempted, and provoked the most high God:
and they kept not his testimonies.
57 And they turned away, and kept not the covenant:
even like their fathers they were turned aside as a crooked bow.
58 They provoked him to anger on their hills:
and moved him to jealousy with their graven things.
59 God heard, and despised them,
and he reduced Israel exceedingly as it were to nothing.
60 And he put away the tabernacle of Silo,
his tabernacle where he dwelt among men.
61 And he delivered their strength into captivity:
and their beauty into the hands of the enemy.
62 And he shut up his people under the sword:
and he despised his inheritance.
63 Fire consumed their young men:
and their maidens were not lamented.
64 Their priests fell by the sword:
and their widows did not mourn.
65 And the Lord was awaked as one out of sleep,
and like a mighty man that hath been surfeited with wine.
66 And he smote his enemies on the hinder parts:
he put them to an everlasting reproach.
67 And he rejected the tabernacle of Joseph:
and chose not the tribe of Ephraim:
68 But he chose the tribe of Juda,
mount Sion which he loved.
69 And he built his sanctuary as of unicorns,
in the land which he founded for ever.

The Psalter

70 And he chose his servant David, and took him from
           the hocks of sheep:
he brought him from following the ewes great with
           young,
71 To feed Jacob his servant,
and Israel his inheritance.
72 And he fed them in the innocence of his heart:
and conducted them by the skilfulness of his hands.

The Psalter

Day 16 - Morning Prayer

Psalm 78(79)
Deus, venerunt gentes

Antiphon:
Be not very angry, O Lord, and remember no longer
   our iniquity;
behold, see we are all Thy people. (Isaiah 64:9)

1 A *psalm for Asaph.*
O God, the heathens are come into thy inheritance,
   they have defiled thy holy temple:
they have made Jerusalem as a place to keep fruit.
2 They have given the dead bodies of thy servants
   to be meat for the fowls of the air:
the flesh of thy saints for the beasts of the earth.
3 They have poured out their blood as water,
round about Jerusalem and there was none to bury
   them.
4 We are become a reproach to our neighbours:
a scorn and derision to them that are round about us.
5 How long, O Lord, wilt thou be angry for ever:
shall thy zeal be kindled like a fire?
6 Pour out thy wrath upon the nations that have not
   known thee:
and upon the kingdoms that have not called upon thy
   name.
7 Because they have devoured Jacob;
and have laid waste his place.
8 Remember not our former iniquities:
let thy mercies speedily prevent us,
   for we are become exceeding poor.
9 Help us, O God, our saviour:
   and for the glory of thy name, O Lord, deliver us:
   and forgive us our sins for thy name's sake:
10 Lest they should say among the Gentiles:
   Where is their God?
And let him be made known among the nations before
our eyes,
   By the revenging the blood of thy servants,
      which hath been shed:

The Psalter

11 let the sighing of the prisoners come in before thee.
    According to the greatness of thy arm,
take possession of the children of them that have been
        put to death.
12 And render to our neighbours sevenfold in their
        bosom:
the reproach wherewith they have reproached thee, O
    Lord.
13 But we thy people, and the sheep of thy pasture,
    will give thanks to thee for ever.
We will shew forth thy praise,
    unto generation and generation.

Psalm 79(80)
Qui regis Israel

Antiphon:
Sing ye to the Lord, for He hath done great things;
shew this forth in all the earth. (Isaiah 12:5)

1 *Unto the end, for them that shall be changed, a
        testimony for Asaph, a psalm.*
2 Give ear, O thou that rulest Israel:
    thou that leadest Joseph like a sheep.
    Thou that sittest upon the cherubims, shine forth
3 before Ephraim, Benjamin, and Manasses.
Stir up thy might, and come to save us.
4 Convert us, O God:
and shew us thy face, and we shall be saved.
5 O Lord God of hosts, how long wilt thou be angry
against the prayer of thy servant?
6 How long wilt thou feed us with the bread of tears:
and give us for our drink tears in measure?
7 Thou hast made us to be a contradiction to our
        neighbours:
and our enemies have scoffed at us.

The Psalter

8 O God of hosts, convert us:
and shew thy face, and we shall be saved.
9 Thou hast brought a vineyard out of Egypt:
thou hast cast out the Gentiles and planted it.
10 Thou wast the guide of its journey in its sight:
thou plantedst the roots thereof, and it filled the land.
11 The shadow of it covered the hills:
and the branches thereof the cedars of God.
12 It stretched forth its branches unto the sea,
and its boughs unto the river.
13 Why hast thou broken down the hedge thereof,
so that all they who pass by the way do pluck it?
14 The boar out of the wood hath laid it waste:
and a singular wild beast hath devoured it.
15 Turn again, O God of hosts, look down from heaven,
and see, and visit this vineyard:
16 And perfect the same which thy right hand hath
    planted:
and upon the son of man whom thou hast confirmed for
    thyself.
17 Things set on fire and dug down shall perish
at the rebuke of thy countenance.
18 Let thy hand be upon the man of thy right hand:
and upon the son of man whom thou hast confirmed for
    thyself.
19 And we depart not from thee, thou shalt quicken us:
and we will call upon thy name.
20 O Lord God of hosts, convert us:
and shew thy face, and we shall be saved.

The Psalter

Day 16 - Evening Prayer

Psalm 80
Exultate Deo

Antiphon:
Rejoice, and praise, O thou habitation of Sion;
 for great is He that is in the midst of thee:
The Holy One of Israel. (Isaiah 12:6)

1 Unto the end, for the winepresses, a psalm for Asaph himself.
2 Rejoice to God our helper:
sing aloud to the God of Jacob.
3 Take a psalm, and bring hither the timbrel:
the pleasant psaltery with the harp.
4 Blow up the trumpet on the new moon,
on the noted day of your solemnity.
5 For it is a commandment in Israel,
and a judgment to the God of Jacob.
6 He ordained it for a testimony in Joseph,
 when he came out of the land of Egypt:
 he heard a tongue which he knew not.
7 He removed his back from the burdens:
his hands had served in baskets.
8 Thou calledst upon me in affliction,
 and I delivered thee:
I heard thee in the secret place of tempest:
 I proved thee at the waters of contradiction.
9 Hear, O my people, and I will testify to thee:
O Israel, if thou wilt hearken to me,
10 there shall be no new god in thee:
neither shalt thou adore a strange god.
11 For I am the Lord thy God,
 who brought thee out of the land of Egypt:
open thy mouth wide, and I will fill it.
12 But my people heard not my voice:
and Israel hearkened not to me.
13 So I let them go according to the desires of their heart:
they shall walk in their own inventions.

The Psalter

14 If my people had heard me:
if Israel had walked in my ways:
15 I should soon have humbled their enemies,
and laid my hand on them that troubled them.
16 The enemies of the Lord have lied to him:
and their time shall be for ever.
17 And he fed them with the fat of wheat,
and filled them with honey out of the rock.

Psalm 81(82)
Deus stetit

Antiphon:
Woe to the shepherds of Israel that fed themselves!
Should not the flocks be fed by the shepherds? ...thus
    saith the Lord God:
Behold I myself will seek my sheep and will visit them.
    (Ezek 34:2b,11)

1 *A psalm for Asaph.*
God hath stood in the congregation of gods:
and being in the midst of them he judgeth gods.
2 How long will you judge unjustly:
and accept the persons of the wicked?
3 Judge for the needy and fatherless:
do justice to the humble and the poor.
4 Rescue the poor;
and deliver the needy out of the hand of the sinner.
5 They have not known nor understood:
    they walk on in darkness:
all the foundations of the earth shall be moved.
6 I have said:
You are gods and all of you the sons of the most High.
7 But you like men shall die:
and shall fall like one of the princes.
8 Arise, O God, judge thou the earth:
for thou shalt inherit among all the nations.

The Psalter

Psalm 82(83)
Deus, quis similis

Antiphon:
I will make my Holy Name known in the midst of my
    people Israel;
and my Holy Name shall be profaned no more.
And the Gentiles shall know that I am the Lord, the
    Holy One of Israel. (Ezek 39:7)

1 A canticle of a psalm for Asaph.
2 O God, who shall be like to thee?
hold not thy peace, neither be thou still, O God.
3 For lo, thy enemies have made a noise:
and they that hate thee have lifted up the head.
4 They have taken a malicious counsel against thy
    people,
and have consulted against thy saints.
5 They have said: Come and let us destroy them,
    so that they be not a nation:
and let the name of Israel be remembered no more.
6 For they have contrived with one consent:
they have made a covenant together against thee,
7 the tabernacles of the Edomites, and the Ismahelites:
Moab, and the Agarens,
8 Gebal, and Ammon and Amalec:
the Philistines, with the inhabitants of Tyre.
9 Yea, and the Assyrian also is joined with them:
they are come to the aid of the sons of Lot.
10 Do to them as thou didst to Madian and to Sisara:
as to Jabin at the brook of Cisson.
11 Who perished at Endor:
and became as dung for the earth.
12 Make their princes like Oreb, and Zeb,
and Zebee, and Salmana. All their princes,
13 who have said:
Let us possess the sanctuary of God for an inheritance.

14 O my God, make them like a wheel;
and as stubble before the wind.
15 As fire which burneth the wood:
and as a flame burning mountains:
16 So shalt thou pursue them with thy tempest:
and shalt trouble them in thy wrath.
17 Fill their faces with shame;
and they shall seek thy name, O Lord.
18 Let them be ashamed and troubled for ever and ever:
and let them be confounded and perish.
19 And let them know that the Lord is thy name:
thou alone art the most High over all the earth.

Psalm 83(84)
Quam dilecta

Antiphon:
The things that were gain to me, the same I have
    counted loss for Christ.
Furthermore, I count all things to be but loss for the
    excellent knowledge of Jesus Christ, my Lord...
    (Phil 3:7-8a)

1 *Unto the end, for the winepresses, a psalm for the
    sons of Core.*
2 How lovely are thy tabernacles,
O Lord of host!
3 my soul longeth and fainteth for the courts of the
    Lord.
My heart and my flesh have rejoiced in the living God.
4 For the sparrow hath found herself a house,
    and the turtle a nest for herself where she may lay
        her young ones:
Thy altars, O Lord of hosts, my king and my God.
5 Blessed are they that dwell in thy house, O Lord:
they shall praise thee for ever and ever.
6 Blessed is the man whose help is from thee:
in his heart he hath disposed to ascend by steps,
7 in the vale of tears, in the place which be hath set.

The Psalter

8 For the lawgiver shall give a blessing,
    they shall go from virtue to virtue:
the God of gods shall be seen in Sion.
9 O Lord God of hosts, hear my prayer:
give ear, O God of Jacob.
10 Behold, O God our protector:
and look on the face of thy Christ.
11 For better is one day in thy courts above thousands.
I have chosen to be an abject in the house of my God,
    rather than to dwell in the tabernacles of sinners.
12 For God loveth mercy and truth:
the Lord will give grace and glory.
13 He will not deprive of good things them that walk in
    innocence :
O Lord of hosts, blessed is the man that trusteth in
    thee.

The Psalter

Day 17 - Morning Prayer

Psalm 84(85)
Benedixisti, Domine

Antiphon:
Behold, God is my saviour; I will deal confidently, and
    will not fear, because the Lord is my strength
    and my praise;
and He is become my salvation. (Isaiah 12:2)

1 *Unto the end, for the sons of Core, a psalm.*
2 Lord, thou hast blessed thy land:
thou hast turned away the captivity of Jacob.
3 Thou hast forgiven the iniquity of thy people:
thou hast covered all their sins.
4 Thou hast mitigated all thy anger:
thou hast turned away from the wrath of thy
    indignation.
5 Convert us, O God our saviour:
and turn off thy anger from us.
6 Wilt thou be angry with us for ever:
or wilt thou extend thy wrath from generation to
    generation?
7 Thou wilt turn, O God, and bring us to life:
and thy people shall rejoice in thee.
8 Shew us, O Lord, thy mercy;
and grant us thy salvation.
9 I will hear what the Lord God will speak in me:
    for he will speak peace unto his people:
And unto his saints:
    and unto them that are converted to the heart.
10 Surely his salvation is near to them that fear him:
that glory may dwell in our land.
11 Mercy and truth have met each other:
justice and peace have kissed.
12 Truth is sprung out of the earth:
and justice hath looked down from heaven.

The Psalter

13 For the Lord will give goodness:
and our earth shall yield her fruit.
14 Justice shall walk before him:
and shall set his steps in the way.

Psalm 85(86)
Inclina, Domine

Antiphon:
Rend your hearts and not your garments, and turn to
    the Lord your God;
for He is gracious and merciful, patient and rich in
    mercy, and ready to repent of the evil. *(Joel 2:13)*

1 *A prayer for David himself.*
Incline thy ear, O Lord, and hear me:
for I am needy and poor.
2 Preserve my soul, for I am holy:
save thy servant, O my God, that trusteth in thee.
3 Have mercy on me, O Lord,
 for I have cried to thee all the day.
4 Give joy to the soul of thy servant,
for to thee, O Lord, I have lifted up my soul.
5 For thou, O Lord, art sweet and mild:
and plenteous in mercy to all that call upon thee.
6 Give ear, O Lord, to my prayer:
and attend to the voice of my petition.
7 I have called upon thee in the day of my trouble:
because thou hast heard me.
8 There is none among the gods like unto thee, O Lord:
and there is none according to thy works.
9 All the nations thou hast made shall come and adore
    before thee, O Lord:
and they shall glorify thy name.
10 For thou art great and dost wonderful things:
thou art God alone.
11 Conduct me, O Lord, in thy way,
    and I will walk in thy truth:
let my heart rejoice that it may fear thy name.

12 I will praise thee, O Lord my God:
    with my whole heart,
and I will glorify thy name for ever:
13 For thy mercy is great towards me:
and thou hast delivered my soul out of the lower hell.
14 O God, the wicked are risen up against me,
    and the assembly of the mighty have sought my
        soul:
    and they have not set thee before their eyes.
15 And thou, O Lord, art a God of compassion,
and merciful, patient, and of much mercy, and true.
16 O look upon me, and have mercy on me:
give thy command to thy servant,
    and save the son of thy handmaid.
17 Shew me a token for good:
    that they who hate me may see, and be confounded,
because thou, O Lord,
    hast helped me and hast comforted me.

Psalm 86(87)
Fundamenta ejus

Antiphon:
Now therefore you are no more strangers and
        foreigners;
but you are fellow citizens with the saints and the
        domestics of God.
Built upon the foundation of the apostles and prophets,
    Jesus Christ Himself being the chief corner
        stone... (Eph 3:19-20)

1 *For the sons of Core, a psalm of a canticle.*
The foundations thereof
are in the holy mountains:
2 The Lord loveth the gates of Sion
above all the tabernacles of Jacob.
3 Glorious things are said of thee,
O city of God.

The Psalter

4 I will be mindful of Rahab and of Babylon knowing me.
Behold the foreigners, and Tyre,
  and the people of the Ethiopians, these were there.
5 Shall not Sion say:
  This man and that man is born in her?
  and the Highest himself hath founded her.
6 The Lord shall tell in his writings of peoples and of princes,
of them that have been in her.
7 The dwelling in thee is as it were of all rejoicing.

The Psalter

Day 17 - Evening Prayer

Psalm 87(88)
Domine, Deus salutis

Antiphon:
And Joseph, buying fine linen and taking him down,
> wrapped Him up in the fine linen and laid him in
> a sepulcher which was hewed out of a rock.

And he rolled a stone to the door of the sepulcher.
> (Mark 15:46)

1 A canticle of a psalm for the sons of Core: unto the
> end, for Maheleth, to answer understanding of
> Eman the Ezrahite.

2 O Lord, the God of my salvation:
I have cried in the day, and in the night before thee.

3 Let my prayer come in before thee:
incline thy ear to my petition.

4 For my soul is filled with evils:
and my life hath drawn nigh to hell.

5 I am counted among them that go down to the pit:
I am become as a man without help,

6 Free among the dead.
Like the slain sleeping in the sepulchres,
> whom thou rememberest no more:
> and they are cast off from thy hand.

7 They have laid me in the lower pit:
in the dark places, and in the shadow of death.

8 Thy wrath is strong over me:
and all thy waves thou hast brought in upon me.

9 Thou hast put away my acquaintance far from me:
> they have set me an abomination to themselves.
I was delivered up, and came not forth:

10 my eyes languished through poverty.
All the day I cried to thee, O Lord:
> I stretched out my hands to thee.

11 Wilt thou shew wonders to the dead?
> or shall physicians raise to life,
> and give praise to thee?

12 Shall any one in the sepulchre declare thy mercy:
and thy truth in destruction?
13 Shall thy wonders be known in the dark;
and thy justice in the land of forgetfulness?
14 But I, O Lord, have cried to thee:
and in the morning my prayer shall prevent thee.
15 Lord, why castest thou off my prayer:
why turnest thou away thy face from me?
16 I am poor, and in labours from my youth:
and being exalted have been humbled and troubled.
17 Thy wrath hath come upon me:
and thy terrors have troubled me.
18 They have come round about me like water all the day:
they have compassed me about together.
19 Friend and neighbour thou hast put far from me:
and my acquaintance, because of misery.

Psalm 88(89)
Misericordias Domini

Antiphon:
And when thy days shall be fulfilled, and thou shalt sleep with thy fathers,
I will raise up thy seed after thee, which shall proceed out of thy loins;
and I will establish his kingdom. (2 Kings 7:12)

1 *Of understanding, for Ethan the Ezrahite.*
2 The mercies of the Lord I will sing for ever.
I will shew forth thy truth with my mouth to generation and generation.
3 For thou hast said:
   Mercy shall be built up for ever in the heavens:
   thy truth shall be prepared in them.
4 I have made a covenant with my elect:
I have sworn to David my servant:
5 Thy seed will I settle for ever.
And I will build up thy throne unto generation and generation.

6 The heavens shall confess thy wonders, O Lord:
and thy truth in the church of the saints.
7 For who in the clouds can be compared to the Lord:
or who among the sons of God shall be like to God?
8 God, who is glorified in the assembly of the saints:
great and terrible above all them that are about him.
9 O Lord God of hosts, who is like to thee?
    thou art mighty, O Lord,
      and thy truth is round about thee.
10 Thou rulest the power of the sea:
and appeasest the motion of the waves thereof.
11 Thou hast humbled the proud one, as one that is slain:
with the arm of thy strength thou hast scattered thy enemies.
12 Thine are the heavens, and thine is the earth:
the world and the fulness thereof thou hast founded:
13 the north and the sea thou hast created.
Thabor and Hermon shall rejoice in thy name:
14 thy arm is with might.
Let thy hand be strengthened,
    and thy right hand exalted:
15 justice and judgment are the preparation of thy throne.
Mercy and truth shall go before thy face:
16 blessed is the people that knoweth jubilation.
They shall walk, O Lord, in the light of thy countenance:
17 and in thy name they shall rejoice all the day,
and in thy justice they shall be exalted.
18 For thou art the glory of their strength:
and in thy good pleasure shall our horn be exalted.
19 For our protection is of the Lord,
and of our king the holy one of Israel.
20 Then thou spokest in a vision to thy saints, and saidst:
I have laid help upon one that is mighty,
    and have exalted one chosen out of my people.
21 I have found David my servant:
with my holy oil I have anointed him.

The Psalter

22 For my hand shall help him:
and my arm shall strengthen him.
23 The enemy shall have no advantage over him:
nor the son of iniquity have power to hurt him.
24 And I will cut down his enemies before his face;
and them that hate him I will put to flight.
25 And my truth and my mercy shall be with him:
and in my name shall his horn be exalted.
26 And I will set his hand in the sea;
and his right hand in the rivers.
27 He shall cry out to me: Thou art my father:
my God, and the support of my salvation.
28 And I will make him my firstborn,
high above the kings of the earth.
29 I will keep my mercy for him for ever:
and my covenant faithful to him.
30 And I will make his seed to endure for evermore:
and his throne as the days of heaven.
31 And if his children forsake my law,
and walk not in my judgments:
32 If they profane my justices:
and keep not my commandments:
33 I will visit their iniquities with a rod:
and their sins with stripes.
34 But my mercy I will not take away from him:
nor will I suffer my truth to fail.
35 Neither will I profane my covenant:
and the words that proceed from my mouth I will not
    make void.
36 Once have I sworn by my holiness:
I will not lie unto David:
37 his seed shall endure for ever.
38 And his throne as the sun before me:
and as the moon perfect for ever,
    and a faithful witness in heaven.
39 But thou hast rejected and despised:
thou hast been angry with thy anointed.
40 Thou hast overthrown the covenant of thy
    servant:
thou hast profaned his sanctuary on the earth.

The Psalter

41 Thou hast broken down all his hedges:
thou hast made his strength fear.
42 All that pass by the way have robbed him:
he is become a reproach to his neighbours.
43 Thou hast set up the right hand of them that
    oppress him:
thou hast made all his enemies to rejoice.
44 Thou hast turned away the help of his sword;
and hast not assisted him in battle.
45 Thou hast made his purification to cease:
and thou hast cast his throne down to the ground.
46 Thou hast shortened the days of his time:
thou hast covered him with confusion.
47 How long, O Lord, turnest thou away unto the
    end?
shall thy anger burn like fire?
48 Remember what my substance is
for hast thou made all the children of men in vain?
49 Who is the man that shall live, and not see death:
that shall deliver his soul from the hand of hell?
50 Lord, where are thy ancient mercies,
according to what thou didst swear to David in thy
    truth?
51 Be mindful, O Lord, of the reproach of thy servants
(which I have held in my bosom) of many nations:
52 Wherewith thy enemies have reproached, O Lord;
wherewith they have reproached the change of thy
    anointed.
53 Blessed be the Lord for evermore.
So be it. So be it.

The Psalter

Day 18 - Morning Prayer

Psalm 89(90)
Domine, refugium

Antiphon:
The number of the days of men at the most are a
    hundred years.
As a drop of water of the sea are they esteemed; and as
    a pebble of the sand.
So are a few years compared to eternity. (Ecclus 18:8)

1 A prayer of Moses the man of God.
Lord, thou hast been our refuge
from generation to generation.
2 Before the mountains were made,
    or the earth and the world was formed;
from eternity and to eternity thou art God.
3 Turn not man away to be brought low:
and thou hast said:
    Be converted, O ye sons of men.
4 For a thousand years in thy sight are as yesterday,
    which is past.
And as a watch in the night,
5 things that are counted nothing,
shall their years be.
6 In the morning man shall grow up like grass;
    in the morning he shall flourish and pass away:
    in the evening he shall fall, grow dry, and wither.
7 For in thy wrath we have fainted away:
and are troubled in thy indignation.
8 Thou hast set our iniquities before thy eyes:
our life in the light of thy countenance.
9 For all our days are spent; and in thy wrath we have
    fainted away.
Our years shall be considered as a spider:
10 the days of our years in them are threescore and
    ten years.
But if in the strong they be fourscore years:
    and what is more of them is labour and sorrow.
For mildness is come upon us: and we shall be corrected.

The Psalter

11 Who knoweth the power of thy anger,
and for thy fear
12 can number thy wrath?
So make thy right hand known:
    and men learned in heart, in wisdom.
13 Return, O Lord, how long?
and be entreated in favour of thy servants.
14 We are filled in the morning with thy mercy:
and we have rejoiced, and are delighted all our days.
15 We have rejoiced for the days in which thou hast
    humbled us:
for the years in which we have seen evils.
16 Look upon thy servants and upon their works: and
    direct their children.
17 And let the brightness of the Lord our God be upon
    us:
and direct thou the works of our hands over us;
yea, the work of our hands do thou direct.

Psalm 90(91)
Qui habitat

Antiphon:
If thou be the Son of God, cast Thyself down, for it is
    written;
that He hath given his angels charge over Thee, and in
    their hands shall they bear Thee up, lest
    perhaps Thou dash thy foot against a stone.
  Jesus said to him: It is written again: *Thou shalt not
  tempt the Lord thy God.* (Matt 4:6-7)

1 *The praise of a canticle for David.*
He that dwelleth in the aid of the most High,
shall abide under the protection of the God of Jacob.
2 He shall say to the Lord:
    Thou art my protector, and my refuge:
    my God, in him will I trust.
3 For he hath delivered me from the snare of the
    hunters:
and from the sharp word.

The Psalter

4 He will overshadow thee with his shoulders:
and under his wings thou shalt trust.
5 His truth shall compass thee with a shield:
thou shalt not be afraid of the terror of the night.
6 Of the arrow that flieth in the day,
    of the business that walketh about in the dark:
    of invasion, or of the noonday devil.
7 A thousand shall fall at thy side,
    and ten thousand at thy right hand:
but it shall not come nigh thee.
8 But thou shalt consider with thy eyes:
and shalt see the reward of the wicked.
9 Because thou, O Lord, art my hope:
thou hast made the most High thy refuge.
10 There shall no evil come to thee:
nor shall the scourge come near thy dwelling.
11 For he hath given his angels charge over thee;
to keep thee in all thy ways.
12 In their hands they shall bear thee up:
lest thou dash thy foot against a stone.
13 Thou shalt walk upon the asp and the basilisk:
and thou shalt trample under foot the lion and the
    dragon.
14 Because he hoped in me I will deliver him:
I will protect him because he hath known my name.
15 He shall cry to me, and I will hear him:
I am with him in tribulation,
    I will deliver him, and I will glorify him.
16 I will fill him with length of days;
and I will shew him my salvation.

The Psalter

Day 18 - Evening Prayer

Psalm 91(92)
Bonum est confiteri

Antiphon:
And when they were come and assembled the Church,
   they related what great things God had done
   with them,
and how He had opened the door of faith to the
   Gentiles. (Acts 14:26)

1 *A psalm of a canticle on the sabbath day.*
2 It is good to give praise to the Lord:
and to sing to thy name, O most High.
3 To shew forth thy mercy in the morning,
and thy truth in the night:
4 Upon an instrument of ten strings, upon the
   psaltery:
with a canticle upon the harp.
5 For thou hast given me, O Lord, a delight in thy
   doings:
and in the works of thy hands I shall rejoice.
6 O Lord, how great are thy works!
thy thoughts are exceeding deep.
7 The senseless man shall not know:
nor will the fool understand these things.
8 When the wicked shall spring up as grass:
   and all the workers of iniquity shall appear:
That they may perish for ever and ever:
9 but thou, O Lord, art most high for evermore.
10 For behold thy enemies,
   O Lord, for behold thy enemies shall perish:
   and all the workers of iniquity shall be scattered.
11 But my horn shall be exalted like that of the unicorn:
and my old age in plentiful mercy.
12 My eye also hath looked down upon my enemies:
and my ear shall hear of the downfall of the malignant
   that rise up against me.
13 The just shall flourish like the palm tree:
he shall grow up like the cedar of Libanus.

The Psalter

14 They that are planted in the house of the Lord
shall flourish in the courts of the house of our God.
15 They shall still increase in a fruitful old age:
and shall be well treated,
16 that they may shew, That the Lord our God is
righteous,
and there is no iniquity in him.

Psalm 92(93)
Dominus regnavit

Antiphon:
Blessed be the kingdom of our Father David that
comes;
Hosanna in the highest. (Mark 11:10)

1 The Lord hath reigned, he is clothed with beauty:
the Lord is clothed with strength,
and hath girded himself.
For he hath established the world which shall not be
moved.
2 Thy throne is prepared from of old:
thou art from everlasting.
3 The floods have lifted up, O Lord:
the floods have lifted up their voice.
The floods have lifted up their waves,
4 with the noise of many waters.
Wonderful are the surges of the sea:
wonderful is the Lord on high.
5 Thy testimonies are become exceedingly credible:
holiness becometh thy house, O Lord,
unto length of days.

The Psalter

Psalm 93(94)
Deus ultionum

Antiphon:
Hearken to me, you that know what is just; my people
    who have my law in your heart:
Fear ye not the reproach of men, and be not afraid of
    their blasphemies.
For the worm shall eat them up as a garment, and the
    moth shall consume them as wool;
but my salvation shall be for ever, and my justice from
    generation to generation. *(Isaiah 51:7-8)*

1 The Lord is the God to whom revenge belongeth:
the God of revenge hath acted freely.
2 Lift up thyself, thou that judgest the earth:
render a reward to the proud.
3 How long shall sinners, O Lord:
how long shall sinners glory?
4 Shall they utter, and speak iniquity:
shall all speak who work injustice?
5 Thy people, O Lord, they have brought low:
and they have afflicted thy inheritance.
6 They have slain the widow and the stranger:
and they have murdered the fatherless.
7 And they have said: The Lord shall not see:
neither shall the God of Jacob understand.
8 Understand, ye senseless among the people:
and, you fools, be wise at last.
9 He that planted the ear, shall he not hear?
or he that formed the eye, doth he not consider?
10 He that chastiseth nations, shall he not rebuke:
he that teacheth man knowledge?
11 The Lord knoweth the thoughts of men,
that they are vain.
12 Blessed is the man whom thou shalt instruct, O
    Lord:
and shalt teach him out of thy law.
13 That thou mayst give him rest from the evil days:
till a pit be dug for the wicked.

The Psalter

14 For the Lord will not cast off his people:
neither will he forsake his own inheritance.
15 Until justice be turned into judgment:
and they that are near it are all the upright in heart.
16 Who shall rise up for me against the evildoers?
or who shall stand with me against the workers of iniquity?
17 Unless the Lord had been my helper,
my soul had almost dwelt in hell.
18 If I said: My foot is moved: thy mercy,
O Lord, assisted me.
19 According to the multitude of my sorrows in my heart,
thy comforts have given joy to my soul.
20 Doth the seat of iniquity stick to thee,
who framest labour in commandment?
21 They will hunt after the soul of the just,
and will condemn innocent blood.
22 But the Lord is my refuge:
and my God the help of my hope.
23 And he will render them their iniquity:
and in their malice he will destroy them:
the Lord our God will destroy them.

The Psalter

Day 19 - Morning Prayer

Psalm 94(95)
Venite exultemus

Antiphon:
Wherefore, as the Holy Ghost saith:
*Today if you shall hear His voice, harden not your
    hearts... (Heb 3:7-8a)*

1 Come let us praise the Lord with joy:
let us joyfully sing to God our saviour.
2 Let us come before his presence with thanksgiving;
and make a joyful noise to him with psalms.
3 For the Lord is a great God,
and a great King above all gods.
4 For in his hand are all the ends of the earth:
and the heights of the mountains are his.
5 For the sea is his, and he made it:
and his hands formed the dry land.
6 Come let us adore and fall down:
and weep before the Lord that made us.
7 For he is the Lord our God:
and we are the people of his pasture and the sheep of
    his hand.
8 To day if you shall hear his voice,
harden not your hearts:
9 As in the provocation, according to the day of
    temptation in the wilderness:
where your fathers tempted me, they proved me, and
    saw my works.
10 Forty years long was I offended with that
    generation, and I said:
These always err in heart.
11 And these men have not known my ways:
so I swore in my wrath that they shall not enter into
    my rest.

The Psalter

Psalm 95(96)
Cantate Domino

Antiphon:
To the only God our Saviour through Jesus Christ our
  Lord, be glory and magnificence, empire and
  power, before all ages, and now, and for all ages
  of ages. Amen. (Jude 25)

1 *A canticle for David himself, when the house was built
  after the captivity.*
Sing ye to the Lord a new canticle:
sing to the Lord, all the earth.
2 Sing ye to the Lord and bless his name:
shew forth his salvation from day to day.
3 Declare his glory among the Gentiles:
his wonders among all people.
4 For the Lord is great, and exceedingly to be praised:
he is to be feared above all gods.
5 For all the gods of the Gentiles are devils:
but the Lord made the heavens.
6 Praise and beauty are before him:
holiness and majesty in his sanctuary.
7 Bring ye to the Lord, O ye kindreds of the Gentiles,
bring ye to the Lord glory and honour:
8 bring to the Lord glory unto his name.
Bring up sacrifices, and come into his courts:
9 adore ye the Lord in his holy court.
Let all the earth be moved at his presence.
10 Say ye among the Gentiles, the Lord hath reigned.
For he hath corrected the world, which shall not be
  moved:
he will judge the people with justice.
11 Let the heavens rejoice, and let the earth be glad,
let the sea be moved, and the fulness thereof:

The Psalter

12 the fields and all things that are in them shall be
    joyful.
Then shall all the trees of the woods rejoice
13 before the face of the Lord, because he cometh:
    because he cometh to judge the earth.
He shall judge the world with justice,
    and the people with his truth.

The Psalter

Day 19 - Evening Prayer

Psalm 96(97)
Dominus regnavit

Antiphon:
Hate evil and love good, and establish judgment in the
   gate;
it may be the Lord, the God of hosts, may have mercy
   on the remnant of Joseph. *(Amos 5:15)*

1 *For the same David, when his land was restored again
   to him.*
The Lord hath reigned, let the earth rejoice:
let many islands be glad.
2 Clouds and darkness are round about him:
justice and judgment are the establishment of his
   throne.
3 A fire shall go before him,
and shall burn his enemies round about.
4 His lightnings have shone forth to the world:
the earth saw and trembled.
5 The mountains melted like wax, at the presence of
   the Lord:
at the presence of the Lord of all the earth.
6 The heavens declared his justice:
and all people saw his glory.
7 Let them be all confounded that adore graven things,
   and that glory in their idols.
Adore him, all you his angels:
8 Sion heard, and was glad.
And the daughters of Juda rejoiced,
   because of thy judgments, O Lord.
9 For thou art the most high Lord over all the earth:
thou art exalted exceedingly above all gods.
10 You that love the Lord, hate evil:
the Lord preserveth the souls of his saints,
   he will deliver them out of the hand of the sinner.

The Psalter

11 Light is risen to the just,
and joy to the right of heart.
12 Rejoice, ye just, in the Lord:
and give praise to the remembrance of his holiness.

Psalm 97(98)
Cantate Domino

Antiphon:
The Lord hath prepared His holy arm in the sight of all
    the Gentiles;
and all the ends of the earth shall see the salvation of
    our God. *(Isaiah 52:10)*

1 *A psalm for David himself.*
Sing ye to the Lord anew canticle:
    because he hath done wonderful things.
His right hand hath wrought for him salvation,
    and his arm is holy.
2 The Lord hath made known his salvation:
he hath revealed his justice in the sight of the Gentiles.
3 He hath remembered his mercy his truth toward the
    house of Israel.
All the ends of the earth have seen the salvation of our
    God.
4 Sing joyfully to God, all the earth;
make melody, rejoice and sing.
5 Sing praise to the Lord on the harp,
on the harp, and with the voice of a psalm:
6 with long trumpets, and sound of cornet.
Make a joyful noise before the Lord our king:
7 let the sea be moved and the fulness thereof:
the world end they that dwell therein.
8 The rivers shall clap their hands,
the mountains shall rejoice together
9 at the presence of the Lord:
    because he cometh to judge the earth.
He shall judge the world with justice,
    and the people with equity.

The Psalter

Psalm 98(99)
Dominus regnavit

Antiphon:
All they that shall be left of all the nations that came
    against Jerusalem shall go up from year to year
    to adore the King,
the Lord of hosts and to keep the feast… *(Zechariah
    14:16)*

1 *A psalm for David himself.*
The Lord hath reigned, let the people be angry:
he that sitteth on the cherubims:
    let the earth be moved.
2 The Lord is great in Sion,
and high above all people.
3 Let them give praise to thy great name:
for it is terrible and holy:
4 and the king's honour loveth judgment.
Thou hast prepared directions:
    thou hast done judgment and justice in Jacob.
5 Exalt ye the Lord our God, and adore his footstool,
for it is holy.
6 Moses and Aaron among his priests:
    and Samuel among them that call upon his name.
They called upon the Lord, and he heard them:
7 he spoke to them in the pillar of the cloud.
They kept his testimonies, and the commandment
    which he gave them.
8 Thou didst hear them, O Lord our God:
thou wast a merciful God to them,
    and taking vengeance on all their inventions.
9 Exalt ye the Lord our God, and adore at his holy
    mountain:
for the Lord our God is holy.

The Psalter

Day 20 - Morning Prayer

Psalm 99(100)
Jubilate Deo

Antiphon:
Rejoice in the Lord always; again, I say, rejoice.
And the Peace of God, which surpasseth all
    understanding, keep your hearts and minds in
    Christ Jesus. *(Phil 4:4,7)*

1 *A psalm of praise.*
2 Sing joyfully to God, all the earth:
    serve ye the Lord with gladness.
Come in before his presence with exceeding great joy.
3 Know ye that the Lord he is God:
    he made us, and not we ourselves.
We are his people and the sheep of his pasture.
4 Go ye into his gates with praise,
    into his courts with hymns:
and give glory to him. Praise ye his name:
5 For the Lord is sweet, his mercy endureth for ever,
and his truth to generation and generation.

Psalm 100(101)
Misericordiam et judicium

Antiphon:
Being justified therefore by faith, let us have peace
    with God, through our Lord Jesus Christ;
by Whom also we have access through faith into this
    grace wherein we stand, and glory in the hope
    of the glory of the sons of God. (Rom 5:1-2)

1 *A psalm for David himself.*
Mercy and judgment I will sing to thee, O Lord:
I will sing,
2 and I will understand in the unspotted way,
    when thou shalt come to me.
I walked in the innocence of my heart, in the midst of
my house.

The Psalter

3 I did not set before my eyes any unjust thing:
I hated the workers of iniquities.
4 The perverse heart did not cleave to me:
and the malignant, that turned aside from me,
    I would not know.
5 The man that in private detracted his neighbour,
    him did I persecute.
With him that had a proud eye,
    and an unsatiable heart, I would not eat.
6 My eyes were upon the faithful of the earth,
    to sit with me:
the man that walked in the perfect way,
    he served me.
7 He that worketh pride shall not dwell in the midst of
    my house:
he that speaketh unjust things did not prosper before
    my eyes.
8 In the morning I put to death all the wicked of the
    land:
that I might cut off all the workers of iniquity from
    the city of the Lord.

The Psalter

Day 20 - Evening Prayer

Psalm 101(102)
Domine, exaudi

Antiphon:
O Lord, thou Son of David, have mercy on us…
O Lord, thou Son of David, have mercy on us! *(Matt 20:30b,31b)*

1 *The prayer of the poor man, when he was anxious, and poured out his supplication before the Lord.*
2 Hear, O Lord, my prayer:
and let my cry come to thee.
3 Turn not away thy face from me:
in the day when I am in trouble,
incline thy ear to me.
In what day soever I shall call upon thee,
hear me speedily.
4 For my days are vanished like smoke:
and my bones are grown dry like fuel for the fire.
5 I am smitten as grass, and my heart is withered:
because I forgot to eat my bread.
6 Through the voice of my groaning,
my bone hath cleaved to my flesh.
7 I am become like to a pelican of the wilderness:
I am like a night raven in the house.
8 I have watched,
and am become as a sparrow all alone on the housetop.
9 All the day long my enemies reproached me:
and they that praised me did swear against me.
10 For I did eat ashes like bread,
and mingled my drink with weeping.
11 Because of thy anger and indignation:
for having lifted me up thou hast thrown me down.
12 My days have declined like a shadow,
and I am withered like grass.
13 But thou, O Lord, endurest for ever:
and thy memorial to all generations.

The Psalter

14 Thou shalt arise and have mercy on Sion:
for it is time to have mercy on it, for the time is come.
15 For the stones thereof have pleased thy servants:
and they shall have pity on the earth thereof.
16 And the Gentiles shall fear thy name, O Lord, and
      all the kings of the earth thy glory.
17 For the Lord hath built up Sion:
and he shall be seen in his glory.
18 He hath had regard to the prayer of the humble:
and he hath not despised their petition.
19 Let these things be written unto another
    generation:
and the people that shall be created shall praise the
    Lord:
20 Because he hath looked forth from his high
    sanctuary:
from heaven the Lord hath looked upon the earth.
21 That he might hear the groans of them that are in
    fetters:
that he might release the children of the slain:
22 That they may declare the name of the Lord in
    Sion:
and his praise in Jerusalem;
23 When the people assemble together,
 and kings, to serve the Lord.
24 He answered him in the way of his strength:
Declare unto me the fewness of my days.
25 Call me not away in the midst of my days:
thy years are unto generation and generation.
26 In the beginning, O Lord, thou foundedst the earth:
end the heavens are the works of thy hands.
27 They shall perish but thou remainest:
    and all of them shall grow old like a garment:
And as a vesture thou shalt change them,
    and they shall be changed.
28 But thou art always the selfsame,
and thy years shall not fail.
29 The children of thy servants shall continue:
and their seed shall be directed for ever.

The Psalter

Psalm 102(103)
Benedic, anima

Antiphon:
The Lord is patient and full of mercy, taking away
 iniquity and wickedness, and leaving no man
 clear.
Who visitest the sins of the fathers upon the children
 unto the third and fourth generation;
Forgive, I beseech Thee, the sins of this people,
 according to the greatness of Thy mercy...
 (Num 14:18-19a)

1 *For David himself.*
Bless the Lord, O my soul:
and let all that is within me bless his holy name.
2 Bless the Lord, O my soul,
and never forget all he hath done for thee.
3 Who forgiveth all thy iniquities:
 who healeth all thy diseases.
4 Who redeemeth thy life from destruction:
who crowneth thee with mercy and compassion.
5 Who satisfieth thy desire with good things:
thy youth shall be renewed like the eagle's.
6 The Lord doth mercies,
and judgment for all that suffer wrong.
7 He hath made his ways known to Moses:
his wills to the children of Israel.
8 The ford is compassionate and merciful:
 longsuffering and plenteous in mercy.
9 He will not always be angry:
nor will he threaten for ever.
10 He hath not dealt with us according to our sins:
nor rewarded us according to our iniquities.
11 For according to the height of the heaven above the
 earth:
he hath strengthened his mercy towards them that
 fear him.

The Psalter

12 As far as the east is from the west,
so far hath he removed our iniquities from us.
13 As a father hath compassion on his children,
so hath the Lord compassion on them that fear him:
14 For he knoweth our frame.
He remembereth that we are dust:
15 man's days are as grass,
as the flower of the field so shall he flourish.
16 For the spirit shall pass in him, and he shall not be:
and he shall know his place no more.
17 But the mercy of the Lord is from eternity
    and unto eternity upon them that fear him:
And his justice unto children's children,
18 to such as keep his covenant,
And are mindful of his commandments to do them.
19 The Lord hath prepared his throne in heaven:
and his kingdom shall rule over all.
20 Bless the Lord, all ye his angels:
you that are mighty in strength,
    and execute his word,
    hearkening to the voice of his orders.
21 Bless the Lord, all ye his hosts:
you ministers of his that do his will.
22 Bless the Lord, all his works:
    in every place of his dominion,
O my soul, bless thou the Lord.

The Psalter

Day 21 - Morning Prayer

Psalm 103(104)
Benedic, anima

Antiphon:
By Him therefore let us offer the sacrifice of praise
 always to God,
that is to say, the fruit of lips confessing to His Name.
 (Heb 13:15)

1 *For David himself.*
Bless the Lord, O my soul:
O Lord my God, thou art exceedingly great.
Thou hast put on praise and beauty:
2 and art clothed with light as with a garment.
Who stretchest out the heaven like a pavilion:
3 who coverest the higher rooms thereof with water.
Who makest the clouds thy chariot:
 who walkest upon the wings of the winds.
4 Who makest thy angels spirits:
and thy ministers a burning fire.
5 Who hast founded the earth upon its own bases:
 it shall not be moved for ever and ever.
6 The deep like a garment is its clothing:
above the mountains shall the waters stand.
7 At thy rebuke they shall flee:
at the voice of thy thunder they shall fear.
8 The mountains ascend, and the plains descend
into the place which thou hast founded for them.
9 Thou hast set a bound which they shall not pass over;
neither shall they return to cover the earth.
10 Thou sendest forth springs in the vales:
between the midst of the hills the waters shall pass.
11 All the beasts of the field shall drink:
the wild asses shall expect in their thirst.
12 Over them the birds of the air shall dwell:
from the midst of the rocks they shall give forth their
 voices.
13 Thou waterest the hills from thy upper rooms:
the earth shall be filled with the fruit of thy works:

The Psalter

14 Bringing forth grass for cattle,
 and herb for the service of men.
That thou mayst bring bread out of the earth:
15 and that wine may cheer the heart of man.
That he may make the face cheerful with oil:
 and that bread may strengthen man's heart.
16 The trees of the field shall be filled,
 and the cedars of Libanus which he hath planted:
17 there the sparrows shall make their nests.
The highest of them is the house of the heron.
18 The high hills are a refuge for the harts,
the rock for the irchins.
19 He hath made the moon for seasons:
the sun knoweth his going down.
20 Thou hast appointed darkness, and it is night:
in it shall all the beasts of the woods go about:
21 The young lions roaring after their prey,
and seeking their meat from God.
22 The sun ariseth, and they are gathered together:
and they shall lie down in their dens.
23 Man shall go forth to his work,
and to his labour until the evening.
24 How great are thy works, O Lord?
 thou hast made all things in wisdom:
 the earth is filled with thy riches.
25 So is this great sea, which stretcheth wide its arms:
 there are creeping things without number:
 Creatures little and great.
26 There the ships shall go.
This sea dragon which thou hast formed to play
    therein.
27 All expect of thee
that thou give them food in season.
28 What thou givest to them they shall gather up:
when thou openest thy hand,
 they shall all be filled with good.
29 But if thou turnest away thy face,
 they shall be troubled:
 thou shalt take away their breath,
  and they shall fail,
  and shall return to their dust.

The Psalter

30 Thou shalt send forth thy spirit,
 and they shall be created:
and thou shalt renew the face of the earth.
31 May the glory of the Lord endure for ever:
the Lord shall rejoice in his works.
32 He looketh upon the earth, and maketh it tremble:
he toucheth the mountains, and they smoke.
33 I will sing to the Lord as long as I live:
 I will sing praise to my God while I have my being.
34 Let my speech be acceptable to him:
but I will take delight in the Lord.
35 Let sinners be consumed out of the earth,
 and the unjust, so that they be no more:
O my soul, bless thou the Lord.

Psalm 104 (105)
Confitemini Domino

Antiphon:
And you shall say in that day: Praise ye the Lord, and
 call upon His Name.
Make His works known among the people; remember
 that His Name is high. *(Isaiah 12:4)*

1 Alleluia.
 Give glory to the Lord, and call upon his name:
declare his deeds among the Gentiles.
2 Sing to him, yea sing praises to him:
relate all his wondrous works.
3 Glory ye in his holy name:
let the heart of them rejoice that seek the Lord.
4 Seek ye the Lord, and be strengthened:
seek his face evermore.
5 Remember his marvellous works which he hath done;
his wonders, and the judgments of his mouth.
6 O ye seed of Abraham his servant;
ye sons of Jacob his chosen.
7 He is the Lord our God:
his judgments are in all the earth.

The Psalter

8 He hath remembered his covenant for ever:
the word which he commanded to a thousand generations.
9 Which he made to Abraham;
and his oath to Isaac:
10 And he appointed the same to Jacob for a law,
and to Israel for an everlasting testament:
11 Saying: To thee will I give the land of Chanaan,
the lot of your inheritance.
12 When they were but a small number:
yea very few, and sojourners therein:
13 And they passed from nation to nation,
and from one kingdom to another people.
14 He suffered no man to hurt them:
and he reproved kings for their sakes.
15 Touch ye not my anointed:
and do no evil to my prophets.
16 And he called a famine upon the land:
and he broke in pieces all the support of bread.
17 He sent a man before them:
Joseph, who was sold for a slave.
18 They humbled his feet in fetters:
the iron pierced his soul,
19 until his word came.
The word of the Lord inflamed him.
20 The king sent, and he released him:
the ruler of the people, and he set him at liberty.
21 He made him master of his house,
and ruler of all his possession.
22 That he might instruct his princes as himself,
and teach his ancients wisdom.
23 And Israel went into Egypt:
and Jacob was a sojourner in the land of Cham.
24 And he increased his people exceedingly:
and strengthened them over their enemies,
25 He turned their heart to hate his people:
and to deal deceitfully with his servants.
26 He sent Moses his servant:
Aaron the man whom he had chosen.
27 He gave them power to shew his signs,
and his wonders in the land of Cham.

The Psalter

28 He sent darkness, and made it obscure:
and grieved not his words.
29 He turned their waters into blood,
and destroyed their fish.
30 Their land brought forth frogs,
in the inner chambers of their kings.
31 He spoke, and there came divers sorts of flies
and sciniphs in all their coasts.
32 He gave them hail for rain,
a burning fire in the land.
33 And he destroyed their vineyards and their fig
   trees:
and he broke in pieces the trees of their coasts.
34 He spoke, and the locust came,
 and the bruchus, of which there was no number.
35 And they devoured all the grass in their land,
and consumed all the fruit of their ground.
36 And he slew all the firstborn in their land:
the firstfruits of all their labour.
37 And he brought them out with silver and gold:
and there was not among their tribes one that was
   feeble.
38 Egypt was glad when they departed:
for the fear of them lay upon them.
39 He spread a cloud for their protection,
and fire to give them light in the night.
40 They asked, and the quail came:
and he filled them with the bread of heaven.
41 He opened the rock, and waters flowed:
rivers ran down in the dry land.
42 Because he remembered his holy word,
which he had spoken to his servant Abraham.
43 And he brought forth his people with joy,
and his chosen with gladness.
44 And he gave them the lands of the Gentiles:
and they possessed the labours of the people:
45 That they might observe his justifications,
and seek after his law.

The Psalter

Day 21 - Evening Prayer

Psalm 105(106)
Confitemini Domino

Antiphon:
This is the Water of contradiction; where the children
  of Israel strove with words against the Lord,
and He was sanctified in them. *(Num 20:13)*

1 Alleluia.
Give glory to the Lord, for he is good:
for his mercy endureth for ever.
2 Who shall declare the powers of the Lord?
who shall set forth all his praises?
3 Blessed are they that keep judgment,
and do justice at all times.
4 Remember us, O Lord, in the favour of thy people:
visit us with thy salvation.
5 That we may see the good of thy chosen,
  that we may rejoice in the joy of thy nation:
that thou mayst be praised with thy inheritance.
6 We have sinned with our fathers:
we have acted unjustly, we have wrought iniquity.
7 Our fathers understood not thy wonders in Egypt:
  they remembered not the multitude of thy mercies:
And they provoked to wrath going up to the sea, even
  the Red Sea.
8 And he saved them for his own name's sake:
that he might make his power known.
9 And he rebuked the Red Sea, and it was dried up:
and he led them through the depths, as in a wilderness.
10 And he saved them from the hand of them that
  hated them:
and he redeemed them from the hand of the enemy.
11 And the water covered them that afflicted them:
there was not one of them left.
12 And they believed his words:
and they sang his praises.
13 They had quickly done, they forgot his works:
and they waited not for his counsels.

The Psalter

14 And they coveted their desire in the desert:
and they tempted God in the place without water.
15 And he gave them their request:
and sent fulness into their souls.
16 And they provoked Moses in the camp,
Aaron the holy one of the Lord.
17 The earth opened and swallowed up Dathan:
and covered the congregation of Abiron.
18 And a fire was kindled in their congregation:
the flame burned the wicked.
19 They made also a calf in Horeb:
and they adored the graven thing.
20 And they changed their glory
into the likeness of a calf that eateth grass.
21 They forgot God, who saved them,
who had done great things in Egypt,
22 wondrous works in the land of Cham:
terrible things in the Red Sea.
23 And he said that he would destroy them:
had not Moses his chosen stood before him in the
       breach:
To turn away his wrath, lest he should destroy them.
24 And they set at nought the desirable land.
They believed not his word,
25 and they murmured in their tents:
they hearkened not to the voice of the Lord.
26 And he lifted up his hand over them:
to overthrow them in the desert;
27 And to cast down their seed among the nations,
and to scatter them in the countries.
28 They also were initiated to Beelphegor:
and ate the sacrifices of the dead.
29 And they provoked him with their inventions:
and destruction was multiplied among them.
30 Then Phinees stood up, and pacified him:
and the slaughter ceased.
31 And it was reputed to him unto justice,
to generation and generation for evermore.
32 They provoked him also at the waters of
       contradiction:
and Moses was afflicted for their sakes:

The Psalter

33 because they exasperated his spirit.
And he distinguished with his lips.
34 They did not destroy the nations
of which the Lord spoke unto them.
35 And they were mingled among the heathens,
and learned their works:
36 and served their idols,
and it became a stumblingblock to them.
37 And they sacrificed their sons,
and their daughters to devils.
38 And they shed innocent blood:
> the blood of their sons and of their daughters
> which they sacrificed to the idols of Chanaan.

And the land was polluted with blood,
39 and was defiled with their works:
and they went aside after their own inventions.
40 And the Lord was exceedingly angry with his
people:
and he abhorred his inheritance.
41 And he delivered them into the hands of the nations:
and they that hated them had dominion over them.
42 And their enemies afflicted them:
and they were humbled under their hands:
43 many times did he deliver them.
But they provoked him with their counsel:
> and they were brought low by their iniquities.

44 And he saw when they were in tribulation:
and he heard their prayer.
45 And he was mindful of his covenant:
and repented according to the multitude of his mercies.
46 And he gave them unto mercies,
in the sight of all those that had made them captives.
47 Save us, O Lord, our God:
> and gather us from among nations:

That we may give thanks to thy holy name,
> and may glory in thy praise.

48 Blessed be the Lord the God of Israel,
> from everlasting to everlasting:

and let all the people say:
> So be it, so be it.

The Psalter

Psalm 106(107)
Confitemini Domino

Antiphon:
Submit thyself then to Him, and be at peace; and
    thereby thou shalt have the best fruits...
For he that hath been humbled shall be in glory; and he
    that shall bow down his eyes, he shall be saved.
    (Job 22:21,29)

1 Give glory to the Lord, for he is good:
for his mercy endureth for ever.
2 Let them say so that have been redeemed by the Lord,
    whom he hath redeemed from the hand of the enemy:
    and gathered out of the countries.
3 From the rising and the setting of the sun,
from the north and from the sea.
4 They wandered in a wilderness, in a place without water:
they found not the way of a city for their habitation.
5 They were hungry and thirsty:
their soul fainted in them.
6 And they cried to the Lord in their tribulation:
and he delivered them out of their distresses.
7 And he led them into the right way:
that they might go to a city of habitation.
8 Let the mercies of the Lord give glory to him:
and his wonderful works to the children of men.
9 For he hath satisfied the empty soul,
 and hath filled the hungry soul with good things.
10 Such as sat in darkness and in the shadow of death:
bound in want and in iron.
11 Because they had exasperated the words of God:
and provoked the counsel of the most High:
12 And their heart was humbled with labours:
they were weakened, and their was none to help them.
13 Then they cried to the Lord in their affliction:
and he delivered them out of their distresses.

The Psalter

14 And he brought them out of darkness, and the shadow of death;
and broke their bonds in sunder.
15 Let the mercies of the Lord give glory to him,
and his wonderful works to the children of men.
16 Because he hath broken gates of brass,
and burst the iron bars.
17 He took them out of the way of their iniquity:
for they were brought low for their injustices.
18 Their soul abhorred all manner of meat:
and they drew nigh even to the gates of death.
19 And they cried to the Lord in their affliction:
and he delivered them out of their distresses.
20 He sent his word, and healed them:
and delivered them from their destructions.
21 Let the mercies of the Lord give glory to him:
and his wonderful works to the children of men.
22 And let them sacrifice the sacrifice of praise:
and declare his works with joy.
23 They that go down to the sea in ships,
doing business in the great waters:
24 These have seen the works of the Lord,
and his wonders in the deep.
25 He said the word, and there arose a storm of wind:
and the waves thereof were lifted up.
26 They mount up to the heavens, and they go down to the depths:
their soul pined away with evils.
27 They were troubled, and reeled like a drunken man;
and all their wisdom was swallowed up.
28 And they cried to the Lord in their affliction:
and he brought them out of their distresses.
29 And he turned the storm into a breeze:
and its waves were still.
30 And they rejoiced because they were still:
and he brought them to the haven which they wished for.
31 Let the mercies of the Lord give glory to him,
and his wonderful works to the children of men.
32 And let them exalt him in the church of the people:
and praise him in the chair of the ancients.

The Psalter

33 He hath turned rivers into a wilderness:
and the sources of water into dry ground:
34 A fruitful land into barrenness,
for the wickedness of them that dwell therein.
35 He hath turned a wilderness into pools of water,
and a dry land into water springs.
36 And hath placed there the hungry;
and they made a city for their habitation.
37 And they sowed fields, and planted vineyards:
and they yielded fruit of birth.
38 And he blessed them, and they were multiplied exceedingly:
and their cattle he suffered not to decrease.
39 Then they were brought to be few:
and they were afflicted through the trouble of evils and sorrow.
40 Contempt was poured forth upon their princes:
and he caused them to wander where there was no passing, and out of the way.
41 And he helped the poor out of poverty:
and made him families like a flock of sheep.
42 The just shall see, and shall rejoice,
and all iniquity shall stop their mouth.
43 Who is wise, and will keep these things:
and will understand the mercies of the Lord?

The Psalter

Day 22 - Morning Prayer

Psalm 107(108)
Paratum cor meum

Antiphon:
For all people will walk, every one, in the name of his god;
but we will walk in the Name of the Lord our God forever and ever. *(Micah 4:5)*

1 *A canticle of a psalm for David himself.*
2 My heart is ready, O God, my heart is ready:
I will sing, and will give praise, with my glory.
3 Arise, my glory; arise, psaltery and harp:
I will arise in the morning early.
4 I will praise thee, O Lord, among the people:
and I will sing unto thee among the populations.
5 For thy mercy is great above the heavens:
and thy truth even unto the clouds.
6 Be thou exalted, O God, above the heavens,
and thy glory over all the earth:
7 that thy beloved may be delivered.
Save with thy right hand and hear me.
8 God hath spoken in his holiness.
I will rejoice, and I will divide Sichem
and I will mete out the vale of tabernacles.
9 Galaad is mine, and Manasses is mine and
Ephraim the protection of my head.
Juda is my king:
10 Moab the pot of my hope.
Over Edom I will stretch out my shoe:
the aliens are become my friends.
11 Who will bring me into the strong city?
who will lead me into Edom?
12 Wilt not thou, O God, who hast cast us off?
and wilt not thou, O God, go forth with our armies?
13 O grant us help from trouble:
for vain is the help of man.
14 Through God we shall do mightily:
and he will bring our enemies to nothing.

The Psalter

Psalm 108(109)
Deus, laudem meam

Antiphon:
As He was yet speaking, behold a multitude; and he that was called Judas, one of the twelve, went before them and drew near to Jesus, for to kiss Him.
And Jesus said to him: Judas, dost thou betray the Son of man with a kiss? *(Lk 22:47-48)*

1 *Unto the end, a psalm for David.*
2 O God, be not thou silent in thy praise:
 for the mouth of the wicked and the mouth of the deceitful man is opened against me.
3 They have spoken against with deceitful tongues;
 and they have compassed me about with words of hatred;
 and have fought against me without cause.
4 Instead of making me a return of love, they detracted me:
but I gave myself to prayer.
5 And they repaid me evil for good:
and hatred for my love.
6 Set thou the sinner over him:
and may the devil stand at his right hand.
7 When he is judged, may he go out condemned;
and may his prayer be turned to sin.
8 May his days be few:
and his bishopric let another take.
9 May his children be fatherless,
and his wife a widow.
10 Let his children be carried about vagabonds, and beg;
and let them be cast out of their dwellings.

The Psalter

11 May the userer search all his substance:
and let strangers plunder his labours.
12 May there be none to help him:
nor none to pity his fatherless offspring.
13 May his posterity be cut off;
in one generation may his name be blotted out.
14 May the iniquity of his fathers be remembered in
    the sight of the Lord:
and let not the sin of his mother be blotted out.
15 May they be before the lord continually,
and let the memory of them perish from the earth:
16 because he remembered not to show mercy,
17 But persecuted the poor man and the beggar;
and the broken in heart, to put him to death.
18 And he loved cursing, and it shall come unto him:
    and he would not have blessing,
    and it shall be far from him.
And he put on cursing, like a garment:
    and it went in like water into his entrails,
    and like oil in his bones.
19 May it be unto him like a garment which covereth
    him;
and like a girdle with which he is girded continually.
20 This is the work of them who detract me before
    the Lord;
and who speak evils against my soul.
21 But thou, O Lord, do with for thy names sake:
because thy mercy is sweet. Do thou deliver me.
22 For I am poor and needy,
and my heart is troubled within me.
23 I am taken away like the shadow when it declineth:
and I am shaken off as locusts.
24 My knees are weakened through fasting:
and my flesh is changed for oil.
25 And I am become a reproach to them:
they saw me and they shaked their heads,
26 Help me, O Lord my God;
save me according to thy mercy.
27 And let them know that this is thy hand:
and that thou, O Lord, hast done it.

28 They will curse and thou will bless:
    let them that rise up against me be confounded:
      but thy servant shall rejoice.
29 Let them that detract me be clothed with shame:
and let them be covered with the their confusion as
        with a double cloak.
30 I will give great thanks to the Lord with my mouth:
and in the midst of many I will praise him.
31 Because he hath stood at the right hand of the poor,
to save my soul from persecutors

Psalm 109(110)
Dixit Dominus

Antiphon:
The multitude answered Him: We have heard out of
      the law, that Christ abideth forever.
And how sayest Thou; The Son of man must be lifted
      up? Who is this Son of man? (John 12:34)

1 The Lord said to my Lord:
Sit thou at my right hand:
Until I make thy enemies thy footstool.
2 The Lord will send forth the sceptre of thy power
      out of Sion:
rule thou in the midst of thy enemies.
3 With thee is the principality in the day of thy
      strength:
    in the brightness of the saints:
from the womb before the day star I begot thee.
4 The Lord hath sworn, and he will not repent:
Thou art a priest for ever according to the order of
        Melchisedech.
5 The Lord at thy right hand
hath broken kings in the day of his wrath.
6 He shall judge among nations, he shall fill ruins:
he shall crush the heads in the land of the many.
7 He shall drink of the torrent in the way:
therefore shall he lift up the head.

The Psalter

Day 22 - Evening Prayer

Psalm 110(111)
Confitebor tibi, Domine

Antiphon:
The fear of the Lord is the beginning of wisdom, and
    was created with the faithful in the womb.
It walketh with chosen women, and is known with the
    just and faithful. *(Ecclus 1:16)*

1 I will praise thee, O Lord, with my whole heart;
in the council of the just: and in the congregation.
2 Great are the works of the Lord:
sought out according to all his wills
3 His work is praise and magnificence:
and his justice continueth for ever and ever.
4 He hath made a remembrance of his wonderful
    works,
being a merciful and gracious Lord:
5 he hath given food to them that fear him.
He will be mindful for ever of his covenant:
6 he will shew forth to his people
the power of his works.
7 That he may give them the inheritance of the
    Gentiles:
the works of his hands are truth and judgment.
8 All his commandments are faithful:
confirmed for ever and ever, made in truth and equity.
9 He hath sent redemption to his people:
    he hath commanded his covenant for ever.
Holy and terrible is his name:
10 the fear of the Lord is the beginning of wisdom.
A good understanding to all that do it:
    his praise continueth for ever and ever.

The Psalter

Psalm 111(112)
Beatus vir

Antiphon:
Continuing daily with one accord I the temple and
  breaking bread from house to house,
    they took their meat with gladness and simplicity of
      heart;
Praising God, and having favour with all the people.
(Acts 2:46-47a)

1 Blessed is the man that feareth the Lord:
he shall delight exceedingly in his commandments.
2 His seed shall be mighty upon earth:
the generation of the righteous shall be blessed.
3 Glory and wealth shall be in his house:
and his justice remaineth for ever and ever.
4 To the righteous a light is risen up in darkness:
he is merciful, and compassionate and just.
5 Acceptable is the man that showeth mercy and
    lendeth:
he shall order his words with judgment:
6 because he shall not be moved for ever.
7 The just shall be in everlasting remembrance:
    he shall not hear the evil hearing.
His heart is ready to hope in the Lord:
8 his heart is strengthened,
he shall not be moved until he look over his enemies.
9 He hath distributed, he hath given to the poor:
    his justice remaineth for ever and ever:
    his horn shall be exalted in glory.
10 The wicked shall see, and shall be angry,
    he shall gnash with his teeth and pine away:
the desire of the wicked shall perish.

The Psalter

Psalm 112(113)
Laudate, pueri

Antiphon:
For from the rising of the sun even to the going down,
    my Name is great among the Gentiles;
and in every place there is sacrifice and there is offered
    to my Name a clean oblation.
For my Name is great among the Gentiles, saith the
    Lord of hosts. (Malachi 1:11)

1 Praise the Lord, ye children:
praise ye the name of the Lord.
2 Blessed be the name of the Lord,
from henceforth now and for ever.
3 From the rising of the sun unto the going down of
    the same,
the name of the Lord is worthy of praise.
4 The Lord is high above all nations;
and his glory above the heavens.
5 Who is as the Lord our God,
who dwelleth on high:
6 and looketh down on the low things
in heaven and in earth?
7 Raising up the needy from the earth,
and lifting up the poor out of the dunghill::
8 That he may place him with princes,
with the princes of his people.
9 Who maketh a barren woman to dwell in a house,
the joyful mother of children.

The Psalter

Day 23 - Morning Prayer

Psalm 113(114,115)
In exitu Israel

Antiphon:
Open thy eyes and behold.
For the dead that are in hell, whose spirit is taken from
    deep within them,
  shall not give glory and justice to the Lord. *(Baruch 2:17)*

1 When Israel went out of Egypt,
the house of Jacob from a barbarous people:
2 Judea made his sanctuary, Israel his dominion.
3 The sea saw and fled: Jordan was turned back.
4 The mountains skipped like rams,
and the hills like the lambs of the flock.
5 What ailed thee, O thou sea, that thou didst flee:
and thou, O Jordan, that thou wast turned back?
6 Ye mountains, that ye skipped like rams,
and ye hills, like lambs of the flock?
7 At the presence of the Lord the earth was moved,
at the presence of the God of Jacob:
8 Who turned the rock into pools of water,
and the stony hill into fountains of waters.
9 Not to us, O Lord, not to us;
but to thy name give glory.
10 For thy mercy, and for thy truth's sake:
lest the gentiles should say: Where is their God?
11 But our God is in heaven:
he hath done all things whatsoever he would.
12 The idols of the gentiles are silver and gold,
the works of the hands of men.
13 They have mouths and speak not:
they have eyes and see not.
14 They have ears and hear not:
they have noses and smell not.
15 They have hands and feel not:
  they have feet and walk not:
  neither shall they cry out through their throat.

The Psalter

16 Let them that make them become like unto them:
and all such as trust in them.
17 The house of Israel hath hoped in the Lord:
he is their helper and their protector.
18 The house of Aaron hath hoped in the Lord:
he is their helper and their protector.
19 They that fear the Lord hath hoped in the Lord:
he is their helper and their protector.
20 The Lord hath been mindful of us,
   and hath blessed us.
He hath blessed the house of Israel:
   he hath blessed the house of Aaron.
21 He hath blessed all that fear the Lord,
both little and great.
22 May the Lord add blessings upon you:
upon you, and upon your children.
23 Blessed be you of the Lord,
who made heaven and earth.
24 The heaven of heaven is the Lord's:
but the earth he has given to the children of men.
25 The dead shall not praise thee, O Lord:
nor any of them that go down to hell.
26 But we that live bless the Lord:
from this time now and for ever.

Psalm 114(116a)
Dilexi

Antiphon:
Let us therefore love God;
because God first hath loved us. (1 John 4:19)

1 I have loved,
because the Lord will hear the voice of my prayer.
2 Because he hath inclined his ear unto me:
and in my days I will call upon him.
3 The sorrows of death have encompassed me:
   and the perils of hell have found me.
I met with trouble and sorrow:
4 and I called upon the name of the Lord.
O Lord, deliver my soul.

The Psalter

5 The Lord is merciful and just,
and our God sheweth mercy.
6 The Lord is the keeper of little ones:
I was little and he delivered me.
7 Turn, O my soul, into thy rest:
for the Lord hath been bountiful to thee.
8 For he hath delivered my soul from death:
my eyes from tears, my feet from falling.
9 I will please the Lord in the land of the living.

Psalm 115(116b)
Credidi

Antiphon:
I beseech you therefore, brethren, by the mercy of God,
    that you present your bodies, a living sacrifice,
holy and pleasing unto God; your reasonable service.
    (Romans 12:1)

10 I have believed, therefore have I spoken;
but I have been humbled exceedingly.
11 I said in my excess:
Every man is a liar.
12 What shall I render to the Lord,
for all the things he hath rendered unto me?
13 I will take the chalice of salvation;
and I will call upon the name of the Lord.
14 I will pay my vows to the Lord
before all his people:
15 precious in the sight of the Lord
is the death of his saints.
16 O Lord, for I am thy servant:
I am thy servant, and the son of thy handmaid.
    Thou hast broken my bonds:
17 I will sacrifice to thee the sacrifice of praise,
and I will call upon the name of the Lord.
18 I will pay my vows to the Lord
in the sight of all his people:
19 in the courts of the house of the Lord,
in the midst of thee, O Jerusalem.

The Psalter

Day 23 - Evening Prayer

Psalm 116(117)
Laudate Dominum

Antiphon:
Behold, I AM with you all days,
even to the consummation of the world. *(Matt 28:20b)*

1 O praise the Lord, all ye nations:
praise him, all ye people.
2 For his mercy is confirmed upon us:
and the truth of the Lord remaineth for ever.

Psalm 117(118)
Confitemini Domino

Antiphon:
To you therefore that believe, He is honor;
but to them that believe not, *the stone which the
    builders rejected; the same is made the head of
    the corner.* (1 Peter 2:7)

1 Give praise to Lord, for he is good:
for his mercy endureth for ever.
2 Let Israel now say that he is good:
that his mercy endureth for ever.
3 Let the house of Aaron now say,
that his mercy endureth for ever.
4 Let them that fear the Lord now say,
that his mercy endureth for ever.
5 In my trouble I called upon the Lord:
and the Lord heard me, and enlarged me.
6 The Lord is my helper,
I will not fear what man can do unto me.
7 The Lord is my helper:
and I will look over my enemies.
8 It is good to confide in the Lord,
rather than to have confidence in man.
9 It is good to trust in the Lord,
rather than to trust in princes.

The Psalter

10 All nations compassed me about;
and in the name of the Lord I have been revenged on them.
11 Surrounding me they compassed me about:
and in the name of the Lord I have been revenged on them.
12 They surrounded me like bees, and they burned like fire among thorns:
and in the name of the Lord I was revenged on them
13 Being pushed I was overturned that I might fall:
but the Lord supported me.
14 The Lord is my strength and my praise:
and he is become my salvation.
15 The voice of rejoicing and of salvation
is in the tabernacles of the just.
16 The right hand of the Lord hath wrought strength:
the right hand of the Lord hath exulted me:
the right hand of the Lord hath wrought strength.
17 I shall not die, but live:
and shall declare the works of the Lord.
18 The Lord chastising hath chastised me:
but he hath not delivered me over to death.
19 Open ye to me the gates of justice:
I will go into them, and give praise to the Lord.
20 This is the gate of the Lord,
the just shall enter into it.
21 I will give glory to thee because thou hast heard me:
and art become my salvation.
22 The stone which the builders rejected;
the same is become the head of the corner.
23 This is the Lord's doing:
and it is wonderful in our eyes.
24 This is the day which the Lord hath made:
let us be glad and rejoice therein.
25 O Lord, save me:
O Lord, give good success.
26 Blessed be he that cometh in the name Lord.
We have blessed you out of the house of the Lord.
27 The Lord is God, and he hath shone upon us.
Appoint a solemn day, with shady boughs,
even to the horn of the alter.

28 Thou art my God, and I will praise thee:
  thou art my God, and I will exalt thee.
I will praise thee, because thou hast heard me,
  and art become my salvation.
29 O praise ye the Lord, for he is good:
for his mercy endureth for ever.

Psalm 118
Beati immaculati

Antiphon:
Observe and hear all the things that I command thee,
  that it may be well with thee and thy children
  after thee for ever;
when thou shalt do what is good and pleasing in the
  sight of the Lord thy God. *(Deut 12:28)*

ALEPH
1 Blessed are the undefiled in the way,
who walk in the law of the Lord.
2 Blessed are they who search his testimonies:
that seek him with their whole heart.
3 For they that work iniquity,
have not walked in his ways.
4 Thou hast commanded thy commandments
to be kept most diligently.
5 O! that my ways may be directed
to keep thy justifications.
6 Then shall I not be confounded,
when I shall look into all thy commandments.
7 I will praise thee with uprightness of heart,
when I shall have learned the judgments of thy justice.
8 I will keep thy justifications:
O! do not thou utterly forsake me.

BETH
9 By what doth a young man correct his way?
by observing thy words.

The Psalter

10 With my whole heart have I sought after thee:
let me not stray from thy commandments.
11 Thy words have I hidden in my heart,
that I may not sin against thee.
12 Blessed art thou, O Lord:
teach me thy justifications.
13 With my lips I have pronounced
all the judgments of thy mouth.
14 I have been delighted
 in the way of thy testimonies, as in all riches.
15 I will meditate on thy commandments:
nd I will consider thy ways.
16 I will think of thy justifications:
I will not forget thy words.

The Psalter

Day 24 - Morning Prayer

Antiphon:
Observe and hear all the things that I command thee,
    that it may be well with thee and thy children
    after thee for ever;
when thou shalt do what is good and pleasing in the
    sight of the Lord thy God. *(Deut 12:28)*

GIMEL

17 Give bountifully to thy servant, enliven me:
and I shall keep thy words.
18 Open thou my eyes:
and I will consider the wondrous things of thy law.
19 I am a sojourner on the earth:
hide not thy commandments from me.
20 My soul hath coveted to long
for thy justifications, at all times.
21 Thou hast rebuked the proud:
they are cursed who decline from thy commandments.
22 Remove from reproach and contempt:
because I have sought after thy testimonies.
23 For princes sat, and spoke against me:
but thy servant was employed in thy justifications.
24 For thy testimonies are my meditation:
and thy justifications my counsel.

DALETH

25 My soul hath cleaved to the pavement:
quicken thou me according to thy word.
26 I have declared my ways, and thou hast heard me:
teach me thy justifications.
27 Make me to understand the way of thy
    justifications:
and I shall be exercised in thy wondrous works.
28 My soul hath slumbered through heaviness:
strengthen thou me in thy words.
29 Remove from me the way of iniquity:
and out of thy law have mercy on me.

30 I have chosen the way of truth:
thy judgments I have not forgotten.
31 I have stuck to thy testimonies, O Lord:
put me not to shame.
32 I have run the way of thy commandments,
when thou didst enlarge my heart.

HE
33 Set before me for a law the way of thy
    justifications,
O Lord: and I will always seek after it.
34 Give me understanding, and I will search thy law;
and I will keep it with my whole heart.
35 Lead me into the path of thy commandments;
for this same I have desired.
36 Incline my heart into thy testimonies
and not to covetousness.
37 Turn away my eyes that they may not behold
    vanity:
quicken me in thy way.
38 Establish thy word to thy servant,
in thy fear.
39 Turn away my reproach, which I have apprehended:
for thy judgments are delightful.
40 Behold I have longed after thy precepts:
quicken me in thy justice.

VAU
41 Let thy mercy also come upon me, O Lord:
thy salvation according to thy word.
42 So shall I answer them that reproach me in any
    thing;
that I have trusted in thy words.
43 And take not thou the word of truth utterly out of
    my mouth:
for in thy words have I hoped exceedingly.
44 So shall I always keep thy law,
for ever and ever.
45 And I walked at large:
because I have sought after thy commandments.

The Psalter

46 And I spoke of thy testimonies before kings: and I was not ashamed.
47 I meditated also on thy commandments, which I loved.
48 And I lifted up my hands to thy commandments, which I loved: and I was exercised in thy justifications.

The Psalter

Day 24 - Evening Prayer

Antiphon:
Observe and hear all the things that I command thee,
    that it may be well with thee and thy children
        after thee for ever;
when thou shalt do what is good and pleasing in the
    sight of the Lord thy God. *(Deut 12:28)*

ZAIN
49 Be thou mindful of thy word to thy servant,
in which thou hast given me hope.
50 This hath comforted me in my humiliation:
because thy word hath enlivened me.
51 The proud did iniquitously altogether:
but I declined not from thy law.
52 I remembered, O Lord, thy judgments of old:
and I was comforted.
53 A fainting hath taken hold of me,
because of the wicked that forsake thy law.
54 Thy justifications were the subject of my song,
in the place of my pilgrimage.
55 In the night I have remembered thy name, O Lord:
and have kept thy law.
56 This happened to me:
because I sought after thy justifications.

HETH
57 O Lord, my portion, I have said,
I would keep the law.
58 I entreated thy face with all my heart:
have mercy on me according to thy word.
59 I have thought on my ways:
and turned my feet unto thy testimonies.
60 I am ready, and am not troubled:
that I may keep thy commandments.
61 The cords of the wicked have encompassed me:
but I have not forgotten thy law.

62 I rose at midnight to give praise to thee;
for the judgments of thy justification.
63 I am a partaker with all them that fear thee,
and that keep thy commandments.
64 The earth, O Lord, is full of thy mercy:
teach me thy justifications.

TETH

65 Thou hast done well with thy servant, O Lord,
according to thy word.
66 Teach me goodness and discipline and knowledge;
for I have believed thy commandments.
67 Before I was humbled I offended;
therefore have I kept thy word.
68 Thou art good;
and in thy goodness teach me thy justifications.
69 The iniquity of the proud hath been multiplied over me:
but I will seek thy commandments with my whole heart.
70 Their heart is curdled like milk:
but I have meditated on thy law.
71 It is good for me that thou hast humbled me,
that I may learn thy justifications.
72 The law of thy mouth is good to me,
above thousands of gold and silver.

JOD

73 Thy hands have made me and formed me:
give me understanding, and I will learn thy commandments.
74 They that fear thee shall see me, and shall be glad:
because I have greatly hoped in thy words.
75 I know, O Lord, that thy judgments are equity:
and in thy truth thou hast humbled me.
76 O! let thy mercy be for my comfort,
according to thy word unto thy servant.

The Psalter

77 Let thy tender mercies come unto me, and I shall
        live:
For thy law is my meditation.
78 Let the proud be ashamed, because they have done
        unjustly towards me:
but I will be employed in thy commandments.
79 Let them that fear thee turn to me"
 and they that know thy testimonies.
80 Let my heart be undefiled in thy justifications,
that I may not be confounded.

CAPH
81 My soul hath fainted after thy salvation:
and in thy word I have very much hoped.
82 My eyes have failed for thy word, saying:
When wilt thou comfort me?
83 For I am become like a bottle in the frost:
I have not forgotten thy justifications.
84 How many are the days of thy servant:
when wilt thou execute judgment on them that
        persecute me?
85 The wicked have told me fables:
but not as thy law.
86 All thy statutes are truth:
they have persecuted me unjustly, do thou help me.
87 They had almost made an end of me upon earth:
but I have not forsaken thy commandments.
88 Quicken thou me according to thy mercy:
and I shall keep the testimonies of thy mouth.

LAMED
89 For ever, O Lord,
thy word standeth firm in heaven.
90 Thy truth unto all generations:
thou hast founded the earth, and it continueth.
91 By thy ordinance the day goeth on:
for all things serve thee.
92 Unless thy law had been my meditation,
I had then perhaps perished in my abjection.

The Psalter

93 Thy justifications I will never forget:
for by them thou hast given me life.
94 I am thine, save thou me:
for I have sought thy justifications.
95 The wicked have waited for me to destroy me:
but I have understood thy testimonies.
96 I have seen an end to all persecution:
thy commandment is exceeding broad.

The Psalter

Day 25 - Morning Prayer

Antiphon:
Observe and hear all the things that I command thee,
 that it may be well with thee and thy children
 after thee for ever;
when thou shalt do what is good and pleasing in the
 sight of the Lord thy God. *(Deut 12:28)*

MEM

97 O how have I loved thy law, O Lord!
it is my meditation all the day.
98 Through thy commandment, thou hast made me
 wiser than my enemies:
for it is ever with me.
99 I have understood more than all my teachers:
because thy testimonies are my meditation.
100 I have had understanding above ancients:
because I have sought thy commandments.
101 I have restrained my feet from every evil way:
that I may keep thy words.
102 I have not declined from thy judgments,
because thou hast set me a law.
103 How sweet are thy words to my palate!
more than honey to my mouth.
104 By thy commandments I have had understanding:
therefore have I hated every way of iniquity.

NUN

105 Thy word is a lamp to my feet,
and a light to my paths.
106 I have sworn and am determined
to keep the judgments of thy justice.
107 I have been humbled, O Lord, exceedingly:
quicken thou me according to thy word.
108 The free offerings of my mouth make acceptable,
 O Lord:
and teach me thy judgments.
109 My soul is continually in my hands:
and I have not forgotten thy law.

110 Sinners have laid a snare for me:
but I have not erred from thy precepts.
111 I have purchased thy testimonies for an inheritance
    for ever:
because they are a joy to my heart.
112 I have inclined my heart to do thy justifications
for ever, for the reward.

SAMECH
113 I have hated the unjust:
and have loved thy law.
114 Thou art my helper and my protector:
and in thy word I have greatly hoped.
115 Depart from me, ye malignant:
and I will search the commandments of my God.
116 Uphold me according to thy word,
and I shall live: and let me not be confounded in my
    expectation.
117 Help me, and I shall be saved:
and I will meditate always on thy justifications.
118 Thou hast despised all them that fall off from thy
    judgments;
for their thought is unjust.
119 I have accounted all the sinners of the earth
    prevaricators:
therefore have I loved thy testimonies.
120 Pierce thou my flesh with thy fear:
for I am afraid of thy judgments.

AIN
121 I have done judgment and justice:
give me not up to them that slander me.
122 Uphold thy servant unto good:
let not the proud calumniate me.
123 My eyes have fainted after thy salvation:
and for the word of thy justice.
124 Deal with thy servant according to thy mercy:
and teach me thy justifications.

The Psalter

125 I am thy servant:
give me understanding that I may know thy
    testimonies.
126 It is time, O Lord, to do:
they have dissipated thy law.
127 Therefore have I loved thy commandments
above gold and the topaz.
128 Therefore was I directed to all thy
    commandments:
I have hated all wicked ways.

The Psalter

Day 25 - Evening Prayer

Antiphon:
Observe and hear all the things that I command thee,
    that it may be well with thee and thy children
    after thee for ever;
when thou shalt do what is good and pleasing in the
    sight of the Lord thy God. *(Deut 12:28)*

PHE
129 Thy testimonies are wonderful:
therefore my soul hath sought them.
130 The declaration of thy words giveth light:
and giveth understanding to little ones.
131 I opened my mouth and panted:
because I longed for thy commandments.
132 Look thou upon me, and have mercy on me,
according to the judgment of them that love thy name.
133 Direct my steps according to thy word:
and let no iniquity have dominion over me.
134 Redeem me from the calumnies of men:
that I may keep thy commandments.
135 Make thy face to shine upon thy servant:
and teach me thy justifications.
136 My eyes have sent forth springs of water:
because they have not kept thy law.

SADE
137 Thou art just, O Lord:
and thy judgment is right.
138 Thou hast commanded justice thy testimonies:
and thy truth exceedingly.
139 My zeal hath made me pine away:
because my enemies forgot thy words.
140 Thy word is exceedingly refined:
and thy servant hath loved it.
141 I am very young and despised;
but I forgot not thy justifications.

142 Thy justice is justice for ever:
and thy law is the truth.
143 Trouble and anguish have found me:
thy commandments are my meditation.
144 Thy testimonies are justice for ever:
give me understanding, and I shall live.

COPH
145 I cried with my whole heart, hear me, O Lord:
I will seek thy justifications.
146 I cried unto thee, save me:
that I may keep thy commandments.
147 I prevented the dawning of the day, and cried:
because in thy words I very much hoped.
148 My eyes to thee have prevented the morning:
that I might meditate on thy words.
149 Hear thou my voice, O Lord, according to thy mercy:
and quicken me according to thy mercy.
150 They that persecute me have drawn nigh to iniquity;
but they are gone far off from the law.
151 Thou art near, O Lord:
and all thy ways are truth.
152 I have known from the beginning concerning thy testimonies:
that thou hast founded them for ever.

RES
153 See my humiliation and deliver me:
for I have not forgotten the law.
154 Judge my judgment and redeem me:
quicken thou me for thy word's sake.
155 Salvation is far from sinners;
because they have not sought thy justifications.
156 Many, O Lord, are thy mercies:
quicken me according to thy judgment.
157 Many are they that persecute me, and afflict me;
but I have not declined from thy testimonies.

158 I beheld the transgressors, and I pined away;
because they kept not thy word.
159 Behold I have loved thy commandments, O Lord;
quicken me thou in thy mercy.
160 The beginning of thy words is truth:
all the judgments of thy justice are for ever.

SIN
161 Princes have persecuted me without cause:
and my heart hath been in awe of thy words.
162 I will rejoice at thy words,
as one that hath found great spoil.
163 I have hated and abhorred iniquity;
but I have loved thy law.
164 Seven times a day I have given praise to thee,
for the judgments of thy justice.
165 Much peace have they that love thy law,
and to them there is no stumbling block
166 I looked to thy salvation, O Lord:
and I loved thy commandments.
167 My soul hath kept thy testimonies:
and hath loved them exceedingly.
168 I have kept thy commandments and thy
    testimonies:
because all my ways are in thy sight.

TAU
169 Let my supplication, O Lord, come near in thy
    sight:
give me understanding according to thy word.
170 Let my request come in before thee;
deliver thou me according to thy word.
171 My lips shall utter a hymn,
 when thou shalt teach me thy justifications.
172 My tongue shall pronounce thy word:
because all thy commandments are justice.
173 Let thy hand be with me to save me;
for I have chosen thy precepts.

The Psalter

174 I have longed for thy salvation, O Lord;
and thy law is my meditation.
175 My soul shall live and shall praise thee:
and thy judgments shall help me.
176 I have gone astray like a sheep that is lost:
seek thy servant, because I have not forgotten thy
       commandments.

The Psalter

Day 26 - Morning Prayer

Psalm 119(120)
Ad Dominum

Antiphon:
And he said to Jesus: Lord, remember me when Thou
 shalt come into Thy kingdom.
And Jesus said to him: Amen I say to thee; This day
 thou shalt be with me in paradise. (Lk 23:42-43)

1 In my trouble I cried to the Lord:
and he heard me.
2 O Lord, deliver my soul from wicked lips,
and a deceitful tongue.
3 What shall be given to thee,
or what shall be added to thee, to a deceitful tongue.
4 The sharp arrows of the mighty,
with coals that lay waste.
5 Woe is me, that my sojourning is prolonged!
I have dwelt with the inhabitants of cedar:
6 my soul hath been long a sojourner.
7 With them that hate peace I was peaceable:
when I spoke to them they fought against me without
 cause.

Psalm 120(121)
Levavi oculos

Antiphon:
Then the king said; Let all the inhabitants of the whole
 earth fear the God of Daniel,
For He is the Saviour, working signs and wonders in the
 earth;
Who hath delivered Daniel out of the lions' den. *(Dan 14:42)*

1 I have lifted up my eyes to the mountains,
from whence help shall come to me.
2 My help is from the Lord,
who made heaven and earth.

3 May he not suffer thy foot to be moved:
neither let him slumber that keepeth thee.
4 Behold he shall neither slumber nor sleep,
that keepeth Israel.
5 The Lord is thy keeper,
the Lord is thy protection upon thy right hand.
6 The sun shall not burn thee by day:
nor the moon by night.
7 The Lord keepeth thee from all evil:
may the Lord keep thy soul.
8 May the Lord keep thy going in and thy going out;
from henceforth now and for ever.

Psalm 121(122)
Laetatus sum in his

Antiphon:
A great multitude, when they heard that Jesus was coming to Jerusalem, took branches of palm trees and went forth to meet Him and cried: Hosanna! Blessed is He that cometh in the Name of the Lord, the King of Israel. *(John 12:12'-13)*

1 I rejoiced at the things that were said to me:
We shall go into the house of the Lord.
2 Our feet were standing in thy courts, O Jerusalem.
3 Jerusalem, which is built as a city,
which is compact together.
4 For thither did the tribes go up, the tribes of the Lord:
the testimony of Israel, to praise the name of the Lord.
5 Because their seats have sat in judgment,
seats upon the house of David.
6 Pray ye for the things that are for the peace of Jerusalem:
and abundance for them that love thee.
7 Let peace be in thy strength:
and abundance in thy towers.

The Psalter

8 For the sake of my brethren, and of my neighbours,
I spoke peace of thee.
9 Because of the house of the Lord our God,
I have sought good things for thee.

The Psalter

Day 26 - Evening Prayer

Psalm 122(123)
Ad te levavi

Antiphon:
Be converted, therefore, ye sinners:
And do justice before God, believing that He will shew
 His mercy to you. (Tobias 14:8)

1 To thee have I lifted up my eyes,
who dwellest in heaven.
2 Behold as the eyes of the servants are on the hands
 of their masters,
As the eyes of the handmaid are on the hands of her
 mistress:
  so are our eyes unto the Lord our God,
  until he have mercy on us.
3 Have mercy on us, O Lord, have mercy on us:
for we are greatly filled with contempt.
4 For our soul is greatly filled:
we are a reproach to the rich, and contempt to the
 proud.

Psalm 123(124)
Nisi quia Domini

Antiphon:
Fear the Lord your God;
and He shall deliver you out of the hand of all your
 enemies. (4 Kings 17:39)

1 If it had not been that the Lord was with us,
let Israel now say:
2 If it had not been that the Lord was with us,
When men rose up against us
3 perhaps they had swallowed us up alive.
When their fury was enkindled against us,
4 perhaps the waters had swallowed us up.

The Psalter

5 Our soul hath passed through a torrent:
perhaps our soul had passed through a water
        insupportable.
6 Blessed be the Lord,
who hath not given us to be a prey to their teeth.
7 Our soul hath been delivered as a sparrow out of the
        snare of the followers.
The snare is broken, and we are delivered.
8 Our help is in the name of the Lord,
who made heaven and earth.

Psalm 124(125)
Qui confidunt

Antiphon:
Let all they enemies perish, O Lord;
but let them that love Thee shine, as the sun shineth in
        his rising. (Judges 5:31)

1 They that trust in the Lord shall be as mount Sion:
he shall not be moved for ever that dwelleth
2 in Jerusalem. Mountains are round about it:
so the Lord is round about his people from henceforth
        now and for ever.
3 For the Lord will not leave the rod of sinners upon
        the lot of the just:
that the just may not stretch forth their hands to
        iniquity.
4 Do good, O Lord, to those that are good,
and to the upright of heart.
5 But such as turn aside into bonds,
    the Lord shall lead out with the workers of iniquity:
    peace upon Israel.

The Psalter

Psalm 125(126)
In convertendo

Antiphon:
Give glory to the Lord for thy good things, and bless
 the God eternal;
that He may rebuild His tabernacle in thee, and may
 call back all the captives to thee;
and thou mayest rejoice for ever and ever. *(Tobias 14:12)*

1 When the lord brought back the captivity of Sion,
we became like men comforted.
2 Then was our mouth filled with gladness;
 and our tongue with joy.
Then shall they say among the Gentiles:
 The Lord hath done great things for them.
3 The Lord hath done great things for us:
we are become joyful.
4 Turn again our captivity, O Lord,
as a stream in the south.
5 They that sow in tears shall reap in joy.
6 Going they went and wept,
casting their seeds.
7 But coming they shall come with joyfulness,
carrying their sheaves.

The Psalter

Day 27 - Morning Prayer

Psalm 126(127)
Nisi Dominus

Antiphon:
Thou therefore, my son,
be strong in the grace which is in Christ Jesus. (2 Tim 2:1)

1 Unless the Lord build the house,
  they labour in vain that build it.
Unless the Lord keep the city,
  he watcheth in vain that keepeth it.
2 It is vain for you to rise before light,
  rise ye after you have sitten,
  you that eat the bread of sorrow.
When he shall give sleep to his beloved,
3 behold the inheritance of the Lord are children:
the reward, the fruit of the womb.
4 As arrows in the hand of the mighty,
so the children of them that have been shaken.
5 Blessed is the man that hath filled the desire with them;
he shall not be confounded when he shall speak to his enemies in the gate.

Psalm 127(128)
Beati omnes

Antiphon:
Be afflicted and mourn and weep; let your laughter be turned into mourning and joy into sorrow.
Be humbled in the sign of the Lord; and He will exalt you. (James 4:9-10)

1 Blessed are all they that fear the Lord:
that walk in his ways.
2 For thou shalt eat the labours of thy hands:
blessed art thou, and it shall be well with thee.

The Psalter

3 Thy wife as a fruitful vine,
on the sides of thy house.
4 Behold, thus shall the man be blessed
that feareth the Lord.
5 May the Lord bless thee out of Sion:
and mayest thou see the good things of Jerusalem all
      the days of thy life.
6 And mayest thou see thy children's children,
peace upon Israel.

Psalm 128(129)
Saepe expugnaverunt

Antiphon:
The Lord liveth, and my God is blessed; and the strong
      God of my salvation shall be exalted;
God who givest me revenge, and bringest down people
      under me, from the wicked man Thou shalt
      deliver me. *(2 Kings 22:47-48, 49b)*

1 Often have they fought against me from my youth,
let Israel now say.
2 Often have they fought against me from my youth:
but they could not prevail over me.
3 The wicked have wrought upon my back:
they have lengthened their iniquity.
4 The Lord who is just will cut the necks of sinners:
5 let them all be confounded and turned back
that hate Sion.
6 Let them be as grass on the tops of houses:
which withered before it be plucked up:
7 Wherewith the mower filleth not his hand:
nor he that gathereth sheaves his bosom.
8 And they that have passed by have not said:
The blessing of the Lord be upon you:
    we have blessed you in the name of the Lord.

The Psalter

Psalm 129(130)
De profundis

Antiphon:
Let us go therefore with confidence to the throne of grace;
that we may obtain mercy and find grace in seasonable aid. (Heb 4:16)

1 Out of the depths I have cried to thee, O Lord:
2 Lord, hear my voice.
Let thy ears be attentive to the voice of my supplication.
3 If thou, O Lord, wilt mark iniquities:
Lord, who shall stand it.
4 For with thee there is merciful forgiveness:
and by reason of thy law, I have waited for thee,
O Lord. My soul hath relied on his word:
5 my soul hath hoped in the Lord.
6 From the morning watch even until night,
let Israel hope in the Lord.
7 Because with the Lord there is mercy:
and with him plentiful redemption.
8 And he shall redeem Israel from all his iniquities.

The Psalter

Day 27 - Evening Prayer

Psalm 130(131)
Domine, none est

Antiphon:
And now, little children, abide in Him,
that when He shall appear, we may have confidence,
    and not be confounded by Him at His coming.
(1 John 2:28)

1 Lord, my heart is not exalted:
    nor are my eyes lofty.
Neither have I walked in great matters,
    nor in wonderful things above me.
2 If I was not humbly minded, but exalted my soul:
As a child that is weaned is towards his mother,
    so reward in my soul.
3 Let Israel hope in the Lord,
from henceforth now and for ever.

Psalm 131(132)
Memento, Domine

Antiphon:
David went up with all the men of Israel to the hill of
    Cariathiarim, which is in Juda,
to bring thence the Ark of the Lord God sitting upon
    the cherubim, where His Name is called upon. (1
    Chron 13:6)

1 O Lord, remember David, and all his meekness.
2 How he swore to the Lord,
he vowed a vow to the God of Jacob:
3 If I shall enter into the tabernacle of my house:
if I shall go up into the bed wherein I lie:
4 If I shall give sleep to my eyes,
or slumber to my eyelids,
5 Or rest to my temples:
    until I find out a place for the Lord, a tabernacle for
        the God of Jacob.

The Psalter

6 Behold we have heard of it in Ephrata:
we have found it in the fields of the wood.
7 We will go into his tabernacle:
We will adore in the place where his feet stood.
8 Arise, O Lord, into thy resting place:
thou and the ark, which thou hast sanctified.
9 Let thy priests be clothed with justice:
and let thy saints rejoice.
10 For thy servant David's sake,
turn not away the face of thy anointed.
11 The Lord hath sworn truth to David,
 and he will not make it void:
of the fruit of thy womb I will set upon thy throne.
12 If thy children will keep thy covenant,
 and these my testimonies which I shall teach them:
Their children also for evermore shall sit upon thy
throne.
13 For the Lord hath chosen Sion:
 he hath chosen it for his dwelling.
14 This is my rest for ever and ever:
here will I dwell, for I have chosen it.
15 Blessing, I will bless her widow:
I will satisfy her poor with bread.
16 I will clothe her priests with salvation:
and her saints shall rejoice with exceeding great joy.
17 There will I bring forth a horn to David:
I have prepared a lamp for my anointed.
18 His enemies I will clothe with confusion:
but upon him will my sanctification flourish.

Psalm 132(133)
Ecce quam bonum

Antiphon:
A new commandment I give unto you:
That you love one another, as I have loved you, that
 you also love one another.
By this shall all men know that you are My disciples;
 if you have love, one for another. (John 13:34-35)

1 Behold how good and how pleasant it is
for brethren to dwell in unity.

The Psalter

2 Like the precious ointment on the head,
    that ran down upon the beard, the beard of Aaron,
Which ran down to the skirt of his garment:
3 as the dew of Hermon, which descendeth upon mount Sion.
For there the Lord hath commandeth blessing,
    and life for evermore.

Psalm 133(134)
Ecce nunc benedicite

Antiphon:
Thanks be to God, Who hath given us the victory through our Lord Jesus Christ. (1 Cor 15:57)

1 Behold now bless ye the Lord,
    all ye servants of the Lord:
Who stand in the house of the Lord,
    in the courts of the house of our God.
2 In the nights lift up your hands to the holy places,
and bless ye the Lord.
3 May the Lord out of Sion bless thee,
he that made heaven and earth.

The Psalter

Day 28 - Morning Prayer

Psalm 134(135)
Laudate nomen

Antiphon:
At His voice He giveth a multitude of waters in the heaven and lifteth up the clouds from the ends of the earth.
He maketh lightnings for rain, and bringeth forth the wind out of His treasures. (Jer 10:13)

1 Praise ye the name of the Lord:
O you his servants, praise the Lord:
2 You that stand in the house of the Lord,
in the courts of the house of our God.
3 Praise ye the Lord, for the Lord is good:
sing ye to his name, for it is sweet.
4 For the Lord hath chosen Jacob unto himself:
Israel for his own possession.
5 For I have known that the Lord is great,
and our God is above all gods.
6 Whatsoever the Lord hath pleased he hath done,
in heaven, in earth, in the sea, and in all the deeps.
7 He bringeth up clouds from the end of the earth:
he hath made lightnings for the rain.
He bringeth forth winds out of his stores:
8 He slew the firstborn of Egypt
from man even unto beast.
9 He sent forth signs and wonders in the midst of thee,
O Egypt: upon Pharao, and upon all his servants.
10 He smote many nations, and slew mighty kings:
11 Sehon king of the Amorrhites, and Og king of Basan,
and all the kingdoms of Chanaan.
12 And gave their land for an inheritance,
for an inheritance to his people Israel.
13 Thy name, O Lord, is for ever:
thy memorial, O Lord, unto all generations.
14 For the Lord will judge his people,
and will be entreated in favour of his servants.

15 The idols of the Gentiles are silver and gold,
the works of men's hands.
16 They have a mouth, but they speak not:
they have eyes, but they see not.
17 They have ears, but they hear not:
neither is there any breath in their mouths.
18 Let them that make them be like to them:
and every one that trusteth in them.
19 Bless the Lord, O house of Israel:
bless the Lord, O house of Aaron.
20 Bless the Lord, O house of Levi:
you that fear the Lord, bless the Lord.
21 Blessed be the Lord out of Sion,
who dwelleth in Jerusalem.

Psalm 135(136)
Confitemini Domino

Antiphon:
In the beginning, God created heaven and earth.
And the earth was void and empty, and darkness was upon the face of the deep;
And the Spirit of God moved over the waters. (Gen 1:1-2)

1 Praise the Lord, for he is good:
for his mercy endureth for ever.
2 Praise ye the God of gods:
for his mercy endureth for ever.
3 Praise ye the Lord of lords:
for his mercy endureth for ever.
4 Who alone doth great wonders:
for his mercy endureth for ever.
5 Who made the heavens in understanding:
for his mercy endureth for ever.
6 Who established the earth above the waters:
for his mercy endureth for ever.
7 Who made the great lights:
for his mercy endureth for ever.
8 The sun to rule over the day:
for his mercy endureth for ever.

The Psalter

9 The moon and the stars to rule the night:
for his mercy endureth for ever.
10 Who smote Egypt with their firstborn:
for his mercy endureth for ever.
11 Who brought Israel from among them:
for his mercy endureth for ever.
12 With a mighty hand and a stretched out arm:
for his mercy endureth for ever.
13 Who divided the Red Sea into parts:
for his mercy endureth for ever.
14 And brought out Israel through the midst thereof:
for his mercy endureth for ever.
15 And overthrew Pharao and his host in the Red Sea:
for his mercy endureth for ever.
16 Who led his people through the desert:
for his mercy endureth for ever.
17 Who smote great kings:
for his mercy endureth for ever.
18 And slew strong kings:
for his mercy endureth for ever.
19 Sehon king of the Amorrhites:
for his mercy endureth for ever.
20 And Og king of Basan:
for his mercy endureth for ever.
21 And he gave their land for an inheritance:
for his mercy endureth for ever.
22 For an inheritance to his servant Israel:
for his mercy endureth for ever.
23 For he was mindful of us in our affliction:
for his mercy endureth for ever.
24 And he redeemed us from our enemies:
for his mercy endureth for ever.
25 Who giveth food to all flesh:
for his mercy endureth for ever.
26 Give glory to the God of heaven:
for his mercy endureth for ever.
27 Give glory to the Lord of lords:
for his mercy endureth for ever.

The Psalter

Day 28 - Evening Prayer

Psalm 136(137)
Super Flumina

Antiphon:
All this land shall be a desolation and an astonishment; and all these nations shall serve the king of Babylon seventy years. (Jer 25:11)

1 Upon the rivers of Babylon, there we sat and wept: when we remembered Sion:
2 On the willows in the midst thereof
 we hung up our instruments.
3 For there they that led us into captivity required of us the words of songs.
And they that carried us away, said:
 Sing ye to us a hymn of the songs of Sion.
4 How shall we sing the song of the Lord
in a strange land?
5 If I forget thee, O Jerusalem,
let my right hand be forgotten.
6 Let my tongue cleave to my jaws, if I do not remember thee:
If I make not Jerusalem the beginning of my joy.
7 Remember, O Lord, the children of Edom, in the day of Jerusalem:
Who say: Rase it, rase it, even to the foundation thereof.
8 O daughter of Babylon, miserable:
blessed shall he be who shall repay thee thy payment which thou hast paid us.
9 Blessed be he that shall take and dash thy little ones against the rock.

The Psalter

Psalm 137(138)
Confitebor tibi

Antiphon:
The Lord is patient and great in power, and will not
    cleanse and acquit the guilty.
The Lord's ways are in a tempest and a whirlwind;
and clouds are the dust of His feet. (Nahum 1:3)

1 I will praise thee, O lord, with my whole heart:
    for thou hast heard the words of my mouth.
I will sing praise to thee in the sight of his angels:
2 I will worship towards thy holy temple,
    and I will give glory to thy name.
For thy mercy, and for thy truth:
    for thou hast magnified thy holy name above all.
3 In what day soever I shall call upon thee, hear me:
thou shall multiply strength in my soul.
4 May all the kings of the earth give glory to thee:
for they have heard all the words of thy mouth.
5 And let them sing in the ways of the Lord:
for great is the glory of the Lord.
6 For the Lord is high, and looketh on the low:
and the high he knoweth afar off.
7 If I shall walk in the midst of tribulation,
    thou wilt quicken me:
and thou hast stretched forth thy hand against the
wrath of my enemies:
    and thy right hand hath saved me.
8 The Lord will repay for me: thy mercy, O Lord,
    endureth for ever:
O despise not the work of thy hands.

Psalm 138(139)
Domine, probasti

Antiphon:
I will raise up the tabernacle of David, that is fallen;
and I will close up the breaches of the walls thereof
and repair what was fallen;
and I will rebuild is as in the days of old. (Amos 9:11)

The Psalter

1 Lord, thou hast proved me,
and known me:
2 thou hast know my sitting down,
and my rising up.
3 Thou hast understood my thoughts afar off:
my path and my line thou hast searched out.
4 And thou hast foreseen all my ways:
for there is no speech in my tongue.
5 Behold, O Lord, thou hast known all things,
    the last and those of old:
thou hast formed me,
    and hast laid thy hand upon me.
6 Thy knowledge is become wonderful to me:
it is high, and I cannot reach to it.
7 Whither shall I go from thy spirit?
or whither shall I flee from thy face?
8 If I ascend into heaven, thou art there:
if I descend into hell, thou art present.
9 If I take my wings early in the morning,
and dwell in the uttermost parts of the sea:
10 Even there also shall thy hand lead me:
and thy right hand shall hold me.
11 And I said: Perhaps darkness shall cover me:
and night shall be my light in my pleasures.
12 But darkness shall not be dark to thee,
    and night shall be light as day: the darkness thereof,
and the light thereof are alike to thee.
13 For thou hast possessed my reins:
thou hast protected me from my mother's womb.
14 I will praise thee, for thou art fearfully magnified:
wonderful are thy works, and my soul knoweth right
        well.
15 My bone is not hidden from thee,
    which thou hast made in secret:
and my substance in the lower parts of the earth.
16 Thy eyes did see my imperfect being,
    and in thy book all shall be written:
days shall be formed, and no one in them.

The Psalter

17 But to me thy friends, O God, are made exceedingly honourable:
their principality is exceedingly strengthened.
18 I will number them, and they shall be multiplied above the sand:
I rose up and am still with thee.
19 If thou wilt kill the wicked, O God:
ye men of blood, depart from me:
20 Because you say in thought:
They shall receive thy cities in vain.
21 Have I not hated them, O Lord, that hated thee:
and pine away because of thy enemies?
22 I have hated them with a perfect hatred:
and they are become enemies to me.
23 Prove me, O God, and know my heart:
examine me, and know my paths.
24 And see if there be in me the way of iniquity:
and lead me in the eternal way.

The Psalter

Day 29 - Morning Prayer

Psalm 139(140)
Eripe me, Domine

Antiphon:
For the wages of sin is death, but of the grace of God; life everlasting in Christ Jesus our Lord.   (Romans 6:23)

1 *Unto the end, a psalm for David.*
2 Deliver me, O Lord, from the evil man:
rescue me from the unjust man.
3 Who have devised iniquities in their hearts:
all the day long they designed battles.
4 They have sharpened their tongues like a serpent:
the venom of saps is under their lips.
5 Keep me, O Lord, from the hand of the wicked:
    and from unjust men deliver me.
Who have proposed to supplant my steps.
6 The proud have hidden a net for me.
And they have stretched out cords for a snare:
    they have laid for me a stumblingblock by the
        wayside.
7 I said to the Lord: Thou art my God:
hear, O Lord, the voice of my supplication.
8 O Lord, Lord, the strength of my salvation:
thou hast overshadowed my head in the day of battle.
9 Give me not up, O Lord, from my desire to the
        wicked:
    they have plotted against me;
do not thou forsake me,
    lest they should triumph.
10 The head of them compassing me about:
the labour of their lips shall overwhelm them.
11 Burning coals shall fall upon them;
    thou wilt cast them down into the fire:
in miseries they shall not be able to stand.
12 A man full of tongue shall not be established in the
        earth:
evil shall catch the unjust man unto destruction.

The Psalter

13 I know that the Lord will do justice to the needy,
and will revenge the poor.
14 But as for the just, they shall give glory to thy name:
and the upright shall dwell with thy countenance.

Psalm 140(141)
Domine, clamavi

Antiphon:
Let not your heart be troubled;
you believe in God, believe also in Me. (John 14:1)

1 I have cried to the, O Lord, hear me:
hearken to my voice, when I cry to thee.
2 Let my prayer be directed as incense in thy sight;
the lifting up of my hands, as evening sacrifice.
3 Set a watch, O Lord, before my mouth:
and a door round about my lips.
4 Incline not my heart to evil words;
to make excuses in sins.
With men that work iniquity:
   and I will not communicate with the choicest of them.
5 The just shall correct me in mercy, and shall reprove me:
but let not the oil of the sinner fatten my head.
For my prayer also shall still be against the things with
   which they are well pleased:
6 their judges falling upon the rock have been
   swallowed up.
They shall hear my words, for they have prevailed:
7 as when the thickness of the earth is broken up upon
   the ground:
Our bones are scattered by the side of hell.
8 But o to thee, O Lord, Lord, are my eyes:
in thee have I put my trust, take not away my soul.

9 Keep me from the snare, which they have laid for me,
and from the stumblingblocks of them that work
iniquity.
10 The wicked shall fall in his net:
I am alone until I pass.

Psalm 141(142)
Voce mea

Antiphon:
Inquire of the former generations, and search diligently
into the memory of the fathers;
For we are but of yesterday, and are ignorant that our
days upon earth are but a shadow. (Job 8:9)

1 *Of understanding for David. A prayer when he was in
the cave. [1 Kings 24].*
2 I cried to the Lord with my voice:
with my voice I made supplication to the Lord.
3 In his sight I pour out my prayer,
and before him I declare my trouble:
4 When my spirit failed me,
then thou newest my paths.
5 I looked on my right hand, and beheld,
and there was no one that would know me.
Flight hath failed me:
and there is no one that hath regard to my soul.
6 I cried to thee, O Lord: I said:
Thou art my hope, my portion in the land of the living.
7 Attend to my supplication:
for I am brought very low.
Deliver me from my persecutors;
for they are stronger than I.
8 Bring my soul out of prison,
that I may praise thy name:
the just wait for me, until thou reward me.

The Psalter

Day 29 - Evening Prayer

Psalm 142(143)
Domine, exaudi

Antiphon:
David arose, and all the people that were with him, and they passed over the Jordan, until it grew light, and not one of them was left that was not gone over the river. (2 Kings 17:22)

1 Hear, O Lord, my prayer:
   give ear to my supplication in thy truth:
   hear me in thy justice.
2 And enter not into judgment with thy servant:
for in thy sight no man living shall be justified.
3 For the enemy hath persecuted my soul:
   he hath brought down my life to the earth.
He hath made me to dwell in darkness
   as those that have been dead of old:
4 and my spirit is in anguish within me:
my heart within me is troubled.
5 I remembered the days of old,
   I meditated on all thy works:
I meditated upon the works of thy hands.
6 I stretched forth my hands to thee:
my soul is as earth without water unto thee.
7 Hear me speedily, O Lord:
   my spirit hath fainted away.
Turn not away thy face from me,
   lest I be like unto them that go down into the pit.
8 Cause me to hear thy mercy in the morning;
   for in thee have I hoped.
Make the way known to me, wherein I should walk:
   for I have lifted up my soul to thee.
9 Deliver me from my enemies, O Lord,
to thee have I fled:
10 teach me to do thy will, for thou art my God.
Thy good spirit shall lead me into the right land:

11 For thy name's sake, O Lord,
    thou wilt quicken me in thy justice.
Thou wilt bring my soul out of trouble:
12 and in thy mercy thou wilt destroy my enemies.
And thou wilt cut off all them that afflict my soul:
    for I am thy servant.

Psalm 143(144)
Benedictus Dominus

Antiphon:
David said: The Lord who delivered me out of the paw
        of the lion, and out of the paw of the bear,
He will deliver me out of the hand of this Philistine.
And Saul said to David; Go, and the Lord be
        with thee. (I Kings 17:37)

1 Blessed be the Lord my God,
    who teacheth my hands to fight,
    and my fingers to war.
2 My mercy, and my refuge:
    my support, and my deliverer:
My protector, and I have hoped in him:
    who subdueth my people under me.
3 Lord, what is man, that thou art made known to
        him?
or the son of man, that thou makest account of him?
4 Man is like to vanity:
his days pass away like a shadow.
5 Lord, bow down thy heavens and descend:
touch the mountains and they shall smoke.
6 Send forth lightning, and thou shalt scatter them:
shoot out thy arrows, and thou shalt trouble them.
7 Put forth thy hand from on high, take me out,
    and deliver me from many waters:
from the hand of strange children:
8 Whose mouth hath spoken vanity:
and their right hand is the right hand of iniquity.
9 To thee, O God, I will sing a new canticle:
on the psaltery and an instrument of ten strings I will

sing praises to thee.
10 Who givest salvation to kings:
who hast redeemed thy servant David from the malicious sword:
11 Deliver me, And rescue me out of the hand of strange children;
    whose mouth hath spoken vanity:
    and their right hand is the right hand of iniquity:
12 Whose sons are as new plants in their youth:
    Their daughters decked out,
    adorned round about after the similitude of a temple:
13 Their storehouses full, flowing out of this into that.
Their sheep fruitful in young,
    abounding in their goings forth:
14 their oxen fat. There is no breach of wall,
nor passage, nor crying out in their streets.
15 They have called the people happy, that hath these things:
but happy is that people whose God is the Lord.

Psalm 144(145)
Exaltabo te, Deus

Antiphon:
Now this is eternal life;
that they may know Thee, the only true God, and Jesus Christ, Whom Thou hast sent. (John 17:3)

1 I will extol thee, O God my king:
    and I will bless thy name for ever;
    yea, for ever and ever.
2 Every day I will bless thee:
    and I will praise thy name for ever;
    yea, for ever and ever.
3 Great is the Lord, and greatly to be praised:
and of his greatness there is no end.
4 Generation and generation shall praise thy works:
and they shall declare thy power.

The Psalter

5 They shall speak of the magnificence of the glory of
    thy holiness:
and shall tell thy wondrous works.
6 And they shall speak of the might of thy terrible
    acts: and shall declare thy greatness.
7 They shall publish the memory of the abundance of
    thy sweetness: and shall rejoice in thy justice.
8 The Lord is gracious and merciful:
patient and plenteous in mercy.
9 The Lord is sweet to all:
and his tender mercies are over all his works.
10 Let all thy works, O lord, praise thee:
and let thy saints bless thee.
11 They shall speak of the glory of thy kingdom:
and shall tell of thy power:
12 To make thy might known to the sons of men:
and the glory of the magnificence of thy kingdom.
13 Thy kingdom is a kingdom of all ages:
and thy dominion endureth throughout all generations.
14 The Lord lifteth up all that fall:
and setteth up all that are cast down.
15 The eyes of all hope in thee, O Lord:
and thou givest them meat in due season.
16 Thou openest thy hand,
and fillest with blessing every living creature.
17 The Lord is just in all his ways:
and holy in all his works.
18 The Lord is nigh unto all them that call upon him:
to all that call upon him in truth.
19 He will do the will of them that fear him:
and he will hear their prayer, and save them.
20 The Lord keepeth all them that love him;
but all the wicked he will destroy.
21 My mouth shall speak the praise of the Lord:
    and let all flesh bless thy holy name for ever;
    yea, for ever and ever.

The Psalter

Day 30 - Morning Prayer

Psalm 145(146)
Lauda, anima

Antiphon:
Fear the Lord and give Him honour, because the hour
    of His judgment is come;
And adore ye Him that made heaven and earth, the sea
    and fountains of waters.   (Rev 14:7)

1 Alleluia, of Aggeus and Zacharias.
2 Praise the Lord, O my soul,
    in my life I will praise the Lord:
I will sing to my God as long as I shall be.
    Put not your trust in princes:
3 in the children of men,
in whom there is no salvation.
4 His spirit shall go forth, and he shall return into his
    earth:
in that day all their thoughts shall perish.
5 Blessed is he who hath the God of Jacob for his
    helper,
whose hope is in the Lord his God:
6 who made heaven and earth, the sea,
and all things that are in them.
7 Who keepeth truth for ever:
    who executeth judgment for them that suffer
        wrong:
    who giveth food to the hungry.
The Lord looseth them that are fettered:
8 the Lord enlighteneth the blind.
The Lord lifteth up them that are cast down:
    the Lord loveth the just.
9 The Lord keepeth the strangers,
    he will support the fatherless and the widow:
    and the ways of sinners he will destroy.
10 The Lord shall reign for ever: thy God, O Sion,
unto generation and generation.

The Psalter

Psalm 146(147a)
Laudate Dominum

Antiphon:
How good and sweet is Thy Spirit, O Lord,
in all things! (Wisdom 12:1)

1 Praise ye the Lord, because psalm is good:
to our God be joyful and comely praise.
2 The Lord buildeth up Jerusalem:
he will gather together the dispersed of Israel.
3 Who healeth the broken of heart,
and bindeth up their bruises.
4 Who telleth the number of the stars:
and calleth them all by their names.
5 Great is our Lord, and great is his power:
and of his wisdom there is no number.
6 The Lord lifteth up the meek,
and bringeth the wicked down even to the ground.
7 Sing ye to the Lord with praise:
sing to our God upon the harp.
8 Who covereth the heaven with clouds,
   and prepareth rain for the earth.
Who maketh grass to grow on the mountains,
   and herbs for the service of men.
9 Who giveth to beasts their food:
and to the young ravens that call upon him.
10 He shall not delight in the strength of the horse:
nor take pleasure in the legs of a man.
11 The Lord taketh pleasure in them that fear him:
and in them that hope in his mercy.

Psalm 147(147b)
Lauda, Jerusalem

Antiphon:
The works of the Lord are perfect, and all His ways
      are judgments;
God is faithful and without any iniquity; He is
      just and right. (Deut 32:4)

The Psalter

12 Praise the Lord, O Jerusalem
praise thy God, O Sion.
13 Because he hath strengthened the bolts of thy
    gates,
he hath blessed thy children within thee.
14 Who hath placed peace in thy borders:
 and filleth thee with the fat of corn.
15 Who sendeth forth his speech to the earth:
 his word runneth swiftly.
16 Who giveth snow like wool:
scattereth mists like ashes.
17 He sendeth his crystal like morsels:
 who shall stand before the face of his cold?
18 He shall send out his word, and shall melt them:
his wind shall blow, and the waters shall run.
19 Who declareth his word to Jacob:
his justices and his judgments to Israel.
20 He hath not done in like manner to every nation:
and his judgments he hath not made manifest to them.
Alleluia.

The Psalter

Day 30 - Evening Prayer

Psalm 148
Laudate Dominum de caelis

Antiphon:
O ye heavens, bless the Lord;
praise and exalt Him above all forever.
O all ye waters that are above the heavens, bless the Lord;
praise and exalt Him above all forever. (Dan 3:59-60)

1 Praise ye the Lord from the heavens:
praise ye him in the high places.
2 Praise ye him, all his angels:
praise ye him, all his hosts.
3 Praise ye him, O sun and moon:
praise him, all ye stars and light.
4 Praise him, ye heavens of heavens:
and let all the waters that are above the heavens
5 praise the name of the Lord.
For he spoke, and they were made:
he commanded, and they were created.
6 He hath established them for ever, and for ages of ages:
he hath made a decree, and it shall not pass away.
7 Praise the Lord from the earth,
ye dragons, and all ye deeps:
8 Fire, hail, snow, ice,
stormy winds which fulfil his word:
9 Mountains and all hills,
fruitful trees and all cedars:
10 Beasts and all cattle:
serpents and feathered fowls:
11 Kings of the earth and all people:
princes and all judges of the earth:
12 Young men and maidens:
let the old with the younger, praise the name of the Lord:

The Psalter

13 For his name alone is exalted.
14 The praise of him is above heaven and earth:
   and he hath exalted the horn of his people.
A hymn to all his saints: to the children of Israel,
   a people approaching to him.
Alleluia.

Psalm 149
Cantate Domino

Antiphon:
Be of good comfort my children; cry to the Lord;
and He will deliver you from the hand of the princes of
   your enemies. (Baruch 4:21)

1 Sing ye to the Lord a new canticle:
let his praise be in the church of the saints.
2 Let Israel rejoice in him that made him:
and let the children of Sion be joyful in their king.
3 Let them praise his name in choir:
let them sing to him with the timbrel and the psaltery.
4 For the Lord is well pleased with his people:
and he will exalt the meek unto salvation.
5 The saints shall rejoice in glory:
they shall be joyful in their beds.
6 The high praise of God shall be in their mouth:
and two-edged swords in their hands:
7 To execute vengeance upon the nations,
chastisements among the people:
8 To bind their kings with fetters,
and their nobles with manacles of iron.
9 To execute upon them the judgment that is written:
this glory is to all his saints.
Alleluia.

The Psalter

Psalm 150
Laudate Dominum in sanctis

Antiphon:
Blessed art Thou, O Lord, the God of our fathers, and Thy Name is worthy of praise, and is glorious forever. (Dan 3:26)

1 Praise ye the Lord in his holy places:
praise ye him in the firmament of his power.
2 Praise ye him for his mighty acts:
praise ye him according to the multitude of his greatness.
3 Praise him with sound of trumpet:
praise him with psaltery and harp.
4 Praise him with timbrel and choir:
praise him with strings and organs.
5 Praise him on high sounding cymbals:
praise him on cymbals of joy:
let every spirit praise the Lord.
Alleluia.

The Psalter

Day 31 - Morning Prayer

Psalm 5
Verba mea auribul

Antiphon:
God is true and every man is a liar, as it is written:
*That thou mayest be justified in Thy words and
   mayest overcome when thou art judged...*
For all have sinned and do need the glory of God.
   (Rom 3:4,23)

1 *Unto the end, For her that obtaineth the inheritance.
   A psalm of David.*

2 Give ear, O Lord, to my words,
understand my cry.

3 Hearken to the voice of my prayer,
O my King and my God.

4 For to thee will I pray:
O Lord, in the morning thou shalt hear my voice.

5 In the morning I will stand before thee,
   and will see:
because thou art not a God that willest iniquity.

6 Neither shall the wicked dwell near thee:
nor shall the unjust abide before thy eyes.

7 Thou hatest all the workers of iniquity:
Thou wilt destroy all that speak a lie.
The bloody and the deceitful man the Lord will abhor.

8 But as for me in the multitude of thy mercy,
   I will come into thy house;
I will worship towards thy holy temple,
   in thy fear.

9 Conduct me, O Lord, in thy justice:
because of my enemies,
   direct my way in thy sight.

10 For there is no truth in their mouth;
their heart is vain.

11 Their throat is an open sepulchre:
   they dealt deceitfully with their tongues:
   judge them, O God.
Let them fall from their devices:
according to the multitude of their wickedness cast
      them out:
for they have provoked thee, O Lord.
12 But let all them be glad that hope in thee:
they shall rejoice for ever,
   and thou shalt dwell in them.
And all they that love thy name
   shall glory in thee:
13 For thou wilt bless the just.
O Lord, thou hast crowned us,
   as with a shield of thy good will.

Psalm 8
Domine, Dominus noster

Antiphon:
For He must reign *until He hath put all his enemies
      under his feet.*
and the last enemy, death, shall be destroyed last: *For
      He hath put all things under his feet. (I Cor
      15:25-26)*

1 *Unto the end, for the presses: a psalm of David.*
2 O Lord our Lord,
   how admirable is thy name in the whole earth!
For thy magnificence is elevated above the heavens.
3 Out of the mouth of infants and of sucklings
   thou hast perfected praise,
   because of thy enemies,
that thou mayst destroy the enemy and the avenger.
4 For I will behold thy heavens,
   the works of thy fingers:
the moon and the stars
   which thou hast founded.

The Psalter

5 What is man that thou art mindful of him?
    or the son of man that thou visitest hi?
6 Thou hast made him a little less than the angels,
    thou hast crowned him with glory and honour:
7 and hast set him over the works of thy hands.
8 Thou hast subjected all things under his feet,
    all sheep and oxen:
moreover the beasts also of the fields.
9 The birds of the air,
    and the fishes of the sea,
        that pass through the paths of the sea.
10 O Lord our Lord,
how admirable is thy name in all the earth!

Psalm 62(63)
Deus Deus meus, ad te

Antiphon:
And if I shall go and prepare a place for you,
  I will come again and will take you to myself;
    that where I am, you also may be. *(John 14:3)*

1 A psalm of David when he was in the desert of Edom.
2 O God, my God, to thee do I watch at break of day.
    For thee my soul hath thirsted;
    for thee my flesh, O how many ways!
3 In a desert land, and where there is no way, and no
        water:
so in the sanctuary have I come before thee,
    to see thy power and thy glory.
4 For thy mercy is better than lives:
thee my lips shall praise.
5 Thus will I bless thee all my life long:
and in thy name I will lift up my hands.
6 Let my soul be filled as with marrow and fatness:
and my mouth shall praise thee with joyful lips.
7 If I have remembered thee upon my bed,
I will meditate on thee in the morning:

The Psalter

8 because thou hast been my helper.
And I will rejoice under the covert of thy wings:
9 my soul hath stuck close to thee:
thy right hand hath received me.
10 But they have sought my soul in vain,
they shall go into the lower parts of the earth:
11 They shall be delivered into the hands of the sword,
they shall be the portions of foxes.
12 But the king shall rejoice in God,
    all they shall be praised that swear by him:
because the mouth is stopped of them that speak
        wicked things.

The Psalter

Day 31 – Evening Prayer

Psalm 15(14)
Conserva me, Domine

Antiphon:
David spoke, foreseeing the resurrection of Christ;
for neither was He left in hell; neither did his flesh see
      corruption. *(Acts 2:31)*

1 *The inscription of a title to David himself.*
Preserve me, O Lord,
for I have put trust in thee.
2 I have said to the Lord,
   thou art my God,
for thou hast no need of my goods.
3 To the saints, who are in his land,
 he hath made wonderful all my desires in them.
4 Their infirmities were multiplied:
    afterwards they made haste.
I will not gather together their meetings for blood
      offerings:
   nor will I be mindful of their names by my lips.
5 The Lord is the portion of my inheritance and of my
      cup:
  it is thou that wilt restore my inheritance to me.
6 The lines are fallen unto me in goodly places:
   for my inheritance is goodly to me.
7 I will bless the Lord,
   who hath given me understanding:
moreover my reins also have corrected me even till
      night.
8 I set the Lord always in my sight:
   for he is at my right hand, that I be not moved.
9 Therefore my heart hath been glad,
   and my tongue hath rejoiced:
moreover my flesh also shall rest in hope.

10 Because thou wilt not leave my soul in hell;
   nor wilt then give thy holy one to see corruption.
11 Thou hast made known to me the ways of life,
   thou shalt fill me with joy with thy countenance:
at thy right hand are delights even to the end.

Psalm 76(77)
Voce mea

Antiphon:
The children of Israel marched through the midst of
   the sea upon dry land;
and the waters were to them as a wall on the right
   hand and on the left.
And the Lord delivered Israel on that day out of the
   hands of the Egyptians. (Exodus 14:29-30)

1 Unto the end, for Idithun, a psalm of Asaph.
2 I cried to the Lord with my voice;
to God with my voice, and he gave ear to me.
3 In the day of my trouble I sought God,
   with my hands lifted up to him in the night,
   and I was not deceived.
My soul refused to be comforted:
4 I remembered God, and was delighted,
and was exercised, and my spirit swooned away.
5 My eyes prevented the watches:
I was troubled, and I spoke not.
6 I thought upon the days of old:
and I had in my mind the eternal years.
7 And I meditated in the night with my own heart:
and I was exercised and I swept my spirit.
8 Will God then cast off for ever?
or will he never be more favourable again?
9 Or will he cut off his mercy for ever,
from generation to generation?
10 Or will God forget to shew mercy?
or will he in his anger shut up his mercies?
11 And I said, Now have I begun:
this is the change of the right hand of the most High.

The Psalter

12 I remembered the works of the Lord:
for I will be mindful of thy wonders from the beginning.
13 And I will meditate on all thy works:
and will be employed in thy inventions.
14 Thy way, O God, is in the holy place:
who is the great God like our God?
15 Thou art the God that dost wonders.
Thou hast made thy power known among the nations:
16 with thy arm thou hast redeemed thy people
the children of Jacob and of Joseph.
17 The waters saw thee, O God, the waters saw thee:
and they were afraid, and the depths were troubled.
18 Great was the noise of the waters:
the clouds sent out a sound. For thy arrows pass:
19 the voice of thy thunder in a wheel.
Thy lightnings enlightened the world:
   the earth shook and trembled.
20 Thy way is in the sea, and thy paths in many
            waters:
and thy footsteps shall not be known.
21 Thou hast conducted thy people like sheep,
by the hand of Moses and Aaron

Psalm 111(112)
Beatus vir

Antiphon:
Continuing daily with one accord I the temple and
            breaking bread from house to house,
      they took their meat with gladness and simplicity of
            heart;
Praising God, and having favour with all the people.
(Acts 2:46-47a)

1 Blessed is the man that feareth the Lord:
he shall delight exceedingly in his commandments.
2 His seed shall be mighty upon earth:
the generation of the righteous shall be blessed.
3 Glory and wealth shall be in his house:
and his justice remaineth for ever and ever.

The Psalter

4 To the righteous a light is risen up in darkness:
he is merciful, and compassionate and just.
5 Acceptable is the man that showeth mercy and
lendeth:
he shall order his words with judgment:
6 because he shall not be moved for ever.
7 The just shall be in everlasting remembrance:
he shall not hear the evil hearing.
His heart is ready to hope in the Lord:
8 his heart is strengthened,
he shall not be moved until he look over his enemies.
9 He hath distributed, he hath given to the poor:
his justice remaineth for ever and ever:
his horn shall be exalted in glory.
10 The wicked shall see, and shall be angry,
he shall gnash with his teeth and pine away:
the desire of the wicked shall perish.

The Lectionary

The Lectionary for the Saint Cuthbert Prayer Book is an adaptation of the Lectionary for the Daily Office from the 1979 Book of Common Prayer.

Year One readings begin on the First Sunday of Advent in even number years; year Two readings begin on the First Sunday of Advent of odd number years.

Year One.

Week of 1 Advent

Sunday Isaiah 1:1-9   2Peter 3:1-10   Matthew 25:1-13
Monday   Isaiah 1:10-20   1Thess 1   Luke 20:1-8
Tuesday   Isaiah 1:21-31   1Thess 2:1-12   Luke 20:9-18
Wednesday   Isaiah 2:1-11   1Thess 2:13-20   Luke 20:19-26
Thursday   Isaiah 2:12-22   1Thess 3   Luke 20:27-40
Friday Isaiah 3:8-15   1Thess 4:1-12   Luke 20:41-21:4
Saturday   Isaiah 4:2-6   1Thess 4:13-18   Luke 21:5-19

Week of 2 Advent

Sunday Isaiah 5:1-7   2Peter 3:11-18   Luke 7:28-35
Monday   Isaiah 5:8-12,18-23   1Thess 5:1-11   Luke 21:20-28
Tuesday   Isaiah 5:13-17,24-25   1Thess 5:12-28   Luke 21:29-38
Wednesday   Isaiah 6   2Thess 1   John 7:53-8:11
Thursday   Isaiah 7:1-9   2Thess 2:1-12   Luke 22:1-13
Friday Isaiah 7:10-25   2Thess 2:13-3:5   Luke 22:14-30
Saturday   Isaiah 8:1-15   2Thess 3:6-18   Luke 22:31-38

Week of 3 Advent

Sunday Isaiah 13:6-13   Hebrews 12:18-29   John 3:22-30
Monday   Isaiah 8:16-9:1   2Peter 1:1-11   Luke 22:39-53
Tuesday   Isaiah 9:1-7   2Peter 1:12-21   Luke 22:54-69
Wednesday   Isaiah 9:8-17   2Peter 2:1-10a   Mark 1:1-8
Thursday   Isaiah 9:18-10:4   2 Peter 2:10b-16   Matthew 3:1-12
Friday Isaiah 10:5-19   2Peter 2:17-22   Matthew 11:2-15
Saturday   Isaiah 10:20-27   Jude 17-25   Luke 3:19

The Lectionary – Year One

Week of 4 Advent

Sunday Isaiah 42:1-12 Ephesians 6:10-20 John 3:16-21

Monday Isaiah 11:1-9 Revelation 20:1-10 John 5:30-47

Tuesday Isaiah 11:10-16 Revelation 20:11-21:8 Luke 1:5-25

Wednesday Isaiah 28:9-22 Revelation 21:9-21 Luke 1:26-38

Thursday Isaiah 29:13-24 Revelation 21:22-22:5 Luke 1:39-48a(48b-56)

Friday Isaiah 33:17-22 Revelation 22:6-11,18-20 Luke 1:57-66

Dec. 24   Isaiah 35 Revelation 22:12-17,21 Luke 1:67-80

Christmas Eve Isaiah. 59:15b-21 Philippians 2:5-11

Christmas Day and Following

Christmas Day   Zechariah 2:10-13 1John 4:7-16 John 3:21-26

First Sunday after Christmas   Isaiah 62:6-7,10-12 Hebrews 2:10-18 Matthew 1:18-25

Dec. 29   Isaiah 12 Revelation 1:1-8 John 7:37-52

Dec. 30   Isaiah 25:1-9 Revelation 1:9-20 John 7:53-8:11

Dec. 31   Isaiah 26:1-9 2Corinth 5:16-6:2 John 8:12-19

Eve of Holy Name   Isaiah. 65:15b-25 Revelation 21:1-6

Holy Name   Genesis 17:1-12a, 15-16 Colossians 2:6-12 John 16:23b-30

Second Sunday after Christmas   Sirach 3:3-9,14-17 1John 2:12-17 John 6:41-47

Jan. 2 Genesis 12:1-7 Hebrews 11:1-12 John 6:35-42,48-51

Jan. 3   Genesis 28:10-22 Hebrews 11:13-22 John 10:7-17

Jan. 4 Ex 3:1-12 Hebrews 11:23-31 John 14:6-14

Jan. 5 Jos 1:1-9 Hebrews 11:32-12:2 John 15:1-16

Eve of Epiphany Isaiah 66:18-23 Romans 15:7-13

The Lectionary – Year One

The Epiphany and Following

Epiphany Isaiah 52:7-10   Revelation 21:22-27   Matthew 12:14-21

Jan. 7   Isaiah 52:3-6   Revelation 2:1-7   John 2:1-11

Jan. 8   Isaiah 59:15-21   Revelation 2:8-17   John 4:46-54

Jan. 9   Isaiah 63:1-5   Revelation 2:18-29   John 5:1-15

Jan. 10   Isaiah 65:1-9   Revelation 3:1-6   John 6:1-14

Jan. 11   Isaiah 65:13-16   Revelation 3:7-13   John 6:15-27

Jan. 12   Isaiah 66:1-2,22-23   Revelation 3:14-22   John 9:1-12,35-38

Eve of 1 Epiphany   Isaiah 61:1-9   Galatians 3:23-29,4:4-7

Week of 1 Epiphany

Sunday Isaiah 40:1-11   Hebrews 1:1-12   John 1:1-7,19-20,29-34

Monday   Isaiah 40:12-23   Ephesians 1:1-14   Mark 1:1-13

Tuesday   Isaiah 40:25-31   Ephesians 1:15-23   Mark 1:14-28

Wednesday Isaiah 41:1-16   Ephesians 2:1-10   Mark 1:29-45

Thursday   Isaiah 41:17-29   Ephesians 2:11-22   Mark 2:1-12

Friday   Isaiah. 42:(1-9)10-17   Ephesians 3:1-13   Mark 2:13-22

Saturday   Isaiah 43:1-13   Ephesians 3:14-21   Mark 2:23-3:6

The Readings for the dated days after the Epiphany are used only until the following Saturday Evening.

Week of 2 Epiphany

Sunday Isaiah 43:14-44:5   Hebrews 6:17-7:10   John 4:27-42

Monday   Isaiah 44:6-8,21-23   Ephesians 4:1-16   Mark 3:7-19a

Tuesday   Isaiah 44:9-20   Ephesians 4:17-32   Mark 3:19b-35

Wednesday   Isaiah 44:24-45:7   Ephesians 5:1-14   Mark 4:1-20

Thursday   Isaiah 45:5-17   Ephesians 5:15-33   Mark 4:21-34

Friday   Isaiah 45:18-25   Ephesians 6:1-9   Mark 4:35-41

Saturday   Isaiah 46   Ephesians 6:10-24   Mark 5:1-20

The Lectionary – Year One

Week of 3 Epiphany

Sunday Isaiah 47   Hebrews 10:19-31   John 5:2-18

Monday   Isaiah 48:1-11   Galatians 1:1-17   Mark 5:21-43

Tuesday   Isaiah 48:12-21   Galatians 1:18-2:10   Mark 6:1-13

Wednesday   Isaiah 49:1-12   Galatians 2:11-21   Mark 6:13-29

Thursday Isaiah 49:13-23   Galatians 3:1-14   Mark 6:30-46

Friday Isaiah 50   Galatians 3:15-22   Mark 6:47-56

Saturday   Isaiah 51:1-8   Galatians 3:23-29   Mark 7:1-23

Week of 4 Epiphany

Sunday Isaiah 51:9-16   Hebrews 11:8-16   John 7:14-31

Monday   Isaiah 51:17-23   Galatians 4:1-11   Mark 7:24-37

Tuesday   Isaiah 52:1-12   Galatians 4:12-20   Mark 8:1-10

Wednesday   Isaiah 54:1-10(11-17)   Galatians 4:21-31   Mark 8:11-26

Thursday Isaiah 55   Galatians 5:1-15   Mark 8:27-9:1

Friday Isaiah 56:1-8   Galatians 5:16-24   Mark 9:2-13

Saturday   Isaiah 57:3-13   Galatians 5:25-6:10   Mark 9:14-29

Week of 5 Epiphany

Sunday Isaiah 57:14-21   Hebrews 12:1-6   John 7:37-46

Monday Isaiah 58:1-12   Galatians 6:11-18   Mark 9:30-41

Tuesday   Isaiah 59:1-15a   2 Timothy 1:1-14   Mark 9:42-50

Wednesday   Isaiah. 59:15b-21   2 Timothy 1:15-2:13   Mark 10:1-16

Thursday Isaiah 60:1-17   2 Timothy 2:14-26   Mark 10:17-31

Friday Isaiah 61:1-9   2 Timothy 3   Mark 10:32-45

Saturday   Isaiah 61:10-62:5   2 Timothy 4:1-8   Mark 10:46-52

The Lectionary – Year One

Week of 6 Epiphany

Sunday Isaiah 62:6-12   1John 2:3-11   John 8:12-19

Monday   Isaiah 63:1-6   1Timothy 1:1-17   Mark 11:1-11

Tuesday   Isaiah 63:7-14   1Timothy 1:18-2:8   Mark 11:12-26

Wednesday   Isaiah 63:15-64:9   1Timothy 3   Mark 11:27-12:12

Thursday   Isaiah 65:1-12   1Timothy 4   Mark 12:13-27

Friday Isaiah 65:17-25   1Timothy 5:17-22(23-25)   Mark 12:28-34

Saturday   Isaiah 66:1-6   1Timothy 6:6-21   Mark 12:35-44

Week of 7 Epiphany

Sunday Isaiah 66:7-14   1John 3:4-10   John 10:7-16

Monday   Ruth 1:1-14   2Corinth 1:1-11   Matthew 5:1-12

Tuesday   Ruth 1:15-22   2Corinth 1:12-22   Matthew 5:13-20

Wednesday   Ruth 2:1-13   2Corinth 1:23-2:17   Matthew 5:21-26

Thursday   Ruth 2:14-23   2Corinth 3   Matthew 5:27-37

Friday Ruth 3   2Corinth 4:1-12   Matthew 5:38-48

Saturday   Ruth 4:1-17   2Corinth 4:13-5:10   Matthew 6:1-16

Week of 8 Epiphany

Sunday Deut 4:1-9   2Timothy 4:1-8   John 12:1-8

Monday   Deut 4:9-14   2Corinth 10   Matthew 6:7-15

Tuesday   Deut 4:15-24   2Corinth 11:1-21a   Matthew 6:16-23

Wednesday   Deut 4:25-31   2 Corinth 11:21b-33   Matthew 6:24-34

Thursday   Deut 4:32-40   2Corinth 12:1-10   Matthew 7:1-12

Friday Deut 5:1-22   2Corinth 12:11-21   Matthew 7:13-21

Saturday Deut 5:22-33   2Corinth 13   Matthew 7:22-29

The Lectionary – Year One

Week of Last Epiphany

Sunday Deut 6:1-9   Hebrews 12:18-29   John 12:24-32

Monday Deut 6:10-15   Hebrews 1   John 1:1-18

Tuesday Deut 6:16-25   Hebrews 2:1-10   John 1:19-28

Ash Wednesday   John 3-4   Hebrews 12:1-14   Luke 18:9-14

Thursday Deut 7:6-11   Titus 1   John 1:29-34

Friday Deut 7:12-16   Titus 2   John 1:35-42

Saturday Deut 7:17-26   Titus 3   John 1:43-51

Week of 1 Lent

Sunday Deut 8:1-10   1 Corinth 1:17-31   Mark 2:18-22

Monday Deut 8:11-20   Hebrews 2:11-18   John 2:1-12

Tuesday Deut 9:4-12   Hebrews 3:1-11   John 2:13-22

Wednesday   Deut 9:13-21   Hebrews 3:12-19   John 2:23-3:15

Thursday Deut 9:23-10:5   Hebrews 4:1-10   John 3:16-21

Friday Deut 10:12-22   Hebrews 4:11-16   John 3:22-36

Saturday Deut 11:18-28   Hebrews 5:1-10   John 4:1-26

Week of 2 Lent

Sunday Jeremiah 1:1-10   1 Corinth 3:11-23   Mark 3:31-4:9

Monday Jeremiah 1:11-19   Romans 1:1-15   John 4:27-42

Tuesday Jeremiah 2:1-13   Romans 1:16-25   John 4:43-54

Wednesday   Jeremiah 3:6-18   Romans 1:28-2:11   John 5:1-18

Thursday Jeremiah 4:9-10,19-28   Romans 2:12-24   John 5:19-29

Friday Jeremiah 5:1-9   Romans 2:25-3:18   John 5:30-47

Saturday Jeremiah 5:20-31   Romans 3:19-31   John 7:1-13

The Lectionary – Year One

Week of 3 Lent

Sunday Jeremiah 6:9-15 1 Corinth 6:12-20 Mark 5:1-20

Monday Jeremiah 7:1-15 Romans 4:1-12 John 7:14-36

Tuesday Jeremiah 7:21-34 Romans 4:13-25 John 7:37-52

Wednesday Jeremiah 8:18-9:6 Romans 5:1-11 John 8:12-20

Thursday Jeremiah 10:11-24 Romans 5:12-21 John 8:21-32

Friday Jeremiah 11:1-8,14-20 Romans 6:1-11 John 8:33-47

Saturday Jeremiah 13:1-11 Romans 6:12-23 John 8:47-59

Week of 4 Lent

Sunday Jeremiah 14:1-9,17-22 Galatians 4:21-5:1 Mark 8:11-21

Monday Jeremiah 16:10-21 Romans 7:1-12 John 6:1-15

Tuesday Jeremiah 17:19-27 Romans 7:13-25 John 6:16-27

Wednesday Jeremiah 18:1-11 Romans 8:1-11 John 6:27-40

Thursday Jeremiah 22:13-23 Romans 8:12-27 John 6:41-51

Friday Jeremiah 23:1-8 Romans 8:28-39 John 6:52-59

Saturday Jeremiah 23:9-15 Romans 9:1-18 John 6:60-71

Week of 5 Lent

Sunday Jeremiah 23:16-32 1 Corinth 9:19-27 Mark 8:31-9:1

Monday Jeremiah 24 Romans 9:19-23 John 9:1-17

Tuesday Jeremiah 25:8-17 Romans 10:1-13 John 9:18-41

Wednesday Jeremiah 25:30-38 Romans 10:14-21 John 10:1-18

Thursday Jeremiah 26:1-16 Romans 11:1-12 John 10:19-42

Friday Jeremiah 29:1,4-13 Romans 11:13-24 John 11:1-27 *or* 12:1-10

Saturday Jeremiah 31:27-34 Romans 11:25-36 John 11:28-44 *or* 12:37-50

The Lectionary – Year One

Holy Week

Palm Sunday Zechariah 9:9-12** 1Timothy 6:12-16**
Zechariah 12:9-11; 13:1,7-9*** Matthew 21:12-17***

Monday Jeremiah 12:1-16 Philippians 3:1-14 John 12:9-19

Tuesday Jeremiah 15:10-21 Philippians 3:15-21 John 12:20-26

Wednesday Jeremiah 17:5-10,14-17 Philippians 4:1-13 John 12:27-36

Maundy Thursday Jeremiah 20:7-11 1Corinth 10:14-17; 11:27-32 John 17:1-11(12-26)

Good Friday Wisdom 1:16-2:1,12-22 1Peter 1:10-20 John 13:36-38**
OR Genesis 22:1-14 John 19:38-42***

Holy Saturday Job 19:21-27a Hebrews 4** Romans 8:1-11***

** Intended for use in the morning
*** Intended for use in the evening

Easter Week

Easter Day Exodus 12:1-14** John 1:1-18**
Isaiah 51:9-11*** Luke 24:13-35***, OR John 20:19-23***

Monday John 2:1-9 Acts 2:14,22-32* John 14:1-14

Tuesday Isaiah 30:18-21 Acts 2:26-41(42-47)* John 14:15-31

Wednesday Micah 7:7-15 Acts 3:1-10* John 15:1-11

Thursday Ezekiel 37:1-14 Acts 3:11-26* John 15:12-27

Friday Daniel 12:1-4,13 Acts 4:1-12* John 16:1-15

Saturday Isaiah 25:1-9 Acts 4:13-21(22-31)* John 16:16-33

Week of 2 Easter

Sunday Isaiah 43:8-13 1Peter 2:2-10 John 14:1-7

Monday Daniel 1 1John 1 John 17:1-11

Tuesday Daniel 2:1-16 1John 2:1-11 John 17:12-19

Wednesday Daniel 2:17-30 1John 2:12-17 John 17:20-26

Thursday Daniel 2:31-49 1John 2:18-29 Luke 3:1-14

The Lectionary – Year One

Friday Daniel 3:1-18   1John 3:1-10   Luke 3:15-22

Saturday Daniel 3:19-30   1John 3:11-18   Luke 4:1-13

" *Intended for use in the morning* * *Duplicates the First Lesson at the Eucharist.*
" Intended for use in the evening Readings from Year Two may be substituted.

Week of 3 Easter

Sunday Daniel 4:1-18   1Peter 4:7-11   John 21:15-25

Monday Daniel 4:19-27   1John 3:19-4:6   Luke 4:14-30

Tuesday Daniel 4:28-37   1John 4:7-21   Luke 4:31-37

Wednesday   Daniel 5:1-12   1John 5:1-12   Luke 4:38-44

Thursday Daniel 5:13-30   1John 5:13-20(21)   Luke 5:1-11

Friday Daniel 6:1-15   2John   Luke 5:12-26

Saturday Daniel 6:16-28   3John   Luke 5:27-39

Week of 4 Easter

Sunday Wisdom 1:1-15   1Peter 5:1-11   Matthew 7:15-29

Monday Wisdom 1:16-2:11,21-24   Colossians 1:1-14   Luke 6:1-11

Tuesday Wisdom 3:1-9   Colossians 1:15-23   Luke 6:12-26

Wednesday Wisdom 4:16-5:8   Colossians 1:24-2:7   Luke 6:27-38

Thursday Wisdom 5:9-23   Colossians 2:8-23   Luke 6:39-49

Friday Wisdom 6:12-23   Colossians 3:1-11   Luke 7:1-17

Saturday Wisdom 7:1-14   Colossians 3:12-17   Luke 7:18-28(29-30)31-35

Week of 5 Easter

Sunday Wisdom 7:22-8:1   2Thess 2:13-17   Matthew 7:7-14

Monday Wisdom 9:1,7-18   Colossians. (3:18-4:1)2-18   Luke 7:36-50

Tuesday   Wisdom 10:1-4(5-12)13-21   Romans 12   Luke 8:1-15

The Lectionary – Year One

Wednesday Wisdom 13:1-9 Romans 13 Luke 8:16-25

Thursday Wisdom 14:27-15:3 Romans 14:1-12 Luke 8:26-39

Friday Wisdom 16:15-17:1 Romans 14:13-23 Luke 8:40-56

Saturday Wisdom 19:1-8,18-22 Romans 15:1-13 Luke 9:1-17

Week of 6 Easter

Sunday Sirach 43:1-12,27-32 1 Timothy 3:14-4:5 Matthew 13:24-34a

Monday Deut 8:1-10 James 1:1-15 Luke 9:18-27

Tuesday Deut 8:11-20 James 1:16-27 Luke 11:1-13

Wednesday Baruch 3:24-37 James 5:13-18 Luke 12:22-31

Eve of Ascension 2Ki 2:1-15 Revelation 5

Ascension Day
Ezekiel 1:1-14,24-28b Hebrews 2:5-18 Matthew 28:16-20

Friday Ezekiel 1:28-3:3 Hebrews 4:14-5:6 Luke 9:28-36

Saturday Ezekiel 3:4-17 Hebrews 5:7-14 Luke 9:37-50

Week of 7 Easter

Sunday Ezekiel 3:16-27 Ephesians 2:1-10 Matthew 10:24-33,40-42

Monday Ezekiel 4 Hebrews 6:1-12 Luke 9:51-62

Tuesday Ezekiel 7:10-15,23b-27 Hebrews 6:13-20 Luke 10:1-17

Wednesday Ezekiel 11:14-25 Hebrews 7:1-17 Luke 10:17-24

Thursday Ezekiel 18:1-4,19-32 Hebrews 7:18-28 Luke 10:25-37

Friday Ezekiel 34:17-31 Hebrews 8 Luke 10:38-42

Saturday
Ezekiel 43:1-12 Hebrews 9:1-14 Luke 11:14-23

Eve of Pentecost Exodus 19:3-8a,16-20 1 Peter 2:4-10

The Day of Pentecost Isaiah 11:1-9 1 Corinth 2:1-13 John 14:21-29

The Lectionary – Year One

On the weekdays which follow, the Readings are taken from the numbered Proper (one through six) which corresponds most closely to the date of Pentecost.

Eve of Trinity Sunday   Sirach 42:15-25   Ephesians 3:14-21

Trinity Sunday   Sirach 43:1-12(27-33)   Ephesians 4:1-16   John 1:1-18

On the weekdays which follow, the Readings are taken from the numbered Proper (two through seven) which corresponds most closely to the date of Trinity Sunday.

The Season after Pentecost

Proper 1 Week of the Sunday closest to May 11

Monday   Isaiah 63:7-14   2 Timothy 1:1-14   Luke 11:24-36

Tuesday   Isaiah 63:15-64:9   2 Timothy 1:15-2:13   Luke 11:37-52

Wednesday   Isaiah 65:1-12   2 Timothy 2:14-26   Luke 11:53-12:12

Thursday   Isaiah 65:17-25   2 Timothy 3   Luke 12:13-31

Friday   Isaiah 66:1-6   2 Timothy 4:1-8   Luke 12:32-48

Saturday   Isaiah 66:7-14   2 Timothy 4:9-22   Luke 12:49-59

Proper 2 Week of the Sunday closest to May 18

Monday   Ruth 1:1-18   1 Timothy 1:1-17   Luke 13:1-9

Tuesday   Ruth 1:19-2:13   1 Timothy 1:18-2:8   Luke 13:10-17

Wednesday   Ruth 2:14-23   1 Timothy 3   Luke 13:18-30

Thursday   Ruth 3   1 Timothy 4   Luke 13:31-35

Friday   Ruth 4:1-17   1 Timothy 5:17-22(23-25)   Luke 14:1-11

Saturday   Deut 1:1-8   1 Timothy 6:6-21   Luke 14:12-24

Proper 3 Week of the Sunday closest to May 25

Sunday   Deut 4:1-9   Revelation 7:1-4,9-17   Matthew 12:33-45

Monday   Deut 4:9-14   2 Corinth 1:1-11   Luke 14:25-35

Tuesday   Deut 4:15-24   2 Corinth 1:12-22   Luke 15:1-10

The Lectionary – Year One

Wednesday Deut 4:25-31 2 Corinth 1:23-2:17 Luke 15:1-2,11-32

Thursday Deut 4:32-40 2 Corinth 3 Luke 16:1-9

Friday Deut 5:1-22 2 Corinth 4:1-12 Luke 16:10-17(18)

Saturday Deut 5:22-33 2 Corinth 4:13-5:10 Luke 16:19-31

Proper 4 *Week of the Sunday closest to June 1*

Sunday Deut 11:1-12 Revelation 10 Matthew 13:44-58

Monday Deut 11:13-19 2 Corinth 5:11-6:2 Luke 17:1-10

Tuesday Deut 12:1-12 2 Corinth 6:3-13(6:14-7:1) Luke 17:11-19

Wednesday Deut 13:1-11 2 Corinth 7:2-16 Luke 17:20-37

Thursday Deut 16:18-20,17:14-20 2 Corinth 8:1-16 Luke 18:1-8

Friday Deut 26:1-11 2 Corinth 8:16-24 Luke 18:9-14

Saturday Deut 29:2-15 2 Corinth 9 Luke 18:15-30

Proper 5 *Week of the Sunday closest to June 8*

Sunday Deut 29:16-29 Revelation 12:1-12 Matthew 15:29-39

Monday Deut 30:1-10 2 Corinth 10 Luke 18:31-43

Tuesday Deut 30:11-20 2 Corinth 11:1-21a Luke 19:1-10

Wednesday Deut 31:30-32:14 2 Corinth. 11:21b-33 Luke 19:11-27

Thursday Sirach 44:19-45:5 2 Corinth 12:1-10 Luke 19:28-40

Friday Sirach 45:6-16 2 Corinth 12:11-21 Luke 19:41-48

Saturday Sirach 46:1-10 2 Corinth 13 Luke 20:1-8

Proper 6 *Week of the Sunday closest to June 15*

Sunday Sirach 46:11-20 Revelation 15 Matthew 18:1-14

Monday 1 Samuel 1:1-20 Acts 1:1-14 Luke 20:9-19

Tuesday 1 Samuel 1:21-2:11 Acts 1:15-26 Luke 20:19-26

Wednesday 1 Samuel 2:12-26 Acts 2:1-21 Luke 20:27-40

The Lectionary – Year One

Thursday 1 Samuel 2:27-36 Acts 2:22-36 Luke 20:41-21:4
Friday 1 Samuel 3 Acts 2:37-47 Luke 21:5-19
Saturday 1 Samuel 4:1b-11 Acts 4:32-5:11 Luke 21:20-28

Proper 7 *Week of the Sunday closest to June 22*
Sunday 1 Samuel 4:12-22 James 1:1-18 Matthew 19:23-30
Monday 1 Samuel 5 Acts 5:12-26 Luke 21:29-36
Tuesday 1 Samuel 6:1-16 Acts 5:27-42 Luke 21:37-22:13
Wednesday 1 Samuel 7:2-17 Acts 6 Luke 22:14-23
Thursday 1 Samuel 8 Acts 6:15-7:16 Luke 22:24-30
Friday 1 Samuel 9:1-14 Acts 7:17-29 Luke 22:31-38
Saturday 1 Samuel 9:15-10:1 Acts 7:30-43 Luke 22:39-51

Proper 8 *Week of Sunday closest to June 29*
Sunday 1 Samuel 10:1-16 Rom 4:13-25 Matthew 21:23-32
Monday 1 Samuel 10:17-27 Acts 7:44-8:1a Luke 22:52-62
Tuesday 1 Samuel 11 Acts 8:1-13 Luke 22:63-71
Wednesday 1 Samuel 12:1-6,16-25 Acts 8:14-25 Luke 23:1-12
Thursday 1 Samuel 13:5-18 Acts 8:26-40 Luke 23:13-25
Friday 1 Samuel 13:19-14:15 Acts 9:1-9 Luke 23:26-31
Saturday 1 Samuel 14:16-30 Acts 9:10-19a Luke 23:32-43

Proper 9 *Week of the Sunday closest to July 6*
Sunday 1 Samuel 14:36-45 Romans 5:1-11 Matthew 22:1-14
Monday 1 Samuel 15:1-3,7-23 Acts 9:19b-31 Luke 23:44-56a
Tuesday 1 Samuel 15:24-35 Acts 9:32-43 Luke 23:56b-24:11
Wednesday 1 Samuel 16:1-13 Acts 10:1-16 Luke 24:12-35
Thursday 1 Samuel 16:14-17:11 Acts 10:17-33 Luke 24:36-53
Friday 1 Samuel 17:17-30 Acts 10:34-48 Mark 1:1-13
Saturday 1 Samuel 17:31-49 Acts 11:1-18 Mark 1:14-28

The Lectionary – Year One

Proper 10 *Week of the Sunday closest to July 13*

Sunday 1Samuel 17:50-18:4   Romans 10:4-17   Matthew 23:29-39

Monday 1Samuel 18:5-16,27b-30   Acts 11:19-30   Mark 1:29-45

Tuesday   1Samuel 19:1-18   Acts 12:1-17   Mark 2:1-12

Wednesday   1Samuel 20:1-23   Acts 12:18-25   Mark 2:13-22

Thursday   1Samuel 20:24-42   Acts 13:1-12   Mark 2:23-3:6

Friday 1Samuel 21   Acts 13:13-25   Mark 3:7-19a

Saturday   1Samuel 22   Acts 23:26-33   Mark 3:19b-35

Proper 11 *Week of the Sunday closest to July 20*

Sunday 1Samuel 23:7-18   Romans 11:33-12:2   Matthew 25:14-30

Monday   1Samuel 24   Acts 13:44-52   Mark 4:1-20

Tuesday   1Samuel 25:1-22   Acts 14:1-18   Mark 4:21-34

Wednesday   1Samuel 25:23-44   Acts 14:19-28   Mark 4:35-41

Thursday   1Samuel 28:3-20   Acts 15:1-11   Mark 5:1-20

Friday 1Samuel 31   Acts 15:12-21   Mark 5:21-43

Saturday   2Samuel 1:1-16   Acts 15:22-35   Mark 6:1-13

Proper 12 *Week of the Sunday closest to July 27*

Sunday 2Samuel 1:17-27   Romans 12:9-21   Matthew 25:31-46

Monday   2Samuel 2:1-11   Acts 15:36-16:5   Mark 6:14-29

Tuesday   2Samuel 3:6-21   Acts 16:6-15   Mark 6:30-46

Wednesday   2Samuel 3:22-39   Acts 16:16-24   Mark 6:47-56

Thursday   2Samuel 4   Acts 16:25-40   Mark 7:1-23

Friday 2Samuel 5:1-12   Acts 17:1-15   Mark 7:24-37

Saturday   2Samuel 5:22-6:11   Acts 17:16-34   Mark 8:1-10

The Lectionary – Year One

Proper 13 *Week of the Sunday closest to August 3*
Sunday 2Samuel 6:12-23 Romans 4:7-12 John 1:43-51
Monday 2Samuel 7:1-17 Acts 18:1-11 Mark 8:11-21
Tuesday 2Samuel 7:18-29 Acts 18:12-28 Mark 8:22-33
Wednesday 2Samuel 9 Acts 19:1-10 Mark 8:34-9:1
Thursday 2Samuel 11 Acts 19:11-20 Mark 9:2-13
Friday 2Samuel 12:1-14 Acts 19:21-41 Mark 9:14-29
Saturday 2Samuel 12:15-31 Acts 20:1-16 Mark 9:30-41

Proper 14 *Week of the Sunday closest to August 10*
Sunday 2Samuel 13:1-22 Romans 15:1-13 John 3:22-36
Monday 2Samuel 13:23-39 Acts 20:17-38 Mark 9:42-50
Tuesday 2Samuel 14:1-20 Acts 21:1-14 Mark 10:1-16
Wednesday 2Samuel 14:21-33 Acts 21:15-26 Mark 10:17-31
Thursday 2Samuel 15:1-18 Acts 21:27-36 Mark 10:32-45
Friday 2Samuel 15:19-37 Acts 21:37-22:16 Mark 10:46-52
Saturday 2Samuel 16 Acts 22:17-29 Mark 11:1-11

Proper 15 *Week of the Sunday closest to August 17*
Sunday 2Samuel 17:1-23 Galatians 3:6-14 John 5:30-47
Monday 2Samuel 17:24-18:8 Acts 22:30-23:11 Mark 11:12-26
Tuesday 2Samuel 18:9-18 Acts 23:12-24 Mark 11:27-12:12
Wednesday 2Samuel 18:19-23 Acts 23:23-35 Mark 12:13-27
Thursday 2Samuel 19:1-23 Acts 24:1-23 Mark 12:28-34
Friday 2Samuel 19:24-43 Acts 24:24-25:12 Mark 12:35-44
Saturday 2Samuel 23:1-17,13-17 Acts 25:13-27 Mark 13:1-13

The Lectionary – Year One

Proper 16 *Week of the Sunday closest to August 24*

Sunday 2Samuel 24:1-2,10-25 Galatians 3:23-4:7 John 8:12-20

Monday 1Kingsngs 1:5-31 Acts 26:1-23 Mark 13:14-27

Tuesday 1Kingsngs 1:38-2:4 Acts 26:24-27:8 Mark 13:28-37

Wednesday 1Kingsngs 3:1-15 Acts 27:9-26 Mark 14:1-11

Thursday 1Kingsngs 3:16-28 Acts 27:27-44 Mark 14:12-26

Friday 1Kingsngs 5:1-6:1,7 Acts 28:1-16 Mark 14:27-42

Saturday 1Kingsngs 7:51-8:21 Acts 28:17-31 Mark 14:43-52

Proper 17 *Week of the Sunday closest to August 31*

Sunday 1Kings 8:22-30(31-40) 1 Timothy. 4:7b-16 John 8:47-59

Monday 2Ch 6:32-7:7 James 2:1-13 Mark 14:53-65

Tuesday 1Kings 8:65-9:9 James 2:14-26 Mark 14:66-72

Wednesday 1Kings 9:24-10:13 James 3:1-12 Mark 15:1-11

Thursday 1Kings 11:1-13 James 3:13-4:12 Mark 15:12-21

Friday 1Kings 11:26-43 James 4:13-5:6 Mark 15:22-32

Saturday 1Kings 12:1-20 James 5:7-12,19-20 Mark 15:33-39

Proper 18 *Week of the Sunday closest to September 7*

Sunday 1Kings 12:21-33 Acts 4:18-31 John 10:31-42

Monday 1Kings 13:1-10 Philippians 1:1-11 Mark 15:40-47

Tuesday 1Kings 16:23-34 Philippians 1:12-30 Mark 16:1-8(9-20)

Wednesday 1Kings 17 Philippians 2:1-11 Matthew 2:1-12

Thursday 1Kings 18:1-19 Philippians 2:12-30 Matthew 2:13-23

Friday 1Kings 18:20-40 Philippians 3:1-16 Matthew 3:1-12

Saturday 1Kings 18:41-19:8 Philippians 3:17-4:7 Matthew 3:13-17

The Lectionary – Year One

Proper 19 *Week of the Sunday closest to September 14*

Sunday 1Kings 19:8-21   Acts 5:34-42   John 11:45-47

Monday 1Kings 21:1-16   1Corinth 1:1-19   Matthew 4:1-11

Tuesday 1Kings 21:17-29   1Corinth 1:20-31   Matthew 4:12-17

Wednesday   1Kings 22:1-28   1Corinth 2:1-13   Matthew 4:18-25

Thursday 1Kings 22:29-45   1Corinth 2:14-3:15   Matthew 5:1-10

Friday 2Kings 1:2-17   1Corinth 3:16-23   Matthew 5:11-16

Saturday 2Kings 2:1-18   1Corinth 4:1-7   Matthew 5:17-20

Proper 20 *Week of the Sunday closest to September 21*

Sunday 2Kings 4:8-37   Acts 9:10-31   Luke 3:7-18

Monday 2Kings 5:1-19   1Corinth 4:8-21   Matthew 5:21-26

Tuesday 2Kings 5:19-27   1Corinth 5:1-8   Matthew 5:27-37

Wednesday   2Kings 6:1-23   1Corinth 5:9-6:8   Matthew 5:38-48

Thursday 2Kings 9:1-16   1Corinth 6:12-20   Matthew 6:1-6,16-18

Friday 2Kings 9:17-37   1Corinth 7:1-9   Matthew 6:7-15

Saturday 2Kings 11:1-20a   1Corinth 7:10-24   Matthew 6:19-24

Proper 21 *Week of the Sunday closest to September 28*

Sunday 2Kings 17:1-18   Acts 9:36-43   Luke 5:1-11

Monday 2Kings 17:24-41   1Corinth 7:25-31   Matthew 6:25-34

Tuesday 2Ch 29:1-3; 30:1(2-9)10-27   1Corinth 7:32-40   Matthew 7:1-12

Wednesday   2Kings 18:9-25   1Corinth 8   Matthew 7:13-21

Thursday 2Kings 18:28-37   1Corinth 9:1-15   Matthew 7:22-29

The Lectionary – Year One

Friday 2 Kings 19:1-20 1 Corinth 9:16-27 Matthew 8:1-17

Saturday 2 Kings 19:21-36 1 Corinth 10:1-13 Matt: 8:18-27

Proper 22 *Week of the Sunday closest to October 5*

Sunday 2 Kings 20 Acts 12:1-17 Luke 7:11-17

Monday 2 Kings 21:1-18 1 Corinth 10:14-11:1 Matthew 8:28-34

Tuesday 2 Kings 22:1-13 1 Corinth 11:2,17-22 Matthew 9:1-8

Wednesday 2 Kings 22:14-23:3 1 Corinth 11:23-34 Matthew 9:9-17

Thursday 2 Kings 23:4-25 1 Corinth 12:1-11 Matthew 9:18-26

Friday 2 Kings 23:36-24:17 1 Corinth 12:12-26 Matthew 9:27-34

Saturday Jeremiah 35 1 Corinth 12:27-13:3 Matthew 9:35-10:4

Proper 23 *Week of the Sunday closest to October 12*

Sunday Jeremiah 36:1-10 Acts 14:8-18 Luke 7:36-50

Monday Jeremiah 36:11-26 1 Corinth 13:(1-3)4-13 Matthew 10:5-15

Tuesday Jeremiah 36:27-37:2 1 Corinth 14:1-12 Matthew 10:16-23

Wednesday Jeremiah 37:3-21 1 Corinth 14:13-25 Matthew 10:24-33

Thursday Jeremiah 38:1-13 1 Corinth 14:26-33a,37-40 Matthew 10:34-42

Friday Jeremiah 38:14-28 1 Corinth 15:1-11 Matthew 11:1-6

Saturday 2 Kings 25:8-12,22-26 1 Corinth 15:12-29 Matthew 11:7-15

Proper 24 *Week of the Sunday closest to October 19*

Sunday Jeremiah 29:1,4-14 Acts 16:6-15 Luke 10:1-12,17-20

Monday Jeremiah 44:1-14 1 Corinth 15:30-41 Matthew 11:16-24

The Lectionary – Year One

Tuesday Lamentations 1:1-5(6-9)10-12 1 Corinth 15:41-50 Matthew 11:25-30

Wednesday Lamentations 2:8-15 1 Corinth 15:51-58 Matthew 12:1-14

Thursday Ezra 1 1 Corinth 16:1-9 Matthew 12:15-21

Friday Ezra 3 1 Corinth 16:10-24 Matthew 12:22-32

Saturday Ezra 4:7,11-24 Philemon Matthew 12:33-42

Proper 25 *Week of the Sunday closest to October 26*

Sunday Hag 1:1-2:9 Acts 18:24-19:7 Luke 10:25-37

Monday Zechariah 1:7-17 Revelation 1:4-20 Matthew 12:43-50

Tuesday Ezra 5 Revelation 4 Matthew 13:1-9

Wednesday Ezra 6 Revelation 5:1-10 Matthew 13:10-17

Thursday Nehemiah 1 Revelation 5:11-6:11 Matthew 13:18-23

Friday Nehemiah 2 Revelation 6:12-7:4 Matthew 13:24-30

Saturday Nehemiah 4 Revelation. 7:(4-8)9-17 Matthew 13:31-35

Proper 26 *Week of the Sunday closest to November 2*

Sunday Nehemiah 5 Acts 20:7-12 Luke 12:22-31

Monday Nehemiah 6 Revelation 10 Matthew 13:36-43

Tuesday Nehemiah 12:27-31a,42b-47 Revelation 11 Matthew 13:44-52

Wednesday Nehemiah 13:4-22 Revelation 12:1-12 Matthew 13:53-58

Thursday Ezra 7:(1-10)11-26 Revelation 14:1-13 Matthew 14:1-12

Friday Ezra 7:27-28; 8:21-36 Revelation 15 Matthew 14:13-21

Saturday Ezra 9 Revelation 17:1-14 Matthew 14:22-36

The Lectionary – Year One

Proper 27 *Week of the Sunday closest to November 9*

Sunday Ezra 10:1-17   Acts 24:10-21   Luke 14:12-24

Monday Nehemiah 9:1-15(16-25)   Revelation 18:1-8   Matthew 15:1-20

Tuesday Nehemiah 9:26-38   Revelation 18:9-20   Matthew 15:21-28

Wednesday Nehemiah 7:73b-8:3,5-18   Revelation 18:21-24   Matthew 15:29-39

Thursday 1 Mac 1:1-28   Revelation 19:1-10   Matthew 16:1-12

Friday 1 Mac 1:41-63   Revelation 19:11-16   Matthew 16:13-20

Saturday 1 Mac 2:1-28   Revelation 20:1-6   Mark 16:21-28

Proper 28 *Week of the Sunday closest to November 16*

Sunday 1 Mac 2:29-43,49-50   Acts 28:14b-23   Luke 16:1-13

Monday 1 Mac 3:1-24   Revelation 20:7-15   Matthew 17:1-13

Tuesday 1 Mac 3:25-41   Revelation 21:1-8   Matthew 17:14-21

Wednesday 1 Mac 3:42-60   Revelation 21:9-21   Matthew 17:22-27

Thursday 1 Mac 4:1-25   Revelation 21:22-22:5   Matthew 18:1-9

Friday 1 Mac 4:36-59   Revelation 22:6-13   Matthew 18:10-20

Saturday Isaiah 65:17-25   Revelation 22:14-21   Matthew 18:21-35

Proper 29 *Week of the Sunday closest to November 23*

Sunday Isaiah 19:19-25   Romans 15:5-13   Luke 19:11-27

Monday Joel 3:1-2,9-17   1Peter 1:1-12   Matthew 19:1-12

Tuesday Na 1:1-13   1Peter 1:13-25   Matthew 19:13-22

Wednesday Obadiah 15-21   1Peter 2:1-10   Matthew 19:23-30

Thursday Zephaniah 3:1-13   1Peter 2:11-25   Matthew 20:1-16

Friday Isaiah 24:14-23   1Peter 3:13-4:6   Matthew 20:17-28

Saturday Micah 7:11-20   1Peter 4:7-19   Matthew 20:29-34

Year Two

Week of 1 Advent

Sunday Amos 1:1-5; 1:13-2:8   1 Thess 5:1-11   Luke 21:5-19

Monday Amos 2:6-16   2 Peter 1:1-11   Matthew 21:1-11

Tuesday Amos 3:1-11   2 Peter 1:12-21   Matthew 21:12-22

Wednesday Amos 3:12-4:5   2 Peter 3:1-10   Matthew 21:23-32

Thursday Amos 4:6-13   2 Peter 3:11-18   Matthew 21:33-46

Friday Amos 5:1-17   Jude 1-16   Matthew 22:1-14

Saturday Amos 5:18-27   Jude 17-25   Matthew 22:15-22

Week of 2 Advent

Sunday Amos 6   1 Thess 5:1-11   Luke 1:57-68

Monday Amos 7:1-9   Revelation 1:1-8   Matthew 22:23-33

Tuesday Amos 7:10-17, 24-25   Revelation 1:9-16   Matthew 22:34-46

Wednesday Amos 8   Revelation 1:17-2:7   Matthew 23:1-12

Thursday Amos 9:1-10   Revelation 2:8-17   Matthew 23:13-26

Friday Haggai 1   Revelation 2:18-29   Matthew 23:27-39

Saturday Haggai 2:1-19   Revelation 3:1-6   Matthew 24:1-14

Week of 3 Advent

Sunday Amos 9:11-15   2 Thess 2:1-3,13-17   John 5:30-47

Monday Zechariah 1:7-17   Revelation 3:7-13   Matthew 24:15-31

Tuesday Zechariah 2   Revelation 3:14-22   Matthew 24:32-44

Wednesday Zechariah 3   Revelation 4:1-8   Matthew 24:45-51

Thursday Zechariah 4   Revelation 4:9-5:5   Matthew 25:1-13

Friday Zechariah 7:8-8:8   Revelation 5:6-14   Matthew 25:14-30

Saturday Zechariah 8:9-17   Revelation 6   Matthew 25:31-46

The Lectionary – Year Two

Week of 4 Advent

Sunday Genesis 3:13-15   Revelation 12:1-10   John 3:16-21

Monday Zephaniah 3:14-20   Titus 1   Luke 1:1-25

Tuesday   1 Samuel 2:1b-10   Titus 2:1-10   Luke 1:26-38

Wednesday   2 Samuel 7:1-17   Titus 2:11-3:8a   Luke 1:39-48a(48b-56)

Thursday   2 Samuel 7:18-29   Galatians 3:1-14   Luke 1:57-66

Friday Baruch 4:21-29   Galatians 3:15-22   Luke 1:67-80 OR Matthew 1:1-17

Dec. 24   Baruch 4:36-5:9   Galatians 3:23-4:7   Matthew 1:18-25

Christmas Eve   Isaiah 59:15b-21   Philippians 2:5-11

Christmas Day and Following

Christmas Day   Micah 4:1-5,5:2-4   1John 4:7-16   John 3:21-26

First Sunday after Christmas   1Samuel 1:1-2,7b-28   Hebrews 2:10-18   Matthew 1:18-25

Dec. 29   2Samuel 23:13-17b   Revelation 1:1-8   John 7:37-52

Dec. 30   1Kings 17:17-24   Revelation 1:9-20   John 7:53-8:11

Dec. 31 1Kings 3:5-14   2Corinth 5:16-6:2   John 8:12-19

Eve of Holy Name Isaiah 65:15b-25   Revelation 21:1-6

Holy Name Isaiah 62:1-5,10-12   Colossians 2:6-12   John 16:23-30

Second Sunday after Christmas   Wisdom 7:3-14   Colossians 3:12-17   John 6:41-47

Jan. 2   1Kings 19:1-8   Ephesians 4:1-16   John 6:1-14

Jan. 3   1Kings 19:9-18   Ephesians 4:17-32   John 6:15-27

Jan. 4   Joshua 3:14-4:7   Ephesians 5:1-20   John 9:1-12,35-38

Jan. 5   Jonah 2:2-9   Ephesians 6:10-20   John 11:17-27,38-44

Eve of Epiphany   Isaiah 66:18-23   Romans 15:7-13

The Lectionary – Year Two

The Epiphany and Following

Epiphany Isaiah 49:1-7   Revelation 21:22-27   Matthew 12:14-21

Jan. 7 * Deut 8:1-3   Colossians 1:1-14   John 6:30-33,48-51

Jan. 8   Exodus 17:1-7   Colossians 1:15-23   John 7:37-52

Jan. 9   Isaiah 45:14-19   Colossians 1:24-2:7   John 8:12-19

Jan. 10   Jeremiah 23:1-8   Colossians 2:8-23   John 10:7-17

Jan. 11   Isaiah 55:3-9   Colossians 3:1-17   John 14:6-14

Jan. 12   Genesis 49:1-2,8-12   Colossians 3:18-4:6   John 15:1-16

Eve of 1 Epiphany Isaiah 61:1-9   Galatians 3:23-29; 4:4-7

Week of 1 Epiphany

Sunday   Genesis 1:1-2:3   Ephesians 1:3-14   John 1:29-34

Monday   Genesis 2:4-9(10-15)16-25   Hebrews 1   John 1:1-18

Tuesday   Genesis 3   Hebrews 2:1-10   John 1:19-28

Wednesday   Genesis 4:1-16   Hebrews 2:11-18   John 1:(29-34)35-42

Thursday   Genesis 4:17-26   Hebrews 3:1-11   John 1:43-51

Friday   Genesis 6:1-8   Hebrews 3:12-19   John 2:1-12

Saturday   Genesis 6:9-22   Hebrews 4:1-13   John 2:13-22

* *The Psalms and Readings for the dated days after the Epiphany are used only until the following Saturday Evening.*

Week of 2 Epiphany

Sunday   Genesis 7:1-10,17-23   Ephesians 4:1-16   Mark 3:7-19

Monday   Genesis 8:6-22   Hebrews 4:14-5:6   John 2:23-3:15

Tuesday   Genesis 9:1-17   Hebrews 5:7-14   John 3:16-21

Wednesday   Genesis 9:18-29   Hebrews 6:1-12   John 3:22-36

Thursday   Genesis 11:1-9   Hebrews 6:13-20   John 4:1-15

Friday   Genesis 11:27-12:8   Hebrews 7:1-17   John 4:16-26

Saturday   Genesis 12:9-13:1   Hebrews 7:18-28   John 4:27-42

The Lectionary – Year Two

Week of 3 Epiphany

Sunday Genesis 13:2-18   Galatians 2:1-10   Mark 7:31-37

Monday   Genesis. 14:(1-7)8-24   Hebrews 8   John 4:43-54

Tuesday   Genesis 15:1-11,17-21   Hebrews 9:1-14   John 5:1-18

Wednesday   Genesis 16:1-14   Hebrews 9:15-28   John 5:19-29

Thursday   Genesis 16:15-17:14   Hebrews 10:1-10   John 5:30-47

Friday Genesis 17:15-27   Hebrews 10:11-25   John 6:1-15

Saturday   Genesis 18:1-16   Hebrews 10:26-39   John 6:16-27

Week of 4 Epiphany

Sunday Genesis 18:16-33   Galatians 5:13-25   Mark 8:22-30

Monday   Genesis 19:1-17(18-23)24-29   Hebrews 11:1-12   John 6:27-40

Tuesday   Genesis 21:1-21   Hebrews 11:13-22   John 6:41-51

Wednesday   Genesis 22:1-18   Hebrews 11:23-31   John 6:52-59

Thursday   Genesis 23   Hebrews 11:32-12:2   John 6:60-71

Friday Genesis 24:1-27   Hebrews 12:3-11   John 7:1-13

Saturday   Genesis 24:28-38,49-51   Hebrews 12:12-29   John 7:14-36

Week of 5 Epiphany

Sunday Genesis 24:50-67   2 Timothy 2:14-21   Mark 10:13-22

Monday   Genesis 25:19-34   Hebrews 13:1-16   John 7:37-52

Tuesday   Genesis 26:1-6,12-33   Hebrews 13:17-25   John 7:53-8:11

Wednesday   Genesis 27:1-29   Romans 12:1-8   John 8:12-20

Thursday   Genesis 27:30-45   Romans 12:9-21   John 8:21-32

Friday Genesis 27:46-28:4,10-22   Romans 13   John 8:33-47

Saturday   Genesis 29:1-20   Romans 14   John 8:47-59

The Lectionary – Year Two

Week of 6 Epiphany

Sunday Genesis 29:20-35 1Timothy 3:14-4:10 Mark 10:23-31

Monday Genesis 30:1-24 1John 1 John 9:1-17

Tuesday Genesis 31:1-24 1John 2:1-11 John 9:18-41

Wednesday Genesis 31:25-50 1John 2:12-17 John 10:1-18

Thursday Genesis 32:3-21 1John 2:18-29 John 10:19-30

Friday Genesis 32:22-33:17 1John 3:1-10 John 10:31-42

Saturday Genesis 35:1-20 1John 3:11-18 John 11:1-16

Week of 7 Epiphany

Sunday Proverbs 1:20-33 2Corinth 5:11-21 Mark 10:35-45

Monday Proverbs 3:11-20 1John 3:18-4:6 John 11:17-29

Tuesday Proverbs 4 1John 4:7-21 John 11:30-44

Wednesday Proverbs 6:1-19 1John 5:1-12 John 11:45-54

Thursday Proverbs 7 1John 5:13-21 John 11:55-12:8

Friday Proverbs 8:1-21 Philemon John 12:9-19

Saturday Proverbs 8:22-36 2Timothy 1:1-14 John 12:20-26

Week of 8 Epiphany

Sunday Proverbs 9:1-12 2Corinth. 9:6b-15 Mark 10:46-52

Monday Proverbs 10:1-12 2Timothy 1:15-2:13 John 12:27-36a

Tuesday Proverbs 15:16-33 2Timothy 2:14-26 John 12:36b-50

Wednesday Proverbs 17:1-20 2Timothy 3 John 13:1-20

Thursday Proverbs 21:30-22:6 2Timothy 4:1-8 John 13:21-30

Friday Proverbs 23:19-21; 23:29-24:2 2Timothy 4:9-22 John 13:31-38

Saturday Proverbs 25:15-28 Philippians 1:1-11 John 18:1-14

The Lectionary – Year Two

Week of Last Epiphany

Sunday Sirach 48:1-11   2 Corinth 3:7-18   Luke 9:18-27

Monday Proverbs 27:1-6,10-12   Philippians 2:1-13   John 18:15-18,25-27

Tuesday Proverbs 30:1-4,24-33   Philippians 3:1-11   John 18:28-38

Ash Wednesday Am 5:6-15   Hebrews 12:1-14   Luke 18:9-14

Thursday Habakkuk 3:1-10(11-15)16-18   Philippians 3:12-21   John 17:1-8

Friday Ezekiel 18:1-4,25-32   Philippians 4:1-9   John 17:9-19

Saturday Ezekiel 39:21-29   Philippians 4:10-20   John 17:20-26

Week of 1 Lent

Sunday Daniel 9:3-10   Hebrews 2:10-18   John 12:44-50

Monday Genesis 37:1-11   1 Corinth 1:1-19   Mark 1:1-13

Tuesday Genesis 37:12-24   1 Corinth 1:20-31   Mark 1:14-28

Wednesday Genesis 37:25-36   1 Corinth 2:1-13   Mark 1:29-45

Thursday Genesis 39   1 Corinth 2:14-3:15   Mark 2:1-12

Friday Genesis 40   1 Corinth 3:16-23   Mark 2:13-22

Saturday Genesis 41:1-13   1 Corinth 4:1-7   Mark 2:23-3:6

Week of 2 Lent

Sunday Genesis 41:14-45   Romans 6:3-14   John 5:19-24

Monday Genesis 41:46-57   1 Corinth 4:8-20(21)   Mark 3:7-19a

Tuesday Genesis 42:1-17   1 Corinth 5:1-8   Mark 3:19b-35

Wednesday Genesis 42:18-28   1 Corinth 5:9-6:8   Mark 4:1-20

Thursday Genesis 42:29-38   1 Corinth 6:12-20   Mark 4:21-34

Friday Genesis 43:1-15   1 Corinth 7:1-9   Mark 4:35-41

Saturday Genesis 43:16-34   1 Corinth 7:10-24   Mark 5:1-20

The Lectionary – Year Two

Week of 3 Lent

Sunday Genesis 44:1-17   Romans 8:1-10   John 5:25-29

Monday   Genesis 44:18-34   1 Corinth 7:25-31   Mark 5:21-43

Tuesday   Genesis 45:1-15   1 Corinth 7:32-40   Mark 6:1-13

Wednesday   Genesis 45:16-28   1 Corinth 8   Mark 6:13-29

Thursday Genesis 46:1-7,28-34   1 Corinth 9:1-15   Mark 6:30-46

Friday Genesis 47:1-26   1 Corinth 9:16-27   Mark 6:47-56

Saturday   Genesis 47:27-48:7   1 Corinth 10:1-13   Mark 7:1-23

Week of 4 Lent

Sunday Genesis 48:8-22   Romans 8:11-25   John 6:27-40

Monday   Genesis 49:1-28   1 Corinth 10:14-11:1   Mark 7:24-37

Tuesday   Genesis 49:29-50:14   1 Corinth 11:17-34   Mark 8:1-10

Wednesday   Genesis 50:15-26   1 Corinth 12:1-11   Mark 8:11-26

Thursday Exodus 1:6-22   1 Corinth 12:12-26   Mark 8:27-9:1

Friday Exodus 2:1-22   1 Corinth 12:27-13:3   Mark 9:2-13

Saturday   Exodus 2:23-3:15   1 Corinth 13   Mark 9:14-29

Week of 5 Lent

Sunday Exodus 3:16-4:12   Romans 12   John 8:46-59

Monday   Exodus 4:10-20(21-26)27-31   1 Corinth 14:1-19   Mark 9:30-41

Tuesday   Exodus 5:1-6:1   1 Corinth 14:20-33a,39-40   Mark 9:42-50

Wednesday   Exodus 7:8-24   2 Corinth 2:14-3:6   Mark 10:1-16

The Lectionary – Year Two

Thursday Exodus 7:25-8:19 2Corinth 3:7-18 Mark 10:17-31

Friday Exodus 9:13-35 2Corinth 4:1-12 Mark 10:32-45

Saturday Exodus 10:21-11:8 2Corinth 4:13-18 Mark 10:46-52

Holy Week

Palm Sunday Zechariah 9:9-12" 1Timothy 6:12-16"
Zechariah 12:9-11,13:1,7-9''' Luke 19:41-48'''

Monday Lamentations 1:1-2,6-12 2Corinth 1:1-7 Mark 11:12-25

Tuesday Lamentations 1:17-22 2Corinth 1:8-22 Mark 11:27-33

Wednesday Lamentations 2:1-9,14-17 2Corinth 1:23-2:11 Mark 12:1-11

Maundy Thursday Lamentations 2:10-18 1Corinth 10:14-17,11:27-32 Mark 14:12-25

Good Friday Lamentations 3:1-9,19-33 1Peter 1:10-20 John 13:36-38"
John 19:38-42'''

Holy Saturday Lamentations 3:37-58 Hebrews 4" Ro 8:1-11'''

" *Intended for use in the morning* ''' *Intended for use in the evening*

Easter Week

Easter Day Exodus 12:1-14" John 1:1-18"
Isa 51:9-11''' Luke 24:13-35''', *or* John 20:19-23'''

Monday Exodus 12:14-27 1Corinth 15:1-11 Mark 16:1-8

Tuesday Exodus 12:28-39 1Corinth 15:12-28 Mark 16:9-20

Wednesday Exodus 12:40-51 1 Corinth:(29)30-41 Matthew 28:1-16

Thursday Exodus 13:3-10 1Corinth 15:41-50 Matthew 28:16-20

Friday Exodus 13:1-2,11-16 1Corinth 15:51-58 Luke 24:1-12

Saturday Exodus 13:17-14:4 2Corinth 4:16-5:10 Mark 12:18-27

The Lectionary – Year Two

Week of 2 Easter

Sunday Exodus 14:5-22   1John 1:1-7   John 14:1-7

Monday Exodus 14:21-31   1Peter 1:1-12   John 14:(1-7)8-17

Tuesday Exodus 15:1-21   1Peter 1:13-25   John 14:18-31

Wednesday Exodus 15:22-16:10   1Peter 2:1-10   John 15:1-11

Thursday Exodus 16:10-22   1Peter 2:11-25   John 15:12-27

Friday Exodus 16:23-36   1Peter 3:13-4:6   John 16:1-15

Saturday Exodus 17   1Peter 4:7-19   John 16:16-33

" Intended for use in the morning "' Intended for use in the evening

Week of 3 Easter

Sunday Exodus 18:1-12   1John 2:7-17   Mark 16:9-20

Monday Exodus 18:13-27   1Peter 5   Matt. (1:1-17),3:1-6

Tuesday Exodus 19:1-16   Colossians 1:1-14   Matthew 3:7-12

Wednesday Exodus 19:16-25   Colossians 1:15-23   Matthew 3:13-17

Thursday Exodus 20:1-21   Colossians 1:24-2:7   Matthew 4:1-11

Friday Exodus 24   Colossians 2:8-23   Matthew 4:12-17

Saturday Exodus 25:1-22   Colossians 3:1-17   Matthew 4:18-25

Week of 4 Easter

Sunday Exodus 28:1-4,30-38   1John 2:18-29   Mark 6:30-44

Monday Exodus 32:1-20   Colossians 3:18-4:6(7-18)   Matthew 5:1-10

Tuesday Exodus 32:21-34   1Thess 1   Matthew 5:11-16

Wednesday Exodus 33   1Thess 2:1-12   Matthew 5:17-20

Thursday Exodus 34:1-17   1Thess 2:13-20   Matthew 5:21-26

The Lectionary – Year Two

Friday Exodus 34:18-35 1Thess 3 Matthew 5:27-37

Saturday Exodus 40:18-38 1Thess 4:1-12 Matthew 5:38-48

Week of 5 Easter

Sunday Leviticus 8:1-13,30-36 Hebrews 12:1-14 Luke 4:16-30

Monday Leviticus 16:1-19 1Thess 4:13-18 Matthew 6:1-6,16-18

Tuesday Leviticus 16:20-34 1Thess 5:1-11 Matthew 6:7-15

Wednesday Leviticus 19:1-18 1Thess 5:12-28 Matthew 6:19-24

Thursday Leviticus 19:26-37 2Thess 1 Matthew 6:25-34

Friday Leviticus 23:1-22 2Thess 2 Matthew 7:1-12

Saturday Leviticus 23:23-44 2Thess 3 Matthew 7:13-21

Week of 6 Easter

Sunday Leviticus 25:1-17 James 2-8,16-18 Luke 12:13-21

Monday Leviticus 25:35-55 Colossians 1:9-14 Matthew 13:1-16

Tuesday Leviticus 26:1-20 1Timothy 2:1-6 Matthew 13:18-23

Wednesday Leviticus 26:27-42 Ephesians 1:1-10 Matthew 22:41-46

Eve of Ascension 2Kings 1-15 Revelation 5

Ascension Day Daniel 7:9-14 Hebrews 2:5-18 Matthew 28:16-20

Friday 1Samuel 2:1-10 Ephesians 2:1-10 Matthew 7:22-27

Saturday Numbers 11:16-17,24-29 Ephesians 2:11-22 Matthew 7:28-8:4

Week of 7 Easter

Sunday Exodus 3:1-12 Hebrews 12:18-29 Matthew. Luke 10:17-24

Monday Joshua 1:1-9 Ephesians 3:1-13 Matthew 8:5-17

The Lectionary – Year Two

Tuesday 1 Samuel 16:1-13a Ephesians 3:14-21 Matthew 8:18-27

Wednesday Isaiah 4:2-6 Ephesians 4:1-16 Matthew 8:28-34

Thursday Zechariah 4 Ephesians 4:17-32 Matthew 9:1-8

Friday Jeremiah 31:27-34 Ephesians 5:1-20 Matthew 9:9-17

Saturday Ezekiel 36:22-27 Ephesians 6:10-24 Matthew 9:18-26

Eve of Pentecost Exodus 19:3-8a,16-20 1 Peter 2:4-10

The Day of Pentecost Deut 16:9-12 Acts 4:18-21,23-33 John 4:19-26

On the weekdays which follow, the Readings are taken from the numbered Proper (one through six) which corresponds most closely to the date of Pentecost.

Eve of Trinity Sunday Sirach 42:15-25 Ephesians 3:14-21

Trinity Sunday Job 38:1-11; 42:1-5 Revelation 19:4-16 John 1:29-34

On the weekdays which follow, the Readings are taken from the numbered Proper (two through seven) which corresponds most closely to the date of Trinity Sunday.

The Season after Pentecost

Proper 1 Week of the Sunday closest to May 11

Monday Ezekiel 33:1-11 1 John 1 Matthew 9:27-34

Tuesday Ezekiel 33:21-33 1 John 2:1-11 Matthew 9:35-10:4

Wednesday Ezekiel 34:1-16 1 John 2:12-17 Matthew 10:5-15

Thursday Ezekiel. 37:21b-28 1 John 2:18-29 Matthew 10:16-23

Friday Ezekiel 39:21-29 1 John 3:1-10 Matthew 10:24-33

Saturday Ezekiel 47:1-12 1 John 3:11-18 Matthew 10:34-42

Proper 2 Week of the Sunday closest to May 18

PrMonday Proverbs 3:11-20 1 John 3:18-4:6 Matthew 11:1-6

Tuesday Proverbs 4 1 John 4:7-21 Matthew 11:7-15

The Lectionary – Year Two

Wednesday   Proverbs 6:1-19   1John 5:1-12   Matthew 11:16-24

Thursday   Proverbs 7   1John 5:13-21   Matthew 11:25-30

Friday   Proverbs 8:1-21   2John   Matthew 12:1-14

Saturday   Proverbs 8:22-36   3John   Matthew 12:15-21

Proper 3 *Week of the Sunday closest to May 25*

Sunday Proverbs 9:1-12   Acts:14-25   Luke 10:25-28,38-42

Monday   Proverbs 10:1-12   1Timothy 1:1-17   Matthew 12:22-32

Tuesday   Proverbs 15:16-33   1Timothy 1:18-2:8   Matthew 12:33-42

Wednesday   Proverbs 17:1-20   1Timothy 3   Matthew 12:43-50

Thursday   Proverbs 21:30-22:6   1Timothy 4   Matthew 13:24-30

Friday Proverbs 23:19-21, 29-24:2   1Timothy 5:17-22(23-25)   Matthew 13:31-35

Saturday   Proverbs 25:15-28   1Timothy 6:6-21   Matthew 13:36-43

Proper 4 *Week of the Sunday closest to June 1*

Sunday   Ecclesiastes 1:1-11   Acts 8:26-40   Luke 11:1-13

Monday   Ecclesiastes 2:1-15   Galatians 1:1-17   Matthew 13:44-52

Tuesday   Ecclesiastes 2:16-26   Galatians 1:18-2:10   Matthew 13:53-58

Wednesday   Ecclesiastes 3:1-15   Galatians 2:11-21   Matthew 14:1-12

Thursday   Ecclesiastes 3:16-4:3   Galatians 3:1-14   Matthew 14:13-21

Friday   Ecclesiastes 5:1-7   Galatians 3:15-22   Matthew 14:22-36

Saturday   Ecclesiastes 5:8-20   Galatians 3:23-4:11   Matthew 15:1-20

The Lectionary – Year Two

Proper 5 *Week of the Sunday closest to June 8*

Sunday Ecclesiastes 6   Ac 10:9-23   Luke 12:32-40

Monday Ecclesiastes 7:1-14   Galatians 4:12-20   Matthew 15:21-28

Tuesday Ecclesiastes 8:14-9:10   Galatians 4:21-31   Matthew 15:29-39

Wednesday Ecclesiastes 9:11-18   Galatians 5:1-15   Matthew 16:1-12

Thursday Ecclesiastes 11:1-8   Galatians 5:16-24   Matthew 16:13-20

Friday Ecclesiastes 11:9-12:14   Galatians 5:25-6:10   Matthew 16:21-28

Saturday Numbersmbers 3:1-13   Galatians 6:11-18   Matthew 17:1-13

Proper 6 *Week of the Sunday closest to June 15*

Sunday Numbers 6:22-27   Acts 13:1-12   Luke 12:41-48

Monday Numbers 9:15-23,10:29-36   Romans 1:1-15   Matthew 17:14-21

Tuesday Numbers 11:1-23   Romans 1:16-25   Matthew 17:22-27

Wednesday Numbers 11:24-33(34-35)   Romans 1:28-2:11   Matthew 18:1-9

Thursday Numbers 12   Romans 2:12-24   Matthew 18:10-20

Friday Numbers 13:1-3,21-30   Romans 2:25-3:8   Matthew 18:21-35

Saturday Numbers 13:31-14:25   Romans 3:9-20   Matthew 19:1-12

Proper 7 *Week of the Sunday closest to June 22*

Sunday Numbers 14:26-45   Acts 15:1-12   Luke 12:49-56

Monday Numbers 16:1-19   Romans 3:21-31   Matthew 19:13-22

The Lectionary – Year Two

Tuesday   Numbers 16:20-35   Romans 4:1-12   Matthew 19:23-30

Wednesday   Numbers 16:36-50   Romans 4:13-25   Matthew 20:1-16

Thursday   Numbers 17:1-11   Romans 5:1-11   Matthew 20:17-28

Friday Numbers 20:1-13   Romans 5:12-21   Matthew 20:29-34

Saturday   Numbers 20:14-29   Romans 6:1-11   Matthew 21:1-11

Proper 8 *Week of Sunday closest to June 29*

Sunday Numbers 21:4-9,21-35   Acts 17:(12-21)22-34   Luke 13:10-17

Monday   Numbers 22:1-21   Romans 6:12-23   Matthew 21:12-22

Tuesday   Numbers 22:21-38   Romans 7:1-12   Matthew 21:23-32

Wednesday   Numbers 22:41-23:12   Romans 7:13-25   Matthew 21:33-46

Thursday   Numbers 23:11-26   Romans 8:1-11   Matthew 22:1-14

Friday Numbers 24:1-13   Romans 8:12-17   Matthew 22:15-22

Saturday   Numbers 24:12-25   Romans 8:18-25   Matthew 22:23-40

Proper 9 *Week of the Sunday closest to July 6*

Sunday Numbers 27:12-23   Acts 19:11-20   Mark 1:14-20

Monday   Numbers 32:1-6,16-27   Romans 8:26-30   Matthew 23:1-12

Tuesday   Numbers 35:1-3,9-15,30-34   Romans 8:31-39   Matthew 23:13-26

Wednesday   Deut 1:1-18   Romans 9:1-18   Matthew 23:27-39

Thursday   Deut 3:18-28   Romans 9:19-33   Matthew 24:1-14

Friday Deut 31:7-13; 31:24-32:4   Romans 10:1-13   Matthew 24:15-31

Saturday   Deut 34   Romans 10:14-21   Matthew 24:32-51

The Lectionary – Year Two

Proper 10 *Week of the Sunday closest to July 13*

Sunday Joshua 1 Acts 21:3-15 Mark 1:21-27

Monday Joshua 2:1-14 Romans 11:1-12 Matthew 25:1-13

Tuesday Joshua 2:15-24 Romans 11:13-24 Matthew 25:14-30

Wednesday Joshua 3:1-13 Romans 11:25-36 Matthew 25:31-46

Thursday Joshua 3:14-4:7 Romans 12:1-8 Matthew 26:1-16

Friday Joshua 4:19-5:1,10-15 Romans 12:9-21 Matthew 26:17-25

Saturday Joshua 6:1-14 Romans 13:1-7 Matthew 26:26-35

Proper 11 *Week of the Sunday closest to July 20*

Sunday Joshua 6:15-27 Acts 22:30-23:11 Mark 2:1-12

Monday Joshua 7:1-13 Romans 13:8-14 Matthew 26:36-46

Tuesday Joshua 8:1-22 Romans 14:1-12 Matthew 26:47-56

Wednesday Joshua 8:30-35 Romans 14:13-23 Matthew 26:57-68

Thursday Joshua 9:3-21 Romans 15:1-13 Matthew 26:69-75

Friday Joshua 9:22-10:15 Romans 15:14-24 Matthew 27:1-10

Saturday Joshua 23 Romans 15:25-33 Matthew 27:11-23

Proper 12 *Week of the Sunday closest to July 27*

Sunday Joshua 24:1-15 Acts 28:23-31 Mark 2:23-28

Monday Joshua 24:16-33 Romans 16:1-16 Matthew 27:24-31

Tuesday Judges 2:1-5,11-23 Romans 16:17-27 Matthew 27:32-44

Wednesday Judges 3:12-30 Acts 1:1-14 Matthew 27:45-54

Thursday Judges 4:4-23 Acts 1:15-26 Matthew 27:55-66

Friday Judges 5:1-18 Acts 2:1-21 Matthew 28:1-10

Saturday Judges 5:19-31 Acts 2:22-36 Matthew 28:11-20

The Lectionary – Year Two

Proper 13 *Week of the Sunday closest to August 3*
Sunday Judges 6:1-24   2 Corinth 9:6-15   Mark 3:20-30
Monday   Judges 6:25-40   Acts 2:37-47   John 1:1-18
Tuesday   Judges 7:1-18   Acts 3:1-11   John 1:19-28
Wednesday   Judges 7:19-8:12   Acts 3:12-26   John 1:29-42
Thursday Judges 8:22-35   Acts 4:1-12   John 1:43-51
Friday Judges 9:1-16,19-21   Acts 4:13-31   John 2:2-12
Saturday   Judges 9:22-25,50-57   Acts 4:32-5:11   John 2:13-25

Proper 14 *Week of the Sunday closest to August 10*
Sunday   Judges 11:1-11,29-40   2 Cor. 11:21b-31   Mark 4:35-41
Monday   Judges 12:1-7   Acts 5:12-26   John 3:1-21
Tuesday   Judges 13:1-15   Acts 5:27-42   John 3:22-36
Wednesday   Judges 13:15-24   Acts 6   John 4:1-26
Thursday Judges 14:1-19   Acts 6:15-7:16   John 4:27-42
Friday Judges 14:20-15:20   Acts 7:17-29   John 4:43-54
Saturday   Judges 16:1-14   Acts 7:30-43   John 5:1-18

Proper 15 *Week of the Sunday closest to August 17*
Sunday Judges 16:15-31   2 Corinth 13:1-11   Mark 5:25-34
Monday   Judges 17   Acts 7:44-8:1a   John 5:19-29
Tuesday   Judges 18:1-15   Acts 8:1-13   John 5:30-47
Wednesday   Judges 18:16-31   Acts 8:14-25   John 6:1-15
Thursday Job 1   Acts 8:26-40   John 6:16-27
Friday Job 2   Acts 9:1-9   John 6:27-40
Saturday   Job 3   Acts 9:10-19a   John 6:41-51

The Lectionary – Year Two

Proper 16 *Week of the Sunday closest to August 24*

Sunday Job 4:1-6,12-21   Revelation 4   Mark 6:1-6a

Monday Job 4:1,5:1-11,17-21,26-27   Acts 9:19b-31   John 6:52-59

Tuesday   Job 6:1-4,8-15,21   Acts 9:32-43   John 6:60-71

Wednesday   Job 6:1,7:1-21   Acts 10:1-16   John 7:1-13

Thursday   Job 6:1,7:1-21   Acts 10:17-33   John 7:14-36

Friday Job 9:1-15,32-35   Acts 10:34-48   John 7:37-52

Saturday Job 9:1,10:1-9,16-22   Acts 11:1-18   John 8:12-20

Proper 17 *Week of the Sunday closest to August 31*

Sunday Job 11:1-9,13-20   Revelation 5   Matthew 5:1-12

Monday Job 12:1-6,13-25   Acts 11:19-30   John 8:21-32

Tuesday Job 12:1,13:3-17,21-27   Acts 12:1-17   John 8:33-47

Wednesday   Job 12:1,14:1-22   Acts 12:18-25   John 8:47-59

Thursday Job 16:16-22,17:1,13-16   Acts 13:1-12   John 9:1-17

Friday Job 19:1-7,14-27   Acts 13:13-25   John 9:18-41

Saturday Job 22:1-4; 22:21-23:7   Acts 13:26-43   John 10:1-18

Proper 18 *Week of the Sunday closest to September 7*

Sunday Job 25; 27:1-6   Revelation 14:1-7,13   Matthew 5:13-20

Monday Job 32:1-10; 32:19-33:1,19-28   Acts 13:44-52   John 10:19-30

Tuesday Job 29:1-20   Acts 14:1-18   John 10:31-42

Wednesday Job 29:1,30:1-2,16-31   Acts 14:19-28   John 11:1-16

Thursday Job 29:1,31:1-23   Acts 15:1-11   John 11:17-29

Friday Job 29:1,31:24-40   Acts 15:12-21   John 11:30-44

Saturday Job 38:1-17   Acts 15:22-35   John 11:45-54

The Lectionary – Year Two

Proper 19 *Week of the Sunday closest to September 14*

Sunday   Job 38:1,18-41   Revelation 18:1-8   Matthew 5:21-26

Monday   Job 40   Acts 15:36-16:5   John 11:55-12:8

Tuesday   Job 40:1,41:1-11   Acts 16:6-15   John 12:9-19

Wednesday   Job 42   Acts 16:16-24   John 12:20-26

Thursday   Job 28   Acts 16:25-40   John 12:27-36a

Friday   Esther 1:1-4,10-19 or Judith 4:1-15   Acts 17:1-15   John 12:36b-43

Saturday   Esther 2:5-8,15-23 or Judith 5:1-21   Acts 17:16-34   John 12:44-50

Proper 20 *Week of the Sunday closest to September 21*

Sunday   Esther 3:1-4:3 or Judith 5:22-6:4,10-21   James 1:19-27   Matthew 6:1-6,16-18

Monday   Esther 4:4-17 or Judith 7:1-7,19-32   Acts 18:1-11   Luke (1:1-4),3:1-14

Tuesday   Esther 5 or Judith 8:9-17,9:1.7-10   Acts 18:12-28   Luke 3:15-22

Wednesday   Esther 6 or Judith 10:1-23   Acts 19:1-10   Luke 4:1-13

Thursday   Esther 7 or Judith 12:1-20   Acts 19:11-20   Luke 4:14-30

Friday   Esther 8:1-8,15-17 or Judith 13:1-20   Acts 19:21-41   Luke 4:31-37

Saturday   Hosea 1:1-2:1   Acts 20:1-16   Luke 4:38-44

Proper 21 *Week of the Sunday closest to September 28*

Sunday   Hosea 2:2-14   Jas 3:1-13   Matthew 13:44-52

Monday   Hosea 2:14-23   Acts 20:17-38   Luke 5:1-11

Tuesday   Hosea 4:1-10   Acts 21:1-14   Luke 5:12-26

Wednesday   Hosea 4:11-19   Acts 21:15-26   Luke 5:27-39

The Lectionary – Year Two

Thursday Hosea 5:8-6:6 Acts 21:27-36 Luke 6:1-11
Friday Hosea 10 Acts 21:37-22:16 Luke 6:12-26
Saturday Hosea 11:1-9 Acts 22:17-29 Luke 6:27-38

Proper 22 *Week of the Sunday closest to October 5*
Sunday Hosea 13:4-14 1Co 2:6-16 Matthew 14:1-12
Monday Hosea 14 Acts 22:30-23:11 Luke 6:39-49
Tuesday Micah 1:1-9 Acts 23:12-24 Luke 7:1-17
Wednesday Micah 2 Acts 23:23-35 Luke 7:18-35
Thursday Micah 3:1-8 Acts 24:1-23 Luke 7:36-50
Friday Micah 3:9-4:5 Acts 24:24-25:12 Luke 8:1-15
Saturday Micah 5:1-4,10-15 Acts 25:13-27 Luke 8:16-25

Proper 23 *Week of the Sunday closest to October 12*
Sunday Micah 6:1-8 1Corinth 4:9-16 Matthew 15:21-28
Monday Micah 7:1-7 Acts 26:1-23 Luke 8:26-39
Tuesday Jonah 1:1-17a Acts 26:24-27:8 Luke 8:40-56
Wednesday Jonah 1:17-2:10 Acts 27:9-26 Luke 9:1-17
Thursday Jonah 3-4 Acts 27:27-44 Luke 9:18-27
Friday Sirach 1:1-10,18-27 Acts 28:1-16 Luke 9:28-36
Saturday Sirach 3:17-31 Acts 28:17-31 Luke 9:37-50

Proper 24 *Week of the Sunday closest to October 19*
Sunday Sirach 4:1-10 1Co 10:1-13 Matthew 16:13-20
Monday Sirach 4:20-5:7 Revelation 7:1-8 Luke 9:51-62
Tuesday Sirach 6:5-17 Revelation 7:9-17 Luke 10:1-16
Wednesday Sirach 7:4-14 Revelation 8 Luke 10:17-24
Thursday Sirach 10:1-18 Revelation 9:1-12 Luke 10:25-37
Friday Sirach 11:2-20 Revelation 9:13-21 Luke 10:38-42
Saturday Sirach 15:9-20 Revelation 10 Luke 11:1-13

The Lectionary – Year Two

Proper 25 *Week of the Sunday closest to October 26*

Sunday Sirach 18:19-33   1 Corinth 10:15-24   Matthew 18:15-20

Monday Sirach 19:4-17   Revelation 11:1-14   Luke 11:14-26

Tuesday Sirach 24:1-12   Revelation 11:14-19   Luke 11:27-36

Wednesday Sirach 28:14-26   Revelation 12:1-6   Luke 11:37-52

Thursday Sirach 31:12-18; 31:25-32:2   Revelation 12:7-17   Luke 11:53-12:12

Friday Sirach 34:1-8,18-22   Revelation 13:1-10   Luke 12:13-31

Saturday Sirach 35:1-17   Revelation 13:11-18   Luke 12:32-48

Proper 26 *Week of the Sunday closest to November 2*

Sunday Sirach 36:1-17   1 Corinth 12:27-13:13   Matthew 18:21-35

Monday Sirach 38:24-34   Revelation 14:1-13   Luke 12:49-59

Tuesday Sirach 43:1-22   Revelation 14:14-15:8   Luke 13:1-9

Wednesday Sirach 43:23-33   Revelation 16:1-11   Luke 13:10-17

Thursday Sirach 44:1-15   Revelation 16:12-21   Luke 14:18-30

Friday Sirach 50:1,11-24   Revelation 17   Luke 13:31-35

Saturday Sirach 51:1-12   Revelation 18:1-14   Luke 14:1-11

Proper 27 *Week of the Sunday closest to November 9*

Sunday Sirach 51:13-22   1 Corinth 14:1-12   Matthew 20:1-16

Monday Joel 1:1-13   Revelation 18:15-24   Luke 14:12-24

Tuesday Joel 1:15-2:2(3-11)   Revelation 19:1-10   Luke 14:25-35

Wednesday Joel 2:12-19   Revelation 19:11-21   Luke 15:1-10

Thursday Joel 2:21-27   James 1:1-15   Luke 15:1-2,11-32

Friday Joel 2:28-3:8   James 1:16-27   Luke 16:1-9

Saturday Joel 3:9-17   James 2:1-13   Luke 16:10-17(18)

The Lectionary – Year Two

Proper 28 *Week of the Sunday closest to November 16*

Sunday Habakkuk 1:1-4(5-11)12-2:1 Philippians 3:13-4:1 Matthew 23:13-24

Monday   Habakkuk 2:1-4,9-20 James 2:14-26 Luke 16:19-31

Tuesday   Habakkuk 3:1-10(11-15)16-18 James 3:1-12 Luke 17:1-10

Wednesday   Malachi 1:1,6-14 James 3:13-4:12 Luke 17:11-19

Thursday Malachi 2:1-16 James 4:13-5:6 Luke 17:20-37

Friday Malachi 3:1-12 James 5:7-12 Luke 18:1-8

Saturday   Malachi 3:13-4:6 James 5:13-20 Luke 18:9-14

Proper 29 *Week of the Sunday closest to November 23*

Sunday Zechariah 9:9-16 1Peter 3:13-22 Matthew 21:1-13

Monday   Zechariah 10 Galatians 6:1-10 Luke 18:15-30

Tuesday   Zechariah 11:4-17 1Corinth 3:10-23 Luke 18:31-43

Wednesday   Zechariah 12:1-10 Ephesians 1:3-14 Luke 19:1-10

Thursday Zechariah 13 Ephesians 1:15-23 Luke 19:11-27

Friday Zechariah 14:1-11 Romans 15:7-13 Luke 19:28-40

Saturday   Zechariah 14:12-21 Philippians 2:1-11 Luke 19:41-48

The Lectionary – Holy Days

Holy Days

St. Andrew - November 30
    Morning: Isaiah 49:1-6   1 Corinth 4:1-16
    Evening: Isaiah 55:1-5   John 1:35-42

St. Thomas - December 21
    Morning: Job 42:1-6   1 Peter 1:3-9
    Evening: Isaiah 43:8-13   John 14:1-7

St. Stephen - December 26
    Morning: 2 Chronicles 17-22   Acts 6:1-7
    Evening: Wisdom 4:7-15   Acts 7:59-8:8

St. John - December 27
    Morning: Proverbs 8:22-30   John 13:20-35
    Evening: Isaiah 44:1-8   1 John 5:1-12

Holy Innocents - December 28
    Morning: Isaiah 49:13-23   Matthew 18:1-14
    Evening: Isaiah 54:1-13   Mark 10:13-16

Confession of St. Peter - January 18
    Morning: Ezekiel 3:4-11   Acts 10:34-44
    Evening: Ezekiel 34:11-16   John 21:15-22

Conversion of St. Paul - Janaury 25
    Morning: Isaiah 45:18-25   Philippians 3:4b-11
    Evening: Sirach 39:1-10   Acts 9:1-22

Eve of the Presentation
        1 Samuel 1:20-28a   Romans 8:14-21

The Presentation - February 2
    Morning: 1 Samuel 2:1-10   John 8:31-36
    Evening: Haggai 2:1-9   1 John 3:1-8

The Lectionary – Holy Days

St. Matthias - February 24
    Morning: 1 Samuel 16:1-13   1 John 2:18-25
    Evening: 1 Samuel 12:1-5   Acts 20:17-35

St. Joseph - March 19
    Morning: Isaiah 63:7-16   Matthew 1:18-25
    Evening: 2 Chronicles 6:12-17 Ephesians 3:14-21

Eve of the Anunciation
        Genesis 3:1-15   Romans 5:12-21 or
                                Galatians 4:1-7

St. Cuthbert - March 20
        2 Corinthians 6:1-10 Matthew 6:24-33

The Anunciation - March 25
    Morning: Isaiah 52:7-12   Hebrews 2:5-10
    Evening   Wisdom 9:1-12   John 1:9-14

St. Mark - April 25
    Morning: Sirach 2:1-11   Acts 12:25-13:3
    Evening: Isaiah 62:6-12   2 Timothy 4:1-11

Ss. Philip and James - May 1
    Morning: Job 23:1-12   John 1:43-51
    Evening: Proverbs 4:7-18 John 12:20-26

Eve of the Visitation
        Isaiah 11:1-10   Hebrews 2:11-18

The Visitation - May 31
    Morning: 1 Samuel 1:1-20   Hebrews 3:1-6
    Evening: Zechariah 2:10-13   John 3:25-30

St. Barnabas - June 11
    Morning: Sirach 31:3-11   Acts 4:32-37
    Evening: Job 29:1-16   Acts 9:26-31

The Lectionary – Holy Days

Eve of St. John the Baptist
        Sirach 48:1-11   Luke 1:5-23

Nativity of St. John the Baptist - June 24
    Morning: Malachi 3:1-5   John 3:22-30
    Evening: Malachi 4:1-6   Matthew 11:2-19

Ss. Peter and Paul - June 29
    Morning: Ezekiel 2:1-7   Acts 11:1-18
    Evening: Isaiah 49:1-6   Galatians 2:1-9

St. Mary Magdalene - July 22
    Morning: Zephaniah 3:14-20   Mark 15:14-20
    Evening: Exodus 15:19-21   2 Corinth 1:3-7

St. James - July 25
    Morning: Jeremiah 16:14-21   Mark 1:14-20
    Evening: Jeremiah 16:1-15   Matthew 10:16-32

Eve of the Transfiguration
        1 Kings 19:1-12   2 Corinth 3:1-9,18

The Transfiguration - August 6
    Morning: Exodus 24:12-18   2 Corinth 4:1-6
    Evening: Daniel 7:9-10,13-14   John 12:27-36a

St. Mary the Virgin - August 15
    Morning: 1 Samuel 2:1-10   John 2:1-12
    Evening: Jeremiah 31:1-14 or   John 1:6-14 or
                Zechariah 2:10-13   Acts 1:6-14

St. Bartholomew - August 24
    Morning: Genesis 28:10-17   John 1:43-51
    Evening: Isaiah 66:1-2,18-23   1 Peter 5:1-11

Eve of Holy Cross
        1 Kings 8:22-30   Ephesians 2:11-22

The Lectionary – Holy Days

Holy Cross Day - September 14
    Morning: Numbers 21:4-9   John 3:11-17
    Evening: Genesis 3:1-15   1 Peter 3:17-22

St. Matthew - September 21
    Morning: Isaiah 8:11-20   Romans 10:1-15
    Evening: Job 28:12-28   Matthew 13:44-52

St. Michael and All Angels - September 29
    Morning: Job 38:1-17   Hebrews 1
    Evening: Daniel 12:1-3 or   Mark 13:21-27 or
              2 Kings 6:8-17   Revelation 5

St. Luke - October 18
    Morning: Ezekiel 47:1-12   Luke 1:1-4
    Evening: Isaiah 52:7-10   Acts 1:1-8

St. James of Jerusalem - October 23
    Morning: Jeremiah 11:18-23   Matthew 10:16-22
    Evening: Isaiah 65:17-25   Hebrews 12:12-24

Ss. Simon and Jude - October 28
    Morning: Isaiah 28:9-16   Ephesians 4:1-16
    Evening: Isaiah 4:2-6   John 14:15-31

Eve of All Saints
              Wisdom 3:1-9   Revelation 19:1,4-10

All Siants' Day - November 1
    Morning: 2 Esdras 2:42-47   Hebrews 11:32-12:2
    Evening: Wisdom 5:1-5,14-16   Revelation 21:1-4,22-22:5

www.ingramcontent.com/pod-product-compliance
Lightning Source LLC
Chambersburg PA
CBHW032017230426
43671CB00005B/110